"*God's Good Earth* is a wonderful resource to celebrate the majesty, mystery, and soul of Earth. The songs, praise, and poetry of creation erupt and stir a spiritual presence both within us as worshippers and an awareness of that presence within the deep domains of Earth. A fantastic resource for celebrating The Season of Creation every Sunday in the year. 'Where can Wisdom be Found?' In creation (Job 28:23-27)!"

> —Norman Habel, editor of the Earth Bible series in Australia, a sponsor of the Season of Creation, and author of works relating to ecology, worship, and the Scriptures

"What a splendid book this is, packed with beautifully chosen prayers, hymns, and reflections that celebrate the sacredness of God's skies and seas, larks and eagles, petals and leaves! I hope that *God's Good Earth* will be widely used, not only as a source of liturgies during Creation Season but also as a wellspring of material for weekly services, for special services throughout the year, and for personal prayer. In this time of climate crisis, species extinction, and collective trauma, when so many of us feel numb or overwhelmed, these liturgies can restore our souls: they give voice to our need to praise and give thanks, to grieve and repent, and to renew our resolve for the long struggle ahead."

> —The Rev. Dr. Margaret Bullitt-Jonas, Missioner for Creation Care, Episcopal Diocese of Western Massachusetts & Massachusetts Conference, United Church of Christ

"Rich, abundant, fertile, and creative—the Rowthorns have drawn from broad and deep seas of wisdom to move hearts and mountains in search of Creation's healing. Worship frames for a year of weeks explore the wonder of God's creation, creatures human and not, and the groaning of all. May these prayers and poems, hymns and scriptures, reflections and blessings work their wondrous transformation in all God's people, for *tikkun olam*, repair of the interconnected world God has made. *Caveat lector*, for you will weep, rejoice, be awed and humbled, and by grace, transformed."

> —The Rt. Rev. Katharine Jefferts Schori
> Assisting Bishop, San Diego
> Formerly XXVI Presiding Bishop of The Episcopal Church

"In *God's Good Earth*, Anne and Jeffery Rowthorn have blessed the churches with a beautiful and timely gift. Representing a rich diversity of traditions and voices, these 52 liturgies invite us to worship the God of creation, ponder our deep communion with all living things, repent of our responsibility for environmental destruction and its devastating consequences for marginalized peoples, and reform our actions in agreement with God's hopeful vision for the renewal of the earth."

—Dr. Thomas John Hastings, Executive Director, Overseas Ministries Study Center, New Haven, Connecticut

"If you have ever been overwhelmed by a panorama from a mountaintop or filled with awe at the heavenly canvas glittering with stars or overcome with wonder at the power of the sea as it rushes against a shore, this book is for you. If you have become concerned about the rising temperatures of our oceans and shorelines and understand that there is a religious dimension to these issues, this book is for you. If the social injustices that accompany environmental degradation are moral concerns, this book is for you. This collection of texts from 28 books of the Bible, 42 other authors, 37 writers of hymns plus 90 supplementary hymns, arranged in 52 thematic liturgies, provides those seeking a means to express their faith in both formal and informal settings. I warmly recommend this book to all who understand environmental issues in religious terms."

—Gregory E. Sterling
The Reverend Henry L. Slack Dean
The Lillian Claus Professor of New Testament
Yale Divinity School

"'In the end we will conserve only what we love,' affirmed Senegalese conservationist Baba Dioum. 'We will love only what we understand, and we will understand only what we are taught.' The liturgies developed by Anne and Jeffery Rowthorn's book provide fifty-two ways to understand and love God's good earth more deeply. Their work leads us from praise and thanks to lament and confession and finally to a renewed commitment to all creation and a new sense of wonder at God's infinite imagination in fashioning this world. The Rowthorns challenge us to pray, sing, and act for the earth. Most of all, they give us the words and worship we need to love this world as God loves it, for the sake of the earth and for generations yet to come. It should be required text for every seminary course on liturgy and the worship leaders of every congregation."

—Rev. Talitha Arnold
Senior Minister
The United Church of Santa Fe

God's Good Earth

Praise and Prayer for Creation

Compiled and Edited by
Anne and Jeffery Rowthorn

LITURGICAL PRESS
Collegeville, Minnesota

www.litpress.org

Cover design by Amy Marc. Photo courtesy of Getty Images.

Unless otherwise noted, Scripture quotations are from New Revised Standard Version Bible © 1989 National Council of the Churches of Christ in the United States of America. Used by permission. All rights reserved worldwide.

Other sources are provided at the end of each liturgy.

© 2018 by Anne and Jeffery Rowthorn
Published by Liturgical Press, Collegeville, Minnesota. All rights reserved. No part of this book may be used or reproduced in any manner whatsoever, except brief quotations in reviews, without written permission of Liturgical Press, Saint John's Abbey, PO Box 7500, Collegeville, MN 56321-7500. Printed in the United States of America.

1   2   3   4   5   6   7   8   9

Library of Congress Cataloging-in-Publication Data

Names: Rowthorn, Anne W., compiler.
Title: God's good earth : praise and prayer for creation / compiled and edited by Anne and Jeffery Rowthorn.
Description: Collegeville, Minnesota : Liturgical Press, 2018. | Includes bibliographical references and index.
Identifiers: LCCN 2018021258 (print) | LCCN 2018039691 (ebook) | ISBN 9780814644362 (ebook) | ISBN 9780814644126
Subjects: LCSH: Creation—Prayers and devotions. | Nature—Prayers and devotions. | Worship programs.
Classification: LCC BT695.5 (ebook) | LCC BT695.5 .G629 2018 (print) | DDC 231.7—dc23
LC record available at https://lccn.loc.gov/2018021258

For our grandchildren

Anna
Jackson
Nathaniel
Beckett
Juliette
Kieran
Hannah

and all the world's grandchildren.

May they cherish the wondrous works of God
and protect the beauty and integrity of all creation.

CONTENTS

Preface xi

Foreword xiii

Introduction xvii

How to Use This Book xxii

God the Creator and God's Glorious Creation
- 1. God the Creator 3
- 2. God's Glorious Creation 9
- 3. Sacred Earth 16
- 4. Living Waters 22
- 5. Wonder 28
- 6. The Song of Creation 34
- 7. God Be Praised 40

God's Physical Universe
- 8. Oceans 49
- 9. Sky 54
- 10. Wilderness 60
- 11. Mountains 67
- 12. Trees and Forests 74
- 13. Deserts 80
- 14. Universe 86

The Diversity of God's Creatures
- 15. God's Gift of Diversity 95
- 16. Biodiversity 101
- 17. The One Human Family 107

18. Children   113
19. The Wisdom of Indigenous Cultures   119
20. Animals   125

The Human Community and Its Needs
21. A Good Society   135
22. Farms   141
23. Agriculture with a Human Face   147
24. Water   154
25. Cities   160
26. Nations   166
27. Work   172
28. Simplicity   178
29. Compassion   184
30. Survival   190
31. The Language of Love   196

The Whole Creation Groaning in Travail
32. Exploitation of the Earth   205
33. The Culture of Death   212
34. The Lure of Money   218
35. Climate Change   224
36. Global Warming   230
37. Forgotten People   235
38. Poverty   241
39. Hunger   247
40. Migrants   253
41. Violence   259
42. Victims of War   265
43. Consequences   271
44. Judgment and Mercy   277
45. Death and Resurrection   283

Hope and the Future
46. Ecological Conversion   291
47. Action   298
48. Science   304

49. Healing Our Nation   311
50. Peace   317
51. Hope   323
52. Replenishing God's Good Earth   329

Index of Psalms and Other Biblical Readings   337

Index of Contemporary Reflections   341

Index of Hymns   343

Supplementary Hymns   345

Acknowledgments   350

PREFACE

The story of creation presents us with a panoramic view of the world. Scripture reveals that, "in the beginning," God intended humanity to cooperate in the preservation and protection of the natural environment. At first, as we read in Genesis, "no plant of the field was yet in the earth and no herb of the field had yet sprung up—for the Lord God had not caused it to rain upon the earth, and there was no one to till the ground" (2:5). The earth was entrusted to us as a sublime gift and legacy, for which all of us share responsibility until, "in the end," all things in heaven and on earth will be restored in Christ (cf. Eph 1:10). Our human dignity and welfare are deeply connected to our care for the whole of creation.

However, "in the meantime," the history of the world presents a very different context. It reveals a morally decaying scenario where our attitude and behavior towards creation obscure our calling as God's co-operators. Our propensity to interrupt the world's delicate and balanced ecosystems, our insatiable desire to manipulate and control the planet's limited resources, and our greed for limitless profit in markets—all these have alienated us from the original purpose of creation. We no longer respect nature as a shared gift; instead, we regard it as a private possession. We no longer associate with nature in order to sustain it; instead, we lord over it to support our own constructs.

The consequences of this alternative worldview are tragic and lasting. The human environment and the natural environment are deteriorating together, and this deterioration of the planet weighs upon the most vulnerable of its people. The impact of climate change affects, first and foremost, those who live in poverty in every corner of the globe. Our obligation to use the earth's goods responsibly implies the recognition of and respect for all people and all living creatures. . . .

We labor in vain if the Lord is not by our side (cf. Ps 126-127), if prayer is not at the center of our reflection and celebration. Indeed, *an objective of our prayer is to change the way we perceive the world in order to change the way we relate to the world.*

—Pope Francis and Ecumenical Patriarch Bartholomew

SOURCE

Pope Francis and Ecumenical Patriarch Bartholomew, "Joint Message on the World Day of Prayer for Creation," *Holy See Press Office*, last modified September 1, 2017, http://press.vatican.va/content/salastampa/en/bollettino/pubblico/2017/09/01/170901a.html. © Libreria Editrice Vaticana. Used by permission. Emphasis added.

FOREWORD

This is a book born out of an immense feeling for our planetary crisis. It is a book that brings forth songs of praise and thanksgiving in an age of mourning and loss. It is an offering of hope for all those seeking a way forward, for it responds to the question of how we may affirm life and create liturgies within the anguish of our times.

We can do this through embracing prayers, poems, hymns, and Scripture that weave us into cosmic time and earth time. Is this not what liturgy has always done? Is this not what is needed now more than ever? Humans long to celebrate life and find themselves as part of a community. They desire to express gratitude for the great powers of the universe that inspire us and the fecund forces of earth that sustain us. They yearn to greet the light of morning and acknowledge the stars at night. In doing so they become part of an earth community and feel their place within a cosmic family. It is through liturgy that we express that unspoken longing of the human heart to belong to something larger. This book provides a way into celebrating the great mystery of life that birthed us and grounds us, that ignites in us wonder, awe, and beauty.

We know that the forces that have given rise to life on this planet arose out of an immense journey of the universe. We are now entering into an understanding of the deep time of its unfolding. How can we imagine the evolution of a universe fourteen billion years old? How might we see this as a story that inspires human creativity and a sense of connection? How does liturgy and prayer help us to do that? By dipping into the wellsprings of nature's capacity for regeneration, these wide-ranging prayers replenish us. By integrating these hymns and Scriptures into the flow of worship, we become inspired for the great work of renewing the face of the earth. These selections will become as essential as water in a desert to assuage our thirst for being alive to life. They will guide us and steady us into an unknown future.

As we feel that steadiness, we can begin to reimagine our lineage as not only our parents and ancestors but also the larger family of life. Words and song link us to the language of the living world—bird song in the morning as the sun rises, insect song in the evening as the sun sets, whale song in the depths of the ocean, wolf song in the thick forests. How can we not rejoice in being part of this chorus of praise that is larger than humans but inclusive of humans? We belong to a great continuity of being where our interdependence is primary, not our independence or dominance. These prayers weave us into the liturgy of the earth community that surrounds us. They illumine our way into the cosmic kinship of acknowledging the stars as our ancestors.

The elements of carbon-based life arose out of the great explosion of stars and thus we are part of a lineage that is as vast and mysterious as our sun star. The way to fully acknowledge this lineage of life is not just by science but by story. All cultures have yearned to tell the story of their origin, their place, their role. In doing so, they create the grounds for meaning and purpose. Such a story is expressed in the cycle of the seasons and in the passage of the day. This book offers a way to find a path amid these changes, just as monastic communities have done throughout history. We can learn once again to abide in reverence, to rejoice in beauty, and to bear the pain of suffering.

This is crucial as the anguish of our moment is vast and complex, ranging from human loss to ecosystem loss. The suffering instigated by our global environmental crisis in its many forms is reaching unsustainable proportions. Climate change is producing rising oceans from Miami to Mumbai and fierce hurricanes from the Philippines to Puerto Rico. Forests and fisheries are being decimated at a rapid rate. In traveling to many parts of the world, especially Asia, I see the levels of pollution of air, water, and soil reaching unbearable levels. And we don't have to travel overseas to see the toxicity in our water causing major problems in places like Flint, Michigan, or post-hurricane Houston.

In North America and abroad we have saturated our environment and our food with chemicals, we have allowed oil pipelines to destroy land and pollute rivers, we have created epidemics of asthma with our dirty air. All of this is causing massive health problems of mind and body. As Thomas Berry often said, "We can't have healthy people on a sick planet." And clearly those most vulnerable are the poor, victims of environmental injustice. In his encyclical *Laudato Si'*, Pope Francis has called for an integral ecology where we listen to both the cry of the earth and the cry of the poor.

How can we not respond to the call of the earth for the continuity of all life and ecosystems? If these great planetary processes have birthed us, should we not care for them for future generations? A sense of urgency has motivated this book; its timeliness is evident. A thematic cycle of prayers and hymns that celebrates creation in all its aspects can reignite mutually enhancing human-earth relations. This is an invitation to one and all to embrace renewing life in all its fullness—within and without. Communities of faith and environmental communities alike can join in healing the earth. This book will light the way into how we can participate together in our singing sentient world.

—Mary Evelyn Tucker
Yale Forum on Religion and Ecology

INTRODUCTION

"In the beginning God created the heavens and the earth." *(Genesis 1:1)*

"God saw everything that [God] had made, and indeed it was very good." *(Genesis 1:31)*

"Yahweh God formed man from the dust of the ground, and breathed into his nostrils the breath of life; and the man became a living being." *(Genesis 2:7)*

"Yahweh God took the man and put him in the Garden of Eden to till it and keep it." *(Genesis 2:15)*

At the very beginning of the biblical story, one thing is made clear: there is an inseparable connection between humans made by God in God's image and the good earth which God has created. Humans are charged with tilling and keeping the ground from which they were all made and to which at the end of life they all return. Because all humans come into being in the same way, there is also an inseparable connection between each one of us. We may speak different languages, belong to different races and nations, and live lives shaped by different cultures, traditions, and beliefs. Nonetheless, we are bound inextricably to each other, just as we are bound inextricably to God's good earth which is our common home.

Pope Francis has written of these two inseparable connections:

> A sense of deep communion with the rest of nature cannot be real if our hearts lack tenderness, compassion and concern for our fellow human beings. It is clearly inconsistent to combat trafficking in endangered species while remaining completely indifferent to human trafficking, unconcerned about the poor, or undertaking to destroy another human being deemed unwanted. Everything is connected. Concern for the environment thus

needs to be joined to a sincere love for our fellow human beings and an unwavering commitment to resolving the problems of society.

Everything is connected. The profound truth expressed in those three words is not self-evident. Over the centuries humankind has again and again taken two steps forward and then one step back on the long journey to understanding that everything is inseparably connected. The twentieth century has been described as the bloodiest in world history, torn by wars and ravaged by epidemics. Yet in the course of the century the United Nations came into being, with a current membership of more than 190 countries. The World Council of Churches has brought together parts of the Christian family long indifferent or actively hostile to one another. Deeply divisive issues of race and gender are being painfully, and in places reluctantly, addressed. Everything is connected.

On September 1, 1989, another step forward of immense significance was taken by Dimitrios I, the Ecumenical Patriarch. Writing to the millions of Eastern Orthodox Christians around the world, he spoke of his great anxiety as he followed "the merciless trampling down and destruction of the natural environment which is caused by man with extremely dangerous consequences for the very survival of the natural world created by God."

He invited the entire Christian world to annual observation of September 1—the first day of the Orthodox church year—"in thanksgiving for the great gift of Creation and in petition for its protection and salvation." Since then the Day of Prayer has blossomed into a Season of Creation, extending from September 1 to October 4—the feast of Francis of Assisi—and observed by increasing numbers of Christians of many traditions.

Meanwhile the world's scientists are each day providing further evidence to support the urgent call for ecological conversion. Many of them have called our era the Anthropocene Era, meaning that human beings are, for the first time in history, altering the shape and destiny of our earth. Our planet is moving toward a time when the future of human life on Earth is called into question.

The deteriorating condition of our earth poses three challenges to Christians.

Challenge number one: The need to recall the ecological basis of our faith tradition.

Human beings are made in the image of God. They reflect the Creator. Hills and streams, mountains, the animals of the deep forest and fish of the sea also reflect the beauty and majesty of the Creator. "Ask the animals, and they will teach you; and the birds of the air, and they will tell you; ask the plants of the earth, and they will teach you; and the fish of the sea will declare to you. Who among all of these does not know that the hand of the Lord has done all this? In God's hand is the life of every living thing and the breath of every human being" (Job 12:7-10). John of Damascus (675-749) expressed this succinctly when he said, "The whole earth is an icon of the face of God." Centuries later Martin Luther said, "God writes the Gospel not in the Bible alone, but also on trees and in the flowers and clouds and stars."

Challenge number two: The need to redefine humanity's relationship with the rest of creation.

We especially need to gain a fresh appreciation of the reality that the physical, animal, and human aspects of creation are all interconnected and interdependent. Rain waters the earth and nourishes the crops which feed the human community. Drought dries the land; the dry land will not grow grain, leading to desertification. Forests support many varieties of animal and plant life, from lichens that live on tree trunks to insects and animals small and large that find their homes in the forest. But when forests are clear-cut, all the plants and animals that depended upon the trees and the forest floor die with the trees. Rising atmospheric temperatures lead to rising sea levels, which force evacuation of people who live on low-lying coastlines and coral atolls. If we disturb one aspect of the natural world, other aspects will suffer; if we allow one species to become extinct, the lives that depended upon it will also be lost.

Challenge number three: The need to employ the liturgical resources of our faith to help Christians address the problems of our earthly home.

We have long regarded the natural world as something apart from ourselves, to be exploited for our own ends. Now we are being called to a conversion of attitude and action, understanding at long last that everything is connected. Yet there are powerful political and economic forces that deny the reality of global warming and climate change and of human responsibility for the degradation of the environment. There is also indifference or confusion on the part of many who regularly attend worship.

To underline our need to repent of our indifference and unwillingness to act, the present Ecumenical Patriarch Bartholomew I has written:

> Responding to the environmental crisis is a matter of truthfulness to God, humanity, and the created order. It is not too far-fetched to speak of environmental damage as being a contemporary heresy or natural terrorism. We have repeatedly condemned this behavior as nothing less than sinful. For humans to cause species to become extinct and to destroy the biological diversity of God's creation; for humans to degrade the integrity of the Earth by causing changes in its climate, by stripping the Earth of its

natural forests, or by destroying its wetlands; for humans to injure other humans with disease by contaminating the Earth's waters, its land, its air, and its life with poisonous substances—all these are sins before God, humanity and the world. We have tended to restrict the notion of sin to the individual sense of guilt or the social sense of wrongdoing. Yet sin also contains a cosmic dimension, and repentance from environmental sin demands a radical transformation of the way we perceive the natural world and a tangible change in the way we choose to live.

How may the churches effectively touch the hearts and minds of Christians so that we accept our God-given responsibility to care for creation in the face of this unprecedented ecological crisis? The United Church of Canada responds to that question in this way:

> Rites of Christian worship have the potential to evoke within the worshipping community a powerful, new appreciation of the created order of which they are an intricately interwoven part, but within which they have unique responsibilities. Prayer and ritual action can help transform how communities and individuals view themselves and instill a hallowing of their relationship with all creation.
>
> All who lead Christian worship have unique opportunities, not only on Environmental Sabbath, but every week, to integrate prayers and services for creation as part of regular worship. Through such integration, all humanity might discover a deeper reverence for God, a more profound awareness of the fragility and oneness of creation, and a greater resolve to mend creation.

God's Good Earth is offered to worship leaders and congregations as a resource shaped by the challenges outlined above and by our conviction that worship is the most powerful means the Holy Spirit uses to transform and equip Christians as they seek to live faithful lives, serving God and caring for God's creation.

We believe that such a transformation is not only possible, but absolutely essential if Planet Earth is to survive healthy and whole as far into the future as we can imagine and beyond. As a contribution to this journey of transformation, we have prepared fifty-two liturgies, each consisting of prayers, Scripture, song, contemporary reflections, and silent contemplation. May those who enter into this journey of praise and prayer have their faith in God the Creator strengthened, their gratitude for the wonders of God's creation deepened, and their commitment to act on behalf of God's good earth enhanced.

SOURCES

Genesis 2:7 and Genesis 2:15 from *The Jerusalem Bible*, ed. Alexander Jones (Garden City, NY: Doubleday, 1966). © 1996 by Darton, Longman & Todd, Ltd. and Doubleday, a division of Penguin Random House LLC. Reprinted by permission.

Pope Francis, *Laudato Si'*, accessed December 1, 2017, Vatican.va, 91. © Libreria Editrice Vaticana. Used by permission.

Dimitrios I, "Message by H.A.H. Ecumenical Patriarch Dimitrios upon the Day of Prayer for the Protection of Creation (01/09/1989)," Ecumenical Patriarchate, accessed February 9, 2017, https://www.patriarchate.org/-/message-by-h-a-h-ecumenical-patriarch-dimitrios-upon-the-day-of-prayer-for-the-protection-of-creation-01-09-1989-.

Patriarch Bartholomew I, "The Orthodox Church and the Environmental Crisis: Spiritual Insights and Personal Reflections," in *Holy Ground: A Gathering of Voices on Caring for Creation*, ed. Lyndsay Moseley et al. (San Francisco: Sierra Club Books, 2008), 37–38. © by the Sierra Club and individual authors as credited. Reprinted by permission of Counterpoint Press.

"To Live with Respect in Creation" in United Church of Canada, *Celebrate God's Presence: A Book of Services for the United Church of Canada*, ed. Karen J. Verveda (Etobicoke, Ontario: United Church Publishing House, 2000), 613. Used with permission.

HOW TO USE THIS BOOK

Each of the fifty-two liturgies in *God's Good Earth* is a complete service of worship centered around a specific theme.

The book is intended as a resource to be used in several possible ways: for supplementing regular public worship every Sunday of the year; for regular use by small groups committed to environmental study and action; for enhancing daily devotion and reflection by individuals; as an anthology of environmental prayers; and for inspiring the design of additional environmental liturgies, especially on topics not addressed in this book.

All the topics addressed by the liturgies are connected. As listed in the contents, they fall into six general categories: God the Creator and God's Glorious Creation (7); God's Physical Universe (7); The Diversity of God's Creatures (6); The Human Community and Its Needs (11); The Whole Creation Groaning in Travail (14); and Hope and the Future (7).

Three topics are deemed so essential that two liturgies are devoted to each of them: *climate* (Climate Change, Global Warming); *food* (Agriculture with a Human Face, Farms); and *water* (Living Waters, Water).

Each liturgy is preceded by a brief epigraph that introduces the theme. It encourages meditation on the material that follows.

The fifty-two liturgies constitute a whole year but are not linked with the seasons of the church year. Begin whenever it makes sense for you and your congregation or group. Small groups and individuals intending to work their way through the book are encouraged to begin with Liturgy 1 (God the Creator).

Specifically, we suggest the following:

Each service may begin with a silent reflection on the theme. Silence may follow the Scripture Reading and the Reflection; it may also precede the times of prayer.

In the case of a small group, a shared response to the Reflection may be invited.

The Psalm or Canticle and the Litany may be recited in a variety of ways: divided between the leader and the community, between two sides of the worship space, or between men and women. Regular type denotes the role of the leader(s); bold type the response by the community.

The Hymn at the close of each liturgy may be sung to the tune suggested or to some other tune of the same meter. Most of the tunes can be found in one or more of the major denominational hymnals currently in use.

The liturgies are enhanced by supplementary material to be found at the end of the book: indexes of hymns and Scripture readings; a list of authors of the contemporary reflections; and a wide range of additional hymns for use when an opening hymn is desired.

Any of these liturgies may include a celebration of the Eucharist: if needed, a passage from one of the Gospels is read. Then, following the Prayers of Confession and Intercession, bread and wine are offered at the altar, prayed over and shared according to the normal practice of the particular congregation. The service then ends with the Hymn and Benediction.

Settings, signs, and symbols: This book provides Scripture, prayers, hymns, and reflections on different aspects of creation. We encourage you to use them as starting points for your own creativity and imagination. In order for congregations to experience the fullest possible impact, we suggest that you see each liturgy in the context of its larger setting, whether it be a church, community building, city park, or empty lot. Worshipping outside in nature's cathedral would be ideal, but recognizing that this is often not possible, efforts can be made to bring the outside indoors. For Trees and Forests, Liturgy 12, for example, the sanctuary can be filled with small trees, ferns of the forest, moss, stones, and dripping water. For Oceans, Liturgy 8, sand, driftwood, dried seaweed, shells, and wave-tossed stones can be brought in. For Deserts, 13, sand and desert plants can be introduced. For Sky, 9, and Universe, 14, images of planets and stars can be projected on the ceiling and walls of darkened sanctuaries.

Incorporating actual artifacts from the environment may not always be possible, but photographs of nature in all its glory, projected throughout the church, would provide a magnificent backdrop for the liturgies in the sections God the Creator and God's Glorious Creation, 1–7, and God's Physical Universe, 8–14. Images of pain, suffering, and violence could poignantly illustrate Liturgies 32–45 in the section The Whole Creation Groaning in Travail. Just one image of a long stream of thousands of migrants struggling along as they carry babies and belongings to a checkpoint would effectively elucidate the substance of Liturgy 40, Migrants. This would enhance the litany whose words include, "O God of all nations and peoples, you watch over a world in turmoil. Walk with us as we wait on your promise. Come, O come, Emmanuel."

Symbolic gestures and offerings, the incorporation into each liturgy of the cultural diversity of the congregation, and especially the participation of children, all deserve careful attention. How best to do this is beyond the space limitations of this book, but it is our hope that you will enliven each liturgy with your own free-flowing ideas, passion, and creativity.

God the Creator and God's Glorious Creation

1. GOD THE CREATOR

The ancient Apostles' and Nicene Creeds both begin by affirming belief in God, "the maker of heaven and earth." Sixteen centuries later, Earth is crying out for this belief to be actualized and all of creation cherished and restored to wholeness and health.

Seek the One who made the Pleiades and Orion, who turns the dusk to dawn, the day to the darkest night, who summons the waters of the sea and pours them over the land. *(Amos 5:8)*

PRAYER OF PRAISE AND THANKSGIVING

How glorious you are in the triumph of the seasons. Every creature awakes to new life and joyfully sings your praises with a thousand tongues: you are the source of life, the conqueror of death. By the light of the moon nightingales sing; the plains and the woods put on their wedding garments, white as snow. Glory to you for bringing from the darkness of the earth an endless variety of colors, tastes, and scents. Glory to you for the warmth and tenderness of the world of nature. Glory to you for surrounding us with tens of thousands of your works. Glory to you for the depth of your wisdom: the whole world is a living sign of it. Glory to you; on our knees we kiss the traces of your unseen hand.

Glory to you for setting before us the dazzling light of your eternal beauty. Glory to you for the hope of the imperishable splendor of immortality. Glory to you, O Holy God, from age to age. **Amen.** *(Metropolitan Tryphon)*

CANTICLE   JUDITH 16:13-16

I will sing to my God a new song:
O Lord, you are great and glorious,
    wonderful in strength, invincible.
Let all your creatures serve you,
    for you spoke, and they were made.
You sent forth your spirit, and it formed them;
    there is none that can resist your voice.
For the mountains shall be shaken to their foundations with the waters;
    before your glance the rocks shall melt like wax.
But to those who fear you,
    you show mercy.
For every sacrifice as a fragrant offering is a small thing, . . .
    but whoever fears the Lord is great forever.

PSALM 147:12-18

Praise the Lord, O Jerusalem!
    Praise your God, O Zion!
For he strengthens the bars of your gates;
    he blesses your children within you.
He grants peace within your borders;
    he fills you with the finest of wheat.
He sends out his command to the earth;
    his word runs swiftly.
He gives snow like wool;
    he scatters frost like ashes.
He hurls down hail like crumbs—
    who can stand before his cold?
He sends out his word, and melts them;
    he makes his wind blow, and the waters flow.

SCRIPTURE   ISAIAH 42:5-8A, 10-12

I am the Lord God. I created the heavens like an open tent above. I made the earth and everything that grows on it. I am the source of life for all who live on this earth, so listen to what I say. I chose you to bring justice, and I am here at your side. I selected you and sent you to bring light and my promise of hope to the nations. You will give sight to the blind; you will set prisoners free from dark dungeons. My name is the Lord! Tell the whole world to sing a new song to the Lord! Tell those who sail the ocean and those who live far away to join in the praise. Tell the tribes of the desert and everyone in the mountains to celebrate and sing. Let them announce his praises everywhere.

LITANY

O most high, omnipotent, good Lord God, to you belong praise, glory, honor, and all blessing. For our brother the sun, who is our day and who brings us the light, who is fair and radiant with a very great splendor:
Praise and bless the Lord.

For our sister the moon, and for all the stars, which you have set clear and lovely in the heavens; for our brother the wind, and for air and clouds, doldrums and all weather:
Praise and bless the Lord.

For our sister water, who serves us and is humble and precious and chaste; for our brother fire, by whom you light up the night, and who is fair and merry, and very mighty and strong:
Praise and bless the Lord.

For our mother the earth, who sustains and keeps us, and brings forth various fruits, and flowers of many colors, and grass; for all who pardon one another for your love's sake, and who bear weakness and tribulation:
Praise and bless the Lord.

Blessed are they who peaceably endure, walking by your most holy will, for you, O Most High, shall give them a crown.
Praise and bless the Lord, and give thanks to God, and serve God with great humility. Amen. *(Attributed to St. Francis of Assisi)*

REFLECTION   FRANCIS S. COLLINS

Scientists like me seek to understand nature using the tools of science. We ask "how" questions. But it is also clear that there are some really important "why" questions that science cannot answer, such as: Why is there something instead of nothing? Why are we here? In those domains I have found that faith provides a far better path.

But it's also true that science can point to God. A close consideration of the universe leads one to marvel at its beauty, and wonder about the source of such awesome elegance. The universe has exquisite order, physical laws that follow precise mathematical formulas, and a breathtaking fine-tuning of physical constants that allows the possibility of complexity. Contemplating this, an open-minded observer is almost forced to conclude that there must be a "mind" behind all this. And that intelligence must be outside of space and time or the Big Bang singularity makes no sense. The evidence from nature thus points to a Creator. Faced with that evidence, the purely naturalistic view I embraced in my early twenties looms like the most irrational of all choices; as Chesterton said, "Atheism is the most daring of all dogmas, since it is the assertion of a universal negative."

I have never encountered an irreconcilable conflict between the truths of science and the truths of faith. They just provide answers to different questions. God can be found in the laboratory or the cathedral. And for a believer, science can be a form of worship.

Francis S. Collins is a physician-geneticist who led the Human Genome Project. He is also the author of the best-seller The Language of God, *and the founder of the BioLogos Foundation, a group that fosters discussions about the intersection of Christianity and science. He currently serves as the director of the National Institutes of Health.*

PRAYERS OF CONFESSION AND INTERCESSION

Omnipotent God, Creator and Sustainer of sacred seas, lands and skies—your loving hand is open wide to satisfy the needs of every living creature, yet we have turned against you and against your creation. We have failed to love your creation and all your creatures. We confess that we have polluted your waters and lands and soiled your heavens; we have ignored the weak and vulnerable and those who lack justice. Our thoughtlessness, passivity and greed have put all creation at the brink of extinction. We repent of our sins against you and your creation, and remembering the account that we must one day give, we vow to work to restore all that is broken, polluted and harmed with the help of Christ our Lord, who with you and the Holy Spirit lives and reigns, one God, for ever and ever. **Amen.** *(Anne Rowthorn)*

Ever fashioning, ever renewing God, may we never lose our sense of awe, wonder and amazement at this universe of which we are so insignificant a part. Yet may we never be so overawed that we forget that, great as you are, and vast and intricate as are your works, you know and love each one of us, and we are ever in your care. **Amen.** *(Edmund Banyard)*

HYMN   THOMAS H. TROEGER

1. Night and day this planet sings:
   peepers peeping in the dark,
   roaring rivers, bubbling springs,
   trills and fanfares from the lark.
   To the richness of earth's song
   add the song our voices raise,
   giving witness we belong
   to the God we love and praise:

2. song whose beauty deepens prayer
   with the Spirit's groans and sighs,
   song that fills the very air
   with joys, laments and cries,
   song that echoes through our hymns,
   music heard in heaven's height,
   song whose gladness over-brims
   with the gospel's truth and light,

3. song that wakens hopes and dreams,
   sacred visions that inspire
   the prophetic word that streams
   from God's holy wind and fire,
   song that strengthens those who yearn
   to embody what is just,
   song that helps us to discern
   how to live by faith and trust,

4. song that honors Christ who lives,
   risen, risen! from the grave,
   song that tells how Christ forgives
   all the world he came to save,
   song the morning stars first sang
   when God made creation new
   and the heavens rang and sang:
   Praise, O Lord, O praise to you!

Tune: SALZBURG, 7.7.7.7.D.

Let the sea roar, and all that fills it;
  the world and those who live in it.
Let the floods clap their hands;
  let the hills sing together for joy *(Psalm 98:7-8)*

SOURCES

Amos 5:8 from *The Inclusive Bible* (Landham, MD: Rowman & Littlefield, 2007). A Sheed & Ward Book published by Rowman & Littlefield Publishers, Inc. All rights reserved. Used by permission.

Metropolitan Tryphon [Prince Boris Petrovich Turkestanov], Ikos 3 of "An Akathist in Praise of God's Creation," in *SYNDESMOS Orthodoxy and Ecology Resource Book*, Annex 1, *Orthodox Services for the Creation*, ed. Alexander Belopopsky and Dmitri Oikonomou (Bialystok, Poland: Orthdruk Orthodox Printing House, 1996), 20–25, alt.

Isaiah 42:5-8a, 10-12 from *Contemporary English Version* (New York: American Bible Society, 1995). © 1995 American Bible Society.

St. Francis of Assisi, "Canticle of the Sun," as altered in *The United Methodist Book of Worship* (Nashville, TN: United Methodist Publishing House, 1992), no. 507. Public domain.

Francis S. Collins, reflection written especially for *God's Good Earth*. © 2018 Francis S. Collins. Used by permission.

Anne Rowthorn, "We Repent of Our Sins against You and Your Creation," inspired by prayers for Rogation Days for Stewardship of Creation in Episcopal Church, *Book of Common Prayer* (New York: Church Publishing, 1979), 259.

Edmund Banyard, "Ever fashioning, ever renewing . . . ," in *Dare to Dream: A Prayer and Worship Anthology from around the World*, ed. Geoffrey Duncan (London: HarperCollins, 1995), 27. © Edmund Banyard. Used by permission.

"Night and Day This Planet Sings" by Thomas Troeger © Oxford University Press 2015. Reproduced by permission. All rights reserved.

2. GOD'S GLORIOUS CREATION

God is revealed through every aspect of creation—human beings, made in God's image; animals, plants, forests, mountains, flowing streams, a single dandelion pushing its way up through a city sidewalk; the blazing sunset before dusk; the gleaming stars enfolding Earth like a blanket. All of God's creation is glorious!

This grand show is eternal. It is always sunrise somewhere; the dew is never dried all at once; a shower is forever falling; vapor ever rising. Eternal God, eternal sunrise, eternal sunset, eternal dawn and gloaming, on seas and continents and islands, each in turn, as the round earth rolls. *(John Muir)*

PRAYERS OF PRAISE AND THANKSGIVING

How glorious, O God, is the universe that you have made. Your ever-creating love encompasses all. You are both near and far. You are as close to us as the air we breathe and the nightingale chanting in the meadow. To reach the nearest star would take several lifetimes, so vast is the distance that separates us. Your act of creation continues as new stars are born amidst a whirl of dust and gases, exploding in an ecstasy of light. Encompass us in your presence as we pray in your Holy Name, in the name of your Son and of the Holy Spirit. **Amen.** *(Adapted from Edward Hays)*

O Holy God, how lovely it is to be your guest: breezes full of scent; mountains reaching to the skies; waters like a boundless mirror, reflecting the sun's golden rays and the scudding clouds. All nature murmurs mysteriously, breathing depths of tenderness; birds and beasts bear the imprint of your love. Blessed are you, Mother Earth, in your overwhelming loveliness, which wakens our yearning for happiness that will last forever. All creation sings to you: **Alleluia!** *(Metropolitan Tryphon)*

PSALM 65:5B-7, 9-13

    O God of our salvation;
you are the hope of all the ends of the earth
    and of the farthest seas.
By your strength you established the mountains;
    you are girded with might.
You silence the roaring of the seas,
    the roaring of their waves,
    the tumult of the peoples. . . .
You visit the earth and water it,
    you greatly enrich it;
the river of God is full of water;
    you provide the people with grain,
    for so you have prepared it.
You water its furrows abundantly,
    settling its ridges,
softening it with showers,
    and blessing its growth.
You crown the year with your bounty;
    your wagon tracks overflow with richness.
The pastures of the wilderness overflow,
    the hills gird themselves with joy,
the meadows clothe themselves with flocks,
    the valleys deck themselves with grain,
    they shout and sing together for joy.

SCRIPTURE   GENESIS 1:1-5, 26-27, 31A

In the beginning when God created the heavens and the earth, the earth was a formless void and darkness covered the face of the deep, while a wind from God swept over the face of the waters. Then God said, "Let there be light"; and there was light. And God saw that the light was good; and God separated the light from the darkness. God called the light Day, and the darkness he called Night. And there was evening and there was morning, the first day. . . . Then God said, "Let us make humankind in our image, according to our likeness; and let them have dominion over the fish of the sea, and over the birds of the air, and over the cattle, and over all the wild animals of the earth, and over every creeping thing that creeps upon the earth."

So God created humankind in his image,
   in the image of God he created them;
   male and female he created them. . . .
God saw everything that he had made, and indeed, it was very good.

LITANY

A Prayer for Air:
   We thank you, God, for the gift of air—
   for cool breezes and brisk winds that refresh us,
   for blue skies and crystal-clear nights,
   for the smells of every season—summer and winter, spring and fall.
   Most of all, we thank you for the air that gives us life.
   You offer your Spirit to us with every breath we take.
   May we protect this gift that gives us life.

A Prayer for Water:
   Thanks be for water
   that sustains the life of animals, fish, and plants,
   that cleans our bodies and blesses our souls.
   For the water of tears that wash away our grief,
   for the water of slides, lakes, pools, and oceans where we can play and
have fun. Thanks be for water.
   Your water gives us new life.
   May we treasure this gift and share it with others.

A Prayer for Fire:
   Thank you for fire and the many ways we use it,
   to cook our food,
   to sterilize and purify,
   to smelt ore and form metal,
   to warm our homes, and
   to light our dark nights.
   You light our way and enlighten our minds.
   May we be open to the fire of your Spirit.

A Prayer for Earth:

Thank you for the ground beneath our feet,

your good earth that gives life to all.

In a mystery we don't understand, green plants spring forth from your darkness. Canyons and mountains, plains and deserts show us your infinite imagination. We thank you for this firm foundation on which to build our homes and our lives.

May we always love this land as you love it.

May we care for this good earth that gives us such good life. *(Talitha Arnold)*

REFLECTION   THOMAS BERRY

The story of the universe is now being told. . . . We begin to understand our human identity with all other modes of existence that constitute with us the single universe community. The one story includes us all. We are, everyone, cousins of one another. Every being is intimately present to and immediately influencing every other being.

We see quite clearly that what happens to the non-human happens to the human; what happens to the outer world happens to the inner world. If the outer world is diminished in its grandeur, then the emotional, imaginative, intellectual, and spiritual life of the human is diminished or extinguished. Without the soaring birds, the great forests, the sounds and coloration of the insects, the free-flowing streams, the flowering fields, the sight of the clouds by day and the stars at night, we become impoverished in all that makes us human.

There is now developing a profound mystique of the natural world. Beyond the technical comprehension of what is happening and the directions in which we need to change, we now experience the deep mysteries of existence through the wonders of the world about us. . . . We are now experiencing a moment of significance far beyond what any of us can imagine.

One of the United States' preeminent advocates for the earth, Thomas Berry (1914–2009) told us that "The Great Work" of us all is to carry out the transition from a period of human devastation of the planet to a period when humans are present to the planet in a mutually beneficial manner. The primary guide to the future, the primary university, becomes the universe itself.

2. God's Glorious Creation

PRAYERS OF CONFESSION AND INTERCESSION

Creator God, breathing your own life into our being, you gave us the gift of life: You placed us on this earth, with its minerals and waters, flowers and fruits, living creatures of grace and beauty! You gave us the care of the earth. Today you call us: "Where are you; what have you done?" O God of love, you gave us the gift of peoples—of cultures, races and colors—to share our lives with. Today you ask: "Where is your brother, your sister?" The refugees, the oppressed and voiceless cry out to you. Forgive us, Creator God, and reconcile us to your creation. Teach us, O God of Love, that the earth and all its fullness is yours, the world and those who dwell in it. Call us yet again to safeguard the gift of life. **Amen.** *(Konrad Raiser)*

Creator of the land, the water, and the sky, come and renew the face of the whole earth. Giver of life, we are the sons and daughters of your holy breath; give us new awareness of our role in the world of your making. Savior of the world, touch us in the power of your new creation, that we might hold in reverence the creation you have given. God of sparrows and wild flowers, open our eyes to the inter-connectedness of all things. Weave us into our rightful place in your great design; strengthen the will of people everywhere to appreciate your creation, and to seek to live in deep and caring harmony within it. So may the whole earth be truly blessed by our hard work and joyful living, by your presence and ours. **Amen.** *(The Anglican Church of Canada)*

HYMN   ST. FRANCIS OF ASSISI, TR. WILLIAM H. DRAPER

1. All creatures of our God most high,
   let praise resound in earth and sky:
   Alleluia, alleluia!
   Bright burning sun with golden beams,
   pale silver moon that gently gleams,

   Refrain:
   O praise God, O praise God,
   Alleluia, alleluia, alleluia!

2. Great rushing winds and breezes soft,
   you clouds that ride the heavens aloft,
   O praise God, Alleluia!
   Fair rising morn, with praise rejoice,
   stars nightly shining, find a voice.
   Refrain.

3. Swift flowing water, pure and clear,
   make music for your Lord to hear,
   Alleluia, alleluia!
   Fire, so intense and fiercely bright,
   you give to us both warmth and light.
   Refrain.

4. Dear mother earth, you day by day
   unfold your blessings on our way;
   Alleluia, alleluia!
   All flowers and fruits that in you grow,
   let them God's glory also show.
   Refrain.

5. All you with mercy in your heart,
   forgiving others, take your part,
   O sing now: Alleluia!
   All you that pain and sorrow bear,
   take heart and cast on God your care.
   Refrain.

6. And even you, most gentle death,
   waiting to hush our final breath,
   Alleluia, alleluia!
   you lead back home the child of God,
   for Christ our Lord that way has trod.
   Refrain.

7. Let all things their creator bless,
   and worship God in humbleness,
   Alleluia, alleluia!
   Praise God the Father, praise the Son,
   and praise the Spirit, Three in One.
   Refrain.

Tune: LASST UNS ERFREUEN, 8.8.4.4.8.8.
and Refrain

God of the galaxies, God of the starburst and sunlit morning, God of the forest and shining sea, God of the blooming desert and rolling grasslands—shine on us today and bless us with your presence. *(Anne Rowthorn)*

2. God's Glorious Creation

SOURCES

John Muir, *John of the Mountains: The Unpublished Journals of John Muir*, ed. Linnie Marsh Wolfe, 2nd ed. (Madison: University of Wisconsin Press, 1979), 438, alt. Public domain.

Edward Hays, "How wondrous, O God . . .," in *Prayers for a Planetary Pilgrim: A Personal Manual for Prayer and Ritual* (Easton, KS: Forest of Peace Books, 1988), 33, alt. © 1989, 2008. Used with the permission of the publisher, Forest of Peace, an imprint of Ave Maria Press, Inc., Notre Dame, Indiana 46556. www.forestofpeace.com.

Metropolitan Tryphon [Prince Boris Petrovich Turkestanov], Kontakion 2 of "An Akathist in Praise of God's Creation," in *SYNDESMOS Orthodoxy and Ecology Resource Book*, Annex 1, *Orthodox Services for the Creation*, ed. Alexander Belopopsky and Dmitri Oikonomou (Bialystok, Poland: Orthdruk Orthodox Printing House, 1996), 20–25, alt.

Talitha Arnold, "A Prayer of Thanks for the Four Elements," incorporating ideas from the children of the United Church of Santa Fe, NM, alt. Used by permission.

Thomas Berry, *The Great Work: Our Way into the Future* (New York: Bell Tower, 1999), 200–201.

Konrad Raiser, "Jesus Christ—The Life of the World: A Meditation on the Theme of the Sixth Assembly," *The Ecumenical Review* 33, no. 3 (1981): 6. Used by permission of World Council of Churches.

"Creator of the land . . . ," in United Church of Canada, *Celebrate God's Presence: A Book of Services for the United Church of Canada*, ed. Karen J. Verveda (Etobicoke, Ontario: United Church Publishing House, 2000), 623. Adapted from Anglican Church of Canada, *Occasional Celebrations of the Anglican Church of Canada* (Toronto: Anglican Book Centre, 1992), 185–86. Used with permission of United Church Publishing House and Anglican Church of Canada.

St. Francis of Assisi, "All Creatures of Our God and King" (1225), trans. and paraphrased by William H. Draper (1910), alt. Public domain.

Anne Rowthorn, "God of the Galaxies" © 2016 Anne Rowthorn.

3. SACRED EARTH

Imagine the transformation that would result if we truly believed that all the earth was sacred—every inch and mile and mountain—and every land a holy land.

Earth is crammed with heaven, and every common bush afire with God; but only those who see take off their shoes. *(Elizabeth Barrett Browning)*

PRAYERS OF PRAISE AND THANKSGIVING

God of the new dawn, all the earth resounds in joyful praise of your mighty deeds. As we sing psalms and hymns to you, keep our hearts humble and remind us daily that true wisdom is found only in obedience to you. **Amen.** *(Nancy M. Raabe)*

Creating God, in you everything on Earth and in the heavens is bound together in perfect harmony. If we lose the sweetness of the waters, we lose the life of the land. If we lose the life of the land, we lose the majesty of the forest. If we lose the majesty of the forest, we lose the purity of the air. If we lose the purity of the air, we lose the creatures of the Earth. Open our eyes to behold your creation. Create in us a new spirit of awareness of our place in your delicate balance; transform our hearts that we may reclaim our sense of awe and wonder. Quicken our understanding that we may acknowledge our responsibility and strengthen our resolve to work with you for the healing of your creation; through our Holy God, Savior of the world. **Amen.** *(Inspired by the Earth Charter)*

3. Sacred Earth

PSALM 66:1-9

Make a joyful noise to God, all the earth;
> **sing the glory of his name;**
> **give to him glorious praise.**

Say to God, "How awesome are your deeds!
> **Because of your great power, your enemies cringe before you.**

All the earth worships you;
> they sing praises to you,
> sing praises to your name.". . .

Come and see what God has done:
> **he is awesome in his deeds among mortals.**

He turned the sea into dry land;
> they passed through the river on foot.

There we rejoiced in him,
> **who rules by his might forever,**

whose eyes keep watch on the nations—
> let the rebellious not exalt themselves. . . .

Bless our God, O peoples,
> **let the sound of his praise be heard,**

who has kept us among the living,
> and has not let our feet slip.

SCRIPTURE   PROVERBS 8:22-31

The Lord created me at the beginning of his work,
> the first of his acts of long ago.

Ages ago I was set up,
> at the first, before the beginning of the earth.

When there were no depths I was brought forth,
> when there were no springs abounding with water.

Before the mountains had been shaped,
> before the hills, I was brought forth—

when he had not yet made earth and fields,
> or the world's first bits of soil.

When he established the heavens, I was there,
> when he drew a circle on the face of the deep,

when he made firm the skies above,
> when he established the fountains of the deep,

when he assigned to the sea its limit,
    so that the waters might not transgress his command,
when he marked out the foundations of the earth,
    then I was beside him, like a master worker;
and I was daily his delight,
    rejoicing before him always,
rejoicing in his inhabited world
    and delighting in the human race.

LITANY

Beloved God, known to your creation by a thousand different names, we thank you for giving us power through your Spirit to reveal your life to the world:
strengthen, bless, and guide all that we do.

We thank you for your creation, and pray for the earth that you have given us to cherish and protect:
nourish us in your love for all that you have made.

Every part of this earth is sacred; every shining pine needle, every sandy shore.
Every mist in the dark woods; every clearing and every humming insect is holy,

The rocky crest, the juices of the meadow, the beasts and all the people,
All belong to the same family.

Teach your children that the earth is our mother. Whatever befalls the earth befalls the children of earth.
The earth's murmur is the voice of our father's father.

We are part of the earth and the earth is part of us.
The rivers are our brothers; they quench our thirst.

The perfumed flowers are our sisters.
The air is precious, for we all share the same breath.

The wind that gave our grandparents breath also receives their last sigh, Give our children the spirit of life.
This we know, the earth does not belong to us; we belong to the earth.

This we know: all things are connected, like the blood that unites one family.
All things are connected.

Our God is the same God whose compassion is equal for all,
For we did not weave the web of life; we are merely strands of it.

Whatever we do to the web, we do to ourselves.
Let us give thanks for the web of life in the circle that connects us.

Thanks be to God, the God of all, the God known by a thousand names.
Amen. *(Attributed to Chief Seattle)*

REFLECTION   WES JACKSON

During the last five hundred years or so, the ratio of the domestic to the wild has been so altered, especially in the Western Hemisphere, that wilderness itself has become an artifact of civilization. Only civilization can save wilderness now; the wild that produced us, that we were dependent upon, is now our dependent.

We pay homage to wildness in the United States by regarding pristine wilderness as a kind of saint. That creates more problems. Either all of the earth is holy or none is. Every square foot of it deserves our respect or none does. Harlem and East Saint Louis and Iowa and Kansas and the rest of the world where wilderness has been destroyed must come to be loved by enough of us, or wilderness, too, is doomed.

Born and raised on a Kansas farm, Wes Jackson (b. 1936) founded the Land Institute in 1976, guided by the simple belief that the model for sound, healthy, organic agriculture is nature itself. The plants and animals that thrive are those that are native to the place. Buffalo, tall grass, and prairie sod kept the soil healthy in the Great Plains for millennia, and only when cattle replaced buffalo and wheat the native prairie grasses did the soil begin to erode.

PRAYERS OF CONFESSION AND INTERCESSION

Eternal God, we confess to our sinfulness. You made the world a paradise but we have turned our lands into places of tears and unhappiness. People are fighting with each other, race against race. The holocaust of chauvinism sweeps through countries devouring humanity, terrorizing us into submission. Liberating One, free us from all bondage so that our faith in you will make us free to create with courage a new world. ***Amen.*** *(Anglican Consultative Council)*

O Lord, grant us grace to grow deeper in respecting and caring for your creation. Help us to recognize the sacredness of all your creatures as signs of your wondrous love. Spark our imagination so we might find new ways to live harmoniously with creation and new technologies to reverse the damage we have done to your creation. Help us turn from selfish consumption of resources meant for all to see the impacts of our choices on the poorest and most vulnerable on our planet. **Amen.** *(Catholic Relief Services)*

HYMN   RUTH DUCK

1. Creative God, you spread the earth
   with life in many forms:
   the deer and elk and columbine,
   the bee in humming swarms.
   Forgive us for each flower and bird
   now vanished by our hand.
   Teach us to treat with loving care
   the creatures of the land.

2. The planet teemed with living things
   before all human birth,
   and even fire and beasts of prey
   renewed the life of earth.
   Forgive us that, the last to come,
   we threaten sea and air.
   Teach us to tend life's fragile web
   with wise and tender care.

3. O playful God, you fill the field
   with lavender and blue.
   You paint the bird with indigo,
   with red or tawny hue.
   Forgive us that we grieve your heart,
   destroying what you do,
   and teach us simpler, gentler ways
   to live on earth with you.

   Tune: KINGSFOLD, C.M.D.

Earth, our mother, set us on the paths of peace in full accord with heaven. Holy God, Wise and Immortal One, forever keep your earth in grace and splendor. *(Atharva Veda)*

3. Sacred Earth

SOURCES

Elizabeth Barrett Browning, *Aurora Leigh*, in *The Oxford Book of English Mystical Verse*, ed. D.H. S. Nicholson and A. H. E. Lee (Oxford: Oxford University Press, 1917), 152. Public domain.

Nancy M. Raabe, "God of the New Dawn," in *Bread for the Day: Daily Bible Readings and Prayers 2016* (Minneapolis: Augsburg Fortress, 2016), 139. Used by permission.

Anne Rowthorn, inspired by Interfaith Coordinating Committee on Religion and the Earth (ICCRE), "An Earth Charter."

Litany developed by Peter Holroyd from words attributed to Chief Seattle, alt. Used by permission of Marcia Holroyd.

Wes Jackson, *Nature as Measure: The Selected Essays of Wes Jackson* (Berkeley: Counterpoint Press, 2011), 63–64. © 2011 by Wes Jackson. Reprinted by permission of Counterpoint Press.

"Eternal God we confess to our . . . ," in *Prayers Encircling the World: An International Anthology* (Louisville, KY: Westminster John Knox, 1998), prayer 184, p. 149. © Anglican Consultative Council. Used by permission of the Anglican Consultative Council.

"Creation," in *Climate Change Prayer Booklet* (n.p.: Caritas, Aotearoa New Zealand, 2017), http://www.caritas.org.nz/resource/2159, alt. Adapted from Catholic Relief Services. Used by permission of Caritas, Aotearoa New Zealand.

Ruth Duck, "Creative God, You Spread the Earth" © 1992, GIA Publications, Inc. Used by permission.

Atharva-Veda XII, "Hymn to the Earth," in *Hymns from the Vedas: Original Text and English Translation*, trans. Abinash Chandra Bose (Bombay: Asia Publishing House, 1966), 363–79, alt.

4. LIVING WATERS

Water, life's most essential compound, circulates through lands and living bodies—refreshing, regulating, cleansing, purifying, nourishing, replenishing, and carrying away waste. Two-thirds of the earth is water (four-fifths if ice is included). Jesus was baptized in the River Jordan and we, too, are baptized into the living waters of life.

Do not be afraid, Upright One, whom I choose! For I will pour down rain on parched ground, showers on dry soil—I will pour my spirit on your descendants and my blessing on your offspring! They will spring up like grass in a spring meadow, like poplar trees by flowing streams. *(Isaiah 44:2b-4)*

PRAYER OF PRAISE AND THANKSGIVING

Holy God, holy and merciful, holy and mighty, you are the river of life, you are the everlasting wellspring, you are the fire of rebirth. Glory to you for oceans and lakes, for rivers and streams. Honor to you for cloud and rain, for dew and snow. Your waters are below us, around us, above us: our life is born in you. You are the fountain of resurrection.

Praise to you for saving waters: Noah and the animals survive the flood, Hagar discovers your well. The Israelites escape through the sea, and they drink from your gushing rock. Naaman washes his leprosy away, and the Samaritan woman will never be thirsty again.

Satisfy all our thirst with your living water, Jesus Christ, our Savior, who lives and reigns with you and the Holy Spirit, one God, now and forever. **Amen.** *(Evangelical Lutheran Church in America)*

4. Living Waters

CANTICLE   ISAIAH 55:1-3A, 5

Ho, everyone who thirsts,
    come to the waters;
and you that have no money,
    come, buy and eat!
Come, buy wine and milk
    without money and without price.
Why do you spend your money for that which is not bread,
    and your labor for that which does not satisfy?
Listen carefully to me, and eat what is good,
    and delight yourselves in rich food.
Incline your ear, and come to me;
    listen, so that you may live.
I will make with you an everlasting covenant. . . .
See, you shall call nations that you do not know,
    and nations that do not know you shall run to you,
because of the LORD your God, the Holy One of Israel,
    for he has glorified you.

SCRIPTURE   PSALM 107:35-38 AND JOHN 4:7-15

1. [God] turns a desert into pools of water,
    a parched land into springs of water.
And there he lets the hungry live,
    and they establish a town to live in;
they sow fields, and plant vineyards,
    and get a fruitful yield.
By his blessing they multiply greatly,
    and he does not let their cattle decrease.

2. A Samaritan woman came to draw water, and Jesus said to her, "Give me a drink." (His disciples had gone to the city to buy food.) The Samaritan woman said to him, "How is it that you, a Jew, ask a drink of me, a woman of Samaria?" (Jews do not share things in common with Samaritans.) Jesus answered her, "If you knew the gift of God, and who it is that is saying to you, 'Give me a drink,' you would have asked him, and he would have given you living water." The woman said to him, "Sir, you have no bucket, and the well is deep. Where do you get that living water? Are you greater than our

ancestor Jacob, who gave us the well, and with his sons and his flocks drank from it?" Jesus said to her, "Everyone who drinks of this water will be thirsty again, but those who drink of the water that I will give them will never be thirsty. The water that I will give will become in them a spring of water gushing up to eternal life." The woman said to him, "Sir, give me this water, so that I may never be thirsty or have to keep coming here to draw water."

LITANY

Creator God of the Universe, have mercy,
Creator, have mercy.

On your waters, that they may be clean and sustain a diverse community of life,
Creator, have mercy.

On coral reefs, on the animals, plants, and fish that inhabit them,
Creator, have mercy.

On ocean deeps teeming with life; on the open seas and all that travel upon them,
Creator, have mercy.

On rivers, bringing water to thirsty places,
Creator, have mercy.

On lakes and streams, home to a diversity of life.
Creator, have mercy.

On ponds and marshes, cradles of life,
Creator, have mercy.

On your wetlands and estuaries, on rocky coasts and beaches,
Creator, have mercy.

On islands and atolls, on oases and all outposts of life,
Creator, have mercy.

On glaciers and ice fields, holding the delicate balance of waters,
Creator, have mercy.

On storms, floods, and tempests, and all fearsome forces of weather,
Creator, have mercy.

On rains that water the earth causing plants to sprout and grow,
Creator, have mercy.

On snow and hail, sleet and winter cold, and the dormant things that wait for spring,
Creator have mercy.

On mists and fog silently watering the ground.
Creator, have mercy *(The Episcopal Church)*

REFLECTION   ANNE ROWTHORN

Water is humanity's cradle; it was our first home deep in our mother's womb. Water is all things to all of life; it is as close to us as the tear in our eye and as distant as the cloud hovering over the open sea. As the Tao reminds us, "Water benefits ten thousand things," though today we surely would not stop at ten thousand. Water is life-force, source of inspiration, wonder, solace and beauty. The water that courses through our bodies is the water that upholds and nourishes all that is created, every animal of the land, fish of the sea, bird of the air; every flower, every fern and great towering sequoia. Water in all its forms shapes the landscape of the world. Water created the mountains, plains and valleys of the earth; water is still creating, never ceasing. Water refreshes the soul and feeds the imagination. Water is life. We need to defend and protect it with our lives. John Muir said, "It is a blessed thing to go free in this world, to see God playing upon everything. His fingers upon the lightning and torrent, on every wave of sea and sky, and every living thing, making all together sing and shine in sweet accord, the one love-harmony of the Universe."

Anne Rowthorn is the editor and compiler of The Wisdom of John Muir *(Wilderness Press, 2012).*

PRAYERS OF CONFESSION AND INTERCESSION

Creator God of the universe who hovers over the waters, we confess that we have become alienated from Earth. We have polluted the rivers, wetlands, and lakes, oceans and estuaries, of our garden planet. We are sorry. We have polluted the waters of our planet with poisons and we have treated them as waste dumps. We have turned living waters into deathtraps. We have wasted precious water through greed, luxury living and carelessness. We are sorry and we beg for forgiveness so that the waters of Earth may once again sparkle and reflect your glory. **Amen.** *(Season of Creation)*

God who called us forth from the dust and watered our lands with countless streams and great rivers, we thank you for the garden you have set us to dwell in. And so, as of old, we turn again to the sky: Send your living waters upon us. Sprinkle us again with your purifying rains. Make your mountains fill with dancing streams; your valleys swell with splashing ponds as fertile as the River Jordan, as renewing as the waters of baptism, as overflowing as the cup of salvation. Feed all living things with your life-sustaining water as you fill them with your grace.

As we gaze upon this land that so thirsts for your water, let it remind us of all the thirsts in this world: the thirst for justice, the thirst for peace, the thirst for opportunity, the thirst for reconciliation, the thirst for hope.

When your blessings rain from the sky, and we kneel again at the pools and fountains, teach us to cup our hands, and gently, gracefully, in solidarity, turn first, and share with one another. **Amen.** *(Edward Hoyt)*

HYMN   ROBERT LOWRY

1. Shall we gather at the river,
   where bright angel feet have trod;
   with its crystal tide forever
   flowing by the throne of God?

   Refrain:
   Yes, we'll gather at the river,
   the beautiful, the beautiful river;
   gather with the saints at the river
   that flows by the throne of God.

2. On the margin of the river,
   washing up its silver spray,
   we will walk and worship ever,
   all the happy golden day. *Refrain.*

3. Ere we reach the shining river,
   lay we ev'ry burden down;
   grace our spirits will deliver,
   and provide a robe and crown. *Refrain.*

4. Soon we'll reach the shining river,
   soon our pilgrimage will cease;
   soon our happy hearts will quiver
   with the melody of peace. *Refrain.*

   Tune: SHALL WE GATHER AT THE RIVER, 8.7.8.7. with Refrain

The Lord will guide you continually, and satisfy your needs in parched places, and make your bones strong; and you shall be like a watered garden, like a spring of water, whose waters never fail. *(Isaiah 58:11)*

SOURCES

Isaiah 44:2b-4 from *The Inclusive Bible* (Landham, MD: Rowman & Littlefield, 2007). A Sheed & Ward Book published by Rowman & Littlefield Publishers, Inc. All rights reserved. Used by permission.

"Thanksgiving at the Font: Form V," in Evangelical Lutheran Church in America, *Evangelical Lutheran Worship*, Leaders Desk ed. (Minneapolis: Augsburg Fortress, 2006), 589, alt. Used by permission.

"A Litany for the Planet," in Standing Commission on Liturgy and Music, "Liturgical Materials Honoring God in Creation and Various Rites and Prayers for Animals," in *Report to the 77th General Convention* (Episcopal Church, July 5–12, 2012), 327–28, alt.

John Muir to Janet Douglass Moores, 23 February 1887, in *The Life and Letters of John Muir*, ed. William Frederic Badè (Boston: Houghton Mifflin, 1924), 2:216. Public domain.

Anne Rowthorn, "The Water Worlds of John Muir," in *The Yale ISM Review* 2, no. 1 (Fall 2015), article 4, *http://ismreview.yale.edu*, alt. Creative Commons 4.0, https://creativecommons.org/licenses/by/4.0/legalcode.

"As I hold these . . . ," in "River Sunday," Australia Version 1, *Season of Creation*, accessed May 12, 2016, http://seasonofcreation.com/wp-content/uploads/2010/04/liturgy-river-sunday-1.pdf, alt. © Season of Creation, developed by Norm Habel and the Uniting Church in Australia, Synod of Victoria and Tasmania, 2004, seasonofcreation.com, used with permission.

Edward Hoyt, "Send Your Living Waters: A Prayer for Those Facing Drought," in "Prayers and General Intercessions for Current Emergencies," *Catholic Relief Services*, last modified August 21, 2015, https://www.crs.org/resource-center/prayer-drought, alt. Reprinted with permission of Catholic Relief Services.

Robert Lowry, "Shall We Gather at the River" (1864). Public domain.

5. WONDER

The rising sun uncovers the layers of the ages as its light flows into the Grand Canyon, revealing its splendor. After a spring shower, the landscape is bathed in green as a rainbow appears on the horizon. Dazzling shades of red and orange flung across the western sky announce the close of another day. This is what wonder looks like! Time seems to stop. For a moment we are awestruck.

If we learn to love the earth, we will find labyrinths, gardens, fountains, and precious jewels! A whole new world will open itself to us. We will discover what it means to truly love. *(Attributed to St. Teresa of Avila)*

PRAYERS OF PRAISE AND THANKSGIVING

For the marvelous grace of your creation, we pour out our thanks to you, our God; for the sun and moon and stars, for rain and dew and winds, for winter cold and summer heat. We pour forth our praise to you for mountains and hills, for springs and valleys, for rivers and seas. We praise you, O Lord, for plants growing in earth and water, for life inhabiting lakes and seas, for life creeping in soils and land, for creatures living in wetlands and waters, for life flying above Earth and sea, for beasts dwelling in woods and fields. How many and wonderful are your works, our God! In wisdom you have made them all! **Amen.** *(The North American Conference on Christianity and Ecology)*

O Holy God of Earth and Sky, in your strength each flower gives out its sweet-scented perfume, delicate color, the beauty of the whole universe revealed in the tiniest thing. Glory and honor to God the Giver of life, who covers the fields with their carpet of flowers, crowns the plains with harvest of gold and the blue of corn-flowers, and our souls with the joy of contemplating the Holy God of earth and sky. O be joyful and sing to God: **Alleluia!** *(Metropolitan Tryphon)*

5. Wonder

PSALM 84:1, 3-8, 10-12

How lovely is your dwelling place,
    O Lord of hosts! . . .
Even the sparrow finds a home,
    and the swallow a nest for herself,
    where she may lay her young,
at your altars, O Lord of hosts,
    my King and my God.
Happy are those who live in your house,
    ever singing your praise. . . .
Happy are those whose strength is in you,
    in whose heart are the highways to Zion.
As they go through the valley of Baca
    they make it a place of springs;
    the early rain also covers it with pools.
They go from strength to strength;
    the God of gods will be seen in Zion.
O Lord God of hosts, hear my prayer;
give ear, O God of Jacob! . . .
For a day in your courts is better
    than a thousand elsewhere.
I would rather be a doorkeeper in the house of my God
    than live in the tents of wickedness.
For the Lord God is a sun and shield;
    he bestows favor and honor.
No good thing does the Lord withhold
    from those who walk uprightly.
O Lord of hosts
    happy is everyone who trusts in you.

SCRIPTURE   JOB 37:5, 14-24

God thunders wondrously with his voice;
    he does great things that we cannot comprehend. . . .
"Hear this, O Job;
    stop and consider the wondrous works of God.
Do you know how God lays his command upon them,
    and causes the lightning of his cloud to shine?

Do you know the balancings of the clouds,
>   the wondrous works of the one whose knowledge is perfect,
you whose garments are hot
>   when the earth is still because of the south wind?
Can you, like him, spread out the skies,
hard as a molten mirror?
Teach us what we shall say to him;
>   we cannot draw up our case because of darkness.
Should he be told that I want to speak?
>   Did anyone ever wish to be swallowed up?
Now, no one can look on the light
>   when it is bright in the skies,
>   when the wind has passed and cleared them.
Out of the north comes golden splendor;
>   around God is awesome majesty.
The Almighty—we cannot find him;
>   he is great in power and justice,
>   and abundant righteousness he will not violate.
Therefore mortals fear him;
>   he does not regard any who are wise in their own conceit."

LITANY

Rainbow God, we praise you for the beauty of planet earth; for the deep blue of the oceans and the splendor of sea creatures—shellfish hidden in crevices, spouting whales majestically riding the waves, playful dolphins trying new games and the vast array of multi-colored fish; for all the variety of sea life we praise your name, good Lord.
How wonderful are your works in all the world.

For the green meadows and heather-covered hills, for orchards abundantly producing apples, red and green, for herds of cows replete with milk, for flocks of sheep caring for playful lambs, for horses, chestnut brown, milk white and coal black; for all the variety of the countryside we praise your name, good Lord.
How wonderful are your works in all the world.

For the sun that shines bright in the sky, for the clouds pregnant with rain, showering blessings, for scent-filled, life-sustaining air, for the majestic eagle

soaring over the mountains, for the lark filling the air with her song, for lines of geese heading home. Rainbow God, for all this loveliness we praise your name and give you thanks.
How wonderful are your works in all the world. *(John Johansen-Berg)*

REFLECTION   RACHEL CARSON

What is the value of preserving and strengthening this sense of awe and wonder, this recognition of something beyond the boundaries of human existence? Is the exploration of the natural world just a pleasant way to pass the golden hours of childhood or is there something deeper?

I am sure there is something much deeper, something lasting and significant. Those who dwell among the beauties and mysteries of the earth are never alone or weary of life. Whatever the vexations or concerns of their personal lives, their thoughts can find paths that lead to inner contentment and to renewed excitement in living. Those who contemplate the beauty of the earth find reserves of strength that will endure as long as life lasts. There is symbolic as well as actual beauty in the migration of the birds, the ebb and flow of the tides, the folded bud ready for the spring. There is something infinitely healing in the repeated refrains of nature—the assurance that dawn comes after night, and spring after the winter.

Rachel Carson (1907–1964) began her illustrious career as a marine biologist employed by the U.S. Fish and Wildlife Service. Her book Silent Spring *created a storm of controversy and brought environmental concerns, especially the widespread use of synthetic pesticides, to the attention of the American public. It was serialized by* The New Yorker *and became an immediate best seller.*

PRAYERS OF CONFESSION AND INTERCESSION

O God, the delicate balance of your creation is slowly being stripped of its riches: your streams of living water are choked with chemicals; your life-giving trees droop and die. Open our eyes to see, and our ears to hear the cry of your creation. Teach us its wonders. Teach us to cherish and protect your world. Teach us how to live in partnership with all things, that we may learn how to live as one body in Christ—dependent on each other's gifts, sharing in each other's hopes. **Amen.** *(Kate McIlhagga)*

Almighty and everlasting God, you made the universe with all its marvelous order, its atoms, worlds, and galaxies, and the infinite complexity of living creatures: Grant that, as we probe the mysteries of your creation, we may come to know you more truly, and more surely fulfill our role in your eternal purpose; in the name of Jesus Christ our Lord. **Amen.** *(The Episcopal Church)*

HYMN   ADAM M. L. TICE

1. Earth is full of wit and wisdom,
   sounding God's delighted laugh,
   from the tiny roly-poly
   to the treetop-tall giraffe.
   All creation sings in wonder;
   even rocks and trees rejoice
   as they join the ringing chorus:
   echoes of our Maker's voice.

2. Earth is full of wit and wisdom,
   woven into harmony.
   Every creature has a purpose,
   every flower and bumblebee.
   Spider, human, redwood, gecko,
   monkey, chicken, mouse, and snake,
   live within a single fabric:
   cloth that only God could make.

3. Earth is full of wit and wisdom:
   penguin, platypus, and snail,
   cactus, sea slug, oak, and algae,
   from the microbe to the whale.
   In this great and strange creation,
   with a breath God gives us birth:
   born of soil to live as stewards,
   called to love and serve the earth.

   Tune: HOLY MANNA, 8.7.8.7.D.

Every spring flower sings the wisdom of your ways. Awaken us to the wonder of life that springs each moment from your divine heart. Open our minds, fill our senses, and teach us your ways. **Amen.** *(David Miller)*

SOURCES

Attributed to Saint Teresa of Avila. Source unknown.

North American Conference on Christianity and Ecology, "For the marvelous grace of Your Creation . . . ," in *Earth Prayers from Around the World: 365 Prayers, Poems, and Invocations Honoring Earth*, ed. Elizabeth Roberts and Elias Amidon (New York: HarperCollins, 1991), 228, alt.

Metropolitan Tryphon [Prince Boris Petrovich Turkestanov], Kontakion 3 of "An Akathist in Praise of God's Creation," in *SYNDESMOS Orthodoxy and Ecology Resource Book,* Annex 1, *Orthodox Services for the Creation*, ed. Alexander Belopopsky and Dmitri Oikonomou (Bialystok, Poland: Orthdruk Orthodox Printing House, 1996), 20–25, alt.

John Johansen-Berg, "Rainbow God," in *Harvest for the World: A Worship Anthology on Sharing in the Work of Creation*, ed. Geoffrey Duncan (Cleveland: Pilgrim Press, 2003), 18–19, alt.

Rachel Carson, *The Sense of Wonder* (New York: Harper & Row, 1956), 101–102. © 1956 by Rachel L. Carson. Reprinted by permission of HarperCollins Publishers.

Kate McIlhagga, "Teach Us (1)," in *Seeing Christ in Others: An Anthology for Worship, Meditation and Mission*, ed. Geoffrey Duncan (Atlanta: Canterbury, 2012), 22–23, alt.

"For Knowledge of God's Creation," in Episcopal Church, *The Book of Common Prayer* (New York: Church Publishing, 1986), 827.

Adam M. L. Tice, "Earth Is Full of Wit and Wisdom," © 2009, GIA Publications, Inc. Used by permission.

David Miller, "Every Spring Flower Sings," in *Bread for the Day: Daily Bible Readings and Prayers 2016* (Minneapolis: Augsburg Fortress, 2016), 170. Used by permission.

6. THE SONG OF CREATION

Can you hear the singing silence deep within the forest night? Can you hear her fragile creatures holding the harmonies of life? Will you come and play your spirit, play in tune with life on Earth? Sing your soul and play your spirit in the symphony called Earth! (Norman Habel)

Let the nations be glad and sing for joy,
> for you judge the peoples with equity
> and guide the nations upon earth. . . . *(Psalm 67:4)*

PRAYERS OF PRAISE AND THANKSGIVING

O Supreme Lord of the Universe, you fill and sustain everything around us. With the touch of your hand you turned chaos into order, darkness into light. Unknown energies you hid in the heart of matter. From you burst forth the splendor of the sun and the mild radiance of the moon. Stars and planets without number you set in ordered movement. You are the source of the fire's heat and the wind's might, of the water's coolness and the earth's stability. Deep and wonderful are the mysteries of your creation. **Amen.** *(New Orders of the Mass in India)*

Living God, you have called us to be present in your holy courts. Open our eyes to see where you are most actively present in your world. Open our lips to sing your praises jubilantly in this world you have made. **Amen.** *(Scott A. Moore)*

6. The Song of Creation

CANTICLE   SONG OF THE THREE YOUNG MEN

Glorify the Lord, all you works of the Lord, praise him and highly exalt him for ever.
In the firmament of his power, glorify the Lord, praise him and highly exalt him for ever.
Glorify the Lord, you angels and all powers of the Lord, O heavens and all waters above the heavens.
Sun and moon and stars of the sky, glorify the Lord, praise him and highly exalt him forever.
Glorify the Lord, every shower of rain and fall of dew, all winds and fire and heat.
Winter and summer, glorify the Lord, praise him and highly exalt him for ever.
Glorify the Lord, O chill and cold, drops of dew and flakes of snow.
Frost and cold, ice and sleet, glorify the Lord, praise him and highly exalt him for ever.
Glorify the Lord, O nights and days, O shining light and enfolding dark.
Storm clouds and thunderbolts, glorify the Lord, praise him and highly exalt him for ever.

SCRIPTURE   ISAIAH 55:6-13

Seek the Lord while he may be found,
    call upon him while he is near;
let the wicked forsake their way,
    and the unrighteous their thoughts;
let them return to the Lord, that he may have mercy on them,
    and to our God, for he will abundantly pardon.
For my thoughts are not your thoughts,
    nor are your ways my ways, says the Lord.
For as the heavens are higher than the earth,
    so are my ways higher than your ways
    and my thoughts than your thoughts.

For as the rain and the snow come down from heaven,
    and do not return there until they have watered the earth,
making it bring forth and sprout,
    giving seed to the sower and bread to the eater,

so shall my word be that goes out from my mouth;
> it shall not return to me empty,
but it shall accomplish that which I purpose,
> and succeed in the thing for which I sent it.

For you shall go out in joy,
> and be led back in peace;
the mountains and the hills before you
> shall burst into song,
> and all the trees of the field shall clap their hands.
Instead of the thorn shall come up the cypress;
> instead of the brier shall come up the myrtle;
and it shall be to the LORD for a memorial,
> for an everlasting sign that shall not be cut off.

LITANY

How wonderful, O Lord, are the works of your hands! The heavens declare your glory, the arch of the sky displays your handiwork.
The heavens declare the glory of God.

In your love you have given us the power to behold the beauty of your world, robed in all its splendor, the sun and the stars, the valleys and hills, the rivers and lakes—all disclose your presence.
The earth reveals God's presence.

The roaring breakers of the sea tell of your awesome might; the beasts of the field and the birds of the air proclaim your wondrous will.
Life comes forth by God's creative will.

In your goodness you have made us able to hear the music of the world, the raging of the winds, the whisperings of trees in the wood; and the precious voices of loved ones reveal to us that you are in our midst.
A divine voice speaks through all creation. *(Central Conference of American Rabbis)*

REFLECTION ERAZIM KOHÁK

It is the privilege and task of humans to recognize and to act out the presence of eternity in time. The golden leaves line the river bottom, setting the water aglow in the autumn sun. The forest dies and is renewed in the order of time; the sparkling river bears away grief. In the pained cherishing of that transient world, the human, a dweller between the embers and the stars, can raise it up to eternity.

There is the order of time, the all-reconciling rhythm of love and labor, of day and night, of the full moon and the starry skies of the new moon, the circle of the seasons and the cycle of life, blossoming, renewing itself, and perishing. The great liberating discovery is that the human is not a stranger to it, but has an integral place therein. The order which governs the life of the forest, the seasons of the trees, the care of the porcupines for their young, the snakes at peace on their boulders and the human in his clearing gives a rhythm and a rightness to human life. Even amid their human-made environments, humans need not feel strangers if they recognize in their works the rhythm of nature of which they are part, and let that vision guide them. Humans cannot live at peace with themselves and their God if they are not at peace with nature.

The Czech-born philosopher Erazim Kohák (b. 1933) writes about humanity's place in the order of nature in his book evocatively titled, The Embers and the Stars. *Kohák was a longtime professor at Boston University, and after the "Velvet Revolution," he returned to his homeland to teach at Charles University in Prague.*

PRAYERS OF CONFESSION AND INTERCESSION

Each leaf, each petal, each grain, each person, sings your praises, Creator God.

Each creature on the earth, all the mountains and great seas show your glory, Spirit of love. And yet the hand of greed has patented and plundered your splendor, has taken and not shared your gift, has lived as owner of the earth, not guest. And so the ice is cracked, the rivers dry, the valleys flooded and the snowcaps melt. Loving God, show us how to step gently, how to live simply, how to walk lightly with respect and love for all that you have made. **Amen.** *(Linda Jones)*

Sovereign of the universe, your first covenant of mercy was with every living creature. When your beloved Son came among us, the waters of the river welcomed him, the heavens opened to greet his arrival, the animals of the wilderness drew near as his companions. With all the world's people, may we who are washed into new life through baptism seek the way of your new creation, the way of justice and care, mercy and peace; through Jesus Christ, our Savior and Lord. **Amen.** *(Evangelical Lutheran Church in America)*

HYMN   THOMAS H. TROEGER

1. Learn from all the songs of earth
   that we never sing alone,
   that our music has its birth
   in what wind and wave intone,
   that before God spoke a word,
   God first blew upon the sea,
   and the breath of music stirred
   everything that came to be.

2. The creation God conceives
   brims with melody and beat.
   From the wind among the leaves
   to the thunderstorm's retreat,
   from the whispering of snow
   to the waterfall that sings—
   psalms and anthems rise and flow
   from the plainest, simplest things.

3. And the songs we daily hear
   in the creatures' chirps and cries,
   from the notes that signal fear
   to the hymns that fill the skies,
   beckon us to join earth's choir
   with our own distinctive parts
   that God's melodies inspire
   as the Spirit fills our hearts.

4. When we harmonize with earth
   and its elemental song,
   we recall who gave us birth
   and to whom we all belong,
   we more deeply understand
   what the living Christ displays:
   we are fashioned by God's hand
   for a life that sings God's praise.

Tune: SALZBURG, 7.7.7.7.D.

Because of the great God of the universe, all things hold together. Awesome is the Holy One and very great. Marvelous is the power of God who has made all that lives. Eternal is the song that echoes through all creation. *(Anne and Jeffery Rowthorn)*

SOURCES

Norman Habel, "Can You Hear the Singing Silence," in *Habel Hymns, Vol. 3: Songs in Support of the Eco-Reformation in 2017 and On-Going Earthcare*, 2016, http://www.earth-link.org.au/userfiles/Habel-Hymns-3.pdf. © 1999 Norman Habel. Used by permission.

"O Supreme Lord . . . ," in World Council of Churches, *Unity and Renewal: A Study Guide for Local Groups* (Faith and Order Paper No. 136, World Council of Churches, 1987), p. 18, no. 16. From "New Orders of the Mass in India," in Asia Sunday Prayer Leaflet of the Christian Conference of Asia, 1982.

Scott A. Moore, "Singing Your Praises Jubilantly," in *Bread for the Day: Daily Bible Readings and Prayers 2016* (Minneapolis: Augsburg Fortress, 2016), 325. Used by permission.

"Song of the Three Young Men," in Episcopal Church, *Book of Common Prayer* (New York: Church Publishing, 1986), 88–89.

"How wonderful, O Lord . . . ," in *Gates of Prayer: The New Union Prayerbook* (New York: Central Conference of American Rabbis, 1975), 651, alt. © 1975, by Central Conference of American Rabbis, under the copyright protection of the Central Conference of American Rabbis and reprinted for use by permission of the CCAR. All rights reserved.

Erazim Kohák, *The Embers and the Stars: A Philosophical Inquiry into the Moral Sense of Nature* (Chicago: University of Chicago Press, 1984), 202 and 81, alt. © 1984 by the University of Chicago. Used by permission.

Linda Jones and CAFOD, "Walk Lightly," in "Three *live*simply Prayers," CAFOD, accessed October 6, 2017, https://cafod.org.uk/content/download/644/5934/file/Prayer_Livesimply_prayers.pdf. Used by permission.

"Creation and New Creation," in Evangelical Lutheran Church in America, *Evangelical Lutheran Worship*, Leaders Desk ed. (Minneapolis: Augsburg Fortress, 2006), 152. Used by permission.

"Learn from all the songs of earth" by Thomas Troeger © Oxford University Press Inc. 2009. Assigned to Oxford University Press 2010. Reproduced by permission. All rights reserved.

Anne and Jeffery Rowthorn, inspired by Ecclesiasticus (Sirach) 43:26, 29, 30. © 2016 Anne and Jeffery Rowthorn.

7. GOD BE PRAISED

God be praised in the dazzling orange sunrise announcing the new dawn, in the glistening waters of the fresh running brook, and in the pounding waterfall. God be praised in the crack of thunder. God be praised through whispering aspens, in the call of the whip-poor-will, and in the arrival of the loon on a cold Minnesota lake. God be praised in the green grass under our feet and in love that binds human beings to one another.

From the rising of the sun to its setting,
> the name of the Lord is to be praised. *(Psalm 113:3)*

PRAYERS OF PRAISE AND THANKSGIVING

Blessed and praised, glorified and exalted, extolled and honored, adored and lauded be the name of the Holy One, blessed be God, beyond all the blessings and hymns, praises and consolations that are ever spoken in the world. *(Mourner's Kaddish)*

Lord, we thank you for our world—for its infinite varieties of peoples, colors, races, and cultures, for the endless opportunities of making new relationships, for the challenge of venturing across new frontiers, creating new things, and discovering new truths, for your call to heal all that is hurt or broken. Forgive our narrowness of vision. Open us to the breadth of your love. **Amen.** *(Women of Guatemala)*

O heavenly Father, you have filled the world with beauty: Open our eyes to behold your gracious hand in all your works; that, rejoicing in your whole creation, we may learn to serve you with gladness; for the sake of him through whom all things were made, your Son Jesus Christ our Lord. **Amen.** *(The Episcopal Church)*

7. God Be Praised

PSALM 100

Make a joyful noise to the Lord, all the earth.
> **Worship the Lord with gladness;**
> **come into his presence with singing.**

Know that the Lord is God.
> **It is he that made us, and we are his;**
> we are his people, and the sheep of his pasture.

Enter his gates with thanksgiving,
> and his courts with praise.
> Give thanks to him, bless his name.

For the Lord is good;
> his steadfast love endures for ever,
> **and his faithfulness to all generations.**

SCRIPTURE   REVELATION 7:9-17

After this I looked, and there was a great multitude that no one could count, from every nation, from all tribes and peoples and languages, standing before the throne and before the Lamb, robed in white, with palm branches in their hands. They cried out in a loud voice, saying,

"Salvation belongs to our God who is seated on the throne, and to the Lamb!"

And all the angels stood around the throne and around the elders and the four living creatures, and they fell on their faces before the throne and worshipped God, singing,

"Amen! Blessing and glory and wisdom
and thanksgiving and honor
and power and might
be to our God for ever and ever! Amen."

Then one of the elders addressed me, saying, "Who are these, robed in white, and where have they come from?" I said to him, "Sir, you are the one that knows." Then he said to me, "These are they who have come out of the great ordeal; they have washed their robes and made them white in the blood of the Lamb.

For this reason they are before the throne of God,
> and worship him day and night within his temple,
> and the one who is seated on the throne will shelter them.

They will hunger no more, and thirst no more;
> the sun will not strike them,
> nor any scorching heat;
for the Lamb at the center of the throne will be their shepherd,
> and he will guide them to springs of the water of life,
and God will wipe away every tear from their eyes."

LITANY

Caring God, we thank you for your gifts in creation:
for our world and the heavens that tell of your glory;

for our land, its beauty and its resources,
for the rich heritage we enjoy.

We pray: for those who make decisions about the resources of the earth,
that we may use your gifts responsibly;

for those who work on land and sea, in cities and in industry,
that all may enjoy the fruits of their labors and marvel at your creation;

for artists, scientists and visionaries,
that through their work we may see creation afresh.

We thank you for giving us life;
for all who enrich our experience.

We pray: for all who are deprived of fullness of life,
for prisoners, refugees, and those who are sick;

for those in politics, medical science, social and relief work, and for your Church,
for all who seek to bring life to others.

We thank you that you have called us to celebrate your creation.
Give us reverence for life in your world.

We thank you for your redeeming love;
may your word and sacrament strengthen us to love as you love us.

God, Creator, bring us new life.
Jesus, Redeemer, renew us.

Holy Spirit, strengthen and guide us. *(Anglican Church of New Zealand)*

7. God Be Praised

REFLECTION   THOMAS MERTON

The forms and individual characters of living and growing things, of inanimate beings, of animals and flowers and all nature, constitute their holiness in the sight of God. The pale flowers of the dogwood outside this window are saints. The little flowers that nobody notices on the edge of that road are saints looking up into the face of God. This leaf has its own texture and its own pattern of veins and its own holy shape, and the bass and trout hiding in the deep pools of the river are canonized by their beauty and their strength.

The lakes hidden among the hills are saints, and the sea too is a saint who praises God without interruption in her majestic dance. The great, gashed, half-naked mountain is another of God's saints. There is no other like Him. Nothing else in the world ever did or ever will imitate God in quite the same way.

Thomas Merton's entire life (1915–1968) was marked by a sense of pilgrimage. He was born in the French Pyrenees, his father a New Zealand painter and his mother an American Quaker. He went to England and Cambridge University, and then on to the United States where he underwent a dramatic conversion to Catholicism. Contemplative, social activist, Trappist monk, Merton found inspiration in the natural world, yet he warned, "The contemplative can never allow himself to become invisible to true human values, whether in society, in others or himself. If he does so, then his contemplation stands condemned as vitiated in its very root."

PRAYERS OF CONFESSION AND INTERCESSION

Almighty God, you love us, but we have not loved you. You call, but we have not listened. We walk away from neighbors in need, wrapped in our own concerns. We condone evil, prejudice, warfare, and greed. God of grace, help us to admit our sin so that, as you come to us in mercy, we may repent, turn to you, and receive forgiveness; through Jesus Christ our Redeemer. **Amen.** *(Presbyterian Church, USA)*

May we join you, cosmic congregation of galaxies, as you dance with delight before our God. You spin and leap with brilliant bursts of light, never tiring of your sacred circle-play. May we join you, star-children of countless constellations, in the worship of our common Creator, in your rotating rituals of planetary energy as you sing cosmic chants of divine fire. May we join you, so that our prayers may also spin with sparkling splendor, spawning long tails of luminous devotion to carry our praise and adoration straight to the heart of our Beloved God. **Amen.** *(Edward Hays)*

HYMN   JOHN L. BELL AND GRAHAM MAULE

1. Sing praise to God on mountain tops
   and in earth's lowest places,
   from blue lagoon to polar waste,
   from ocean to oasis.
   No random rock produced this world,
   but God's own will and wonder.
   Thus hills rejoice and valleys sing
   and clouds concur with thunder

2. Sing praise to God where grasses grow
   and flowers display their beauty,
   where nature weaves her complex web
   through love as much as duty.
   The seasons in their cycle speak
   of earth's complete provision.
   Let nothing mock inherent good,
   nor treat it with derision.

3. Sing praise to God where fishes swim
   and birds fly in formation,
   where animals of every kind
   diversify creation.
   All life that finds its home on earth
   is meant to be respected.
   Let nothing threaten, for base ends,
   what God through grace perfected.

4. Sing praise to God where humankind
   its majesty embraces,
   where different races, creeds, and tongues
   distinguish different faces.
   God's image in each child of earth
   shall never pale or perish.
   So treat with love each human soul,
   and thus God's goodness cherish.

Tune: THE VICAR OF BRAY, 8.7.8.7.D.

May the God of the Earth give us the milk of her blessing. Bearers of your bounty, may our lives be lives of unceasing thanksgiving for all the blessings of earth. *(Atharva Veda)*

SOURCES

"Mourner's Kaddish," in *The Authorized Daily Prayer Book*, ed. and trans. Joseph H. Hertz, rev. ed. (New York: Bloch, 1974), 399, alt.

"Lord, we thank you . . . ," in United Church of Canada, *Celebrate God's Presence: A Book of Services for The United Church of Canada*, ed. Karen J. Verveda (Etobicoke, Ontario: United Church Publishing House, 2000), p. 523. Attributed to women of Guatemala, in God's People: Instruments of Healing.

"For Joy in God's Creation," in Episcopal Church, *Book of Common Prayer* (New York: Church Publishing, 1979), 814.

"Caring God, we thank you . . . ," in Church of the Province of New Zealand, *A New Zealand Prayer Book: He Karakia Mihinare o Aotearoa* (Auckland, New Zealand: William Collins, 1989), 463–64. © 1989 The Provincial Secretary, The Church of the Province of New Zealand, Box 2148, Rotorua. Used by permission.

Thomas Merton, *New Seeds of Contemplation* ([Norfolk, CT]: New Directions, 1962), 30–31. © 1961 by The Abbey of Gethsemani, Inc. Reprinted by permission of New Directions Publishing Corp.

"Almighty God, you love us . . . ," in Presbyterian Church (USA), *Book of Common Worship* (Louisville, KY: Westminster John Knox, 1993), 89. Reprinted by permission from *Book of Common Worship*, © 1993 Westminster John Knox Press.

Edward Hays, "A Psalm of Cosmic Communion," in *Prayers for a Planetary Pilgrim: A Personal Manual for Prayer and Ritual* (Easton, KS: Forest of Peace Books, 1988), 184, alt. © 1989, 2008. Used with the permission of the publisher, Forest of Peace, an imprint of Ave Maria Press, Inc., Notre Dame, Indiana 46556. www.forestofpeace.com.

John L. Bell and Graham Maule, "Sing Praise to God on Mountain Tops" © WGRG c/o The Iona Community, Scotland. GIA Publications, Inc., exclusive North American agent. Used by permission.

Atharva-Veda XII, "Hymn to the Earth," in *Hymns from the Vedas: Original Text and English Translation*, trans. Abinash Chandra Bose (Bombay: Asia Publishing House, 1966), 363–79, alt.

God's Physical Universe

8. OCEANS

Cradle of life—the oceans' flow links islands and empires, archipelagos and continents. A message placed in a bottle and tossed in the ocean off Vancouver Island comes ashore in Valparaiso or Suva. Uncorking the bottle, the message reads: "The seas belong to us all. They are rising and becoming more acidic; they are endangered. Save the seas."

Yonder is the sea, great and wide,
>   creeping things innumerable are there,
>   living things both small and great. *(Psalm 104:25)*

PRAYERS OF PRAISE AND THANKSGIVING

O God of the majestic oceans, we thank you for the beauty of your shining waters. Waves rise up to praise you; rolling tides reveal the rhythm of the universe. Crabs and cod, sharks and whales, dolphins and flying fish, sea grass and seaweed glide in your currents. We praise you for the solace of the seas; when your waters rage, we stand in awe of your power. Honor and glory and thanks to you, great God of the oceans. **Amen.** *(Anne Rowthorn)*

From the ocean comes all life. Fish and all creatures of the sea remind us of God's acts of salvation. In the beginning, the Spirit of God swept over the face of the waters, bringing light and life to all. God parted the waters of the Sea of Reeds, graciously giving life to Miriam, Moses, and all of God's people. In the belly of a great fish, Jonah found life and thus God. Witnessing for Jesus Christ, Paul endured a storm-tossed sea before finding safety on shore. We ask for God's blessing upon all who travel over the waters and upon all fishing fleets and the life they harvest from the ocean's sacred depths. **Amen.** *(Betty Lynn Schwab)*

CANTICLE   SONG OF THE THREE YOUNG MEN

Let the earth glorify the Lord,
>   praise him and highly exalt him for ever.

Glorify the Lord, O mountains and hills,
>   **and all that grows upon the earth,**
>   **praise him and highly exalt him for ever.**

Glorify the Lord, O springs of water, seas, and streams,
>   O whales and all that move in the waters.
>   All birds of the air, glorify the Lord,
>   praise him and highly exalt him for ever.

Glorify the Lord, O beasts of the wild,
>   **and all you flocks and herds.**

O men and women everywhere, glorify the Lord,
>   praise him and highly exalt him for ever.

SCRIPTURE   GENESIS 1:9-10, 20-23

God said, "Let the waters under the sky be gathered together into one place, and let the dry land appear." And it was so. God called the dry land Earth, and the waters that were gathered together he called Seas. And God saw that it was good. . . . And God said, "Let the waters bring forth swarms of living creatures, and let birds fly above the earth across the dome of the sky." So God created the great sea monsters and every living creature that moves, of every kind, with which the waters swarm, and every winged bird of every kind. And God saw that it was good. God blessed them, saying, "Be fruitful and multiply and fill the waters in the seas, and let birds multiply on the earth." And there was evening and there was morning, the fifth day.

LITANY

O God, how magnificent are your works! In wisdom you have made them all. All the earth is your creation.

Before us lies the great and wide sea with its living things too many to number, creatures and plants both small and great.

Upon it move the ships, boats and vessels. All look to you to give food in due season.

You give it; we gather it; you open your hand and all are fed.

We pray for good weather on the seas, for an abundant catch this year.
We pray for the safety of those who labor in the waters, for clean and life-filled waters, and for the life they sustain.

We pray for all entrusted with policy decisions about the oceans, for all who have economic power over the harvest of the oceans.
We pray for ourselves, that we may have the grace to seek your will, and be saved from false choices and harmful decisions.

Remind us always that we are your vessels of life and hope for your world.
(The Anglican Church of Canada)

REFLECTION   THOR HEYERDAHL

What are we doing to the ocean? The ocean covers 71 percent of the surface of the planet. An important part of the human food supply comes directly from the sea. If we kill the plankton, we lose the fish and thus drastically reduce the protein available for human sustenance. If we kill the plankton, we reduce to less than half the supply of oxygen available to humans and beasts, and this at a time when forests are becoming scarcer than ever before. We, like all breathing species, will be increasingly dependent on the plants of the ocean since green landscapes rapidly recede before the spread of urbanization, industry, and the onslaught of modern farming, while asphalt, concrete, and barren sand dunes advance on previously fertile land. Since life on land is so utterly dependent on life in the sea, we can safely deduce that a dead sea means a dead planet.

The explorer and ethnologist Thor Heyerdahl (1914–2002) led the celebrated Kon-Tiki Expedition in 1947. Heyerdahl and five companions sailed across the Pacific in 101 days to illustrate how ancient people could travel great distances navigating by the stars and ocean currents in boats made of natural materials. Building on his Kon-Tiki fame, Heyerdahl became an outspoken defender of the world's oceans, influencing the United Nations and twenty-three countries to address the issue of marine contamination.

PRAYERS OF CONFESSION AND INTERCESSION

We remember and confess that we have become alienated from Earth and viewed this planet as disposable, a source of endless resources, a mere stopping place en route to heaven. We are sorry. We have polluted Earth's waters with toxins, and killed millions of species in the ocean. We have turned our greed into global warming. We have helped cause arctic regions to melt. We have loved progress more than the planet. We are sorry. We are sorry. We are sorry. **Amen.** *(Season of Creation)*

God, our Creator, as we reflect on the mysteries of the ocean depths, we celebrate the wondrous design of the seas that surround us. Help us to discern how we have polluted our oceans and to empathize with the groaning of creation beneath us. Teach us to sense the presence of God in the tides and currents of the surging seas. Teach us to care for the oceans and all our waterways. In the name of the Wisdom of God, the creative force that designs and governs all creation. **Amen.** *(Season of Creation)*

HYMN   ANDREW PRATT

1. In the beginning God played with the planets,
   set them a-spinning in time and in space,
   stars in the night sky, while sun lit the daytime,
   blue was the globe that was formed for our race.

2. God saw the seas and the fish that swam in them,
   formed the dry land where the trees soon would grow,
   animals now could inhabit the countries
   warmed by the oceans or covered in snow.

3. After the animals, people were coming
   made in God's likeness to live on the earth;
   big the blue planet God gave them to live on
   sharing its riches, its wonder and worth.

   Tune: WAS LEBET, 11.10.11.10.
   Words © 1999 Stainer & Bell, Ltd. (admin. Hope Publishing)

Yonder is the sea, great and wide,
creeping things innumerable are there,
living things both small and great. . . . People will stand fishing beside the sea . . . it will be a place for the spreading of nets; its fish will be of a great many kinds, like the fish of the Great Sea. *(Psalm 104:25 and Ezekiel 47:10)*

SOURCES

Anne Rowthorn, "O God of the Majestic Oceans" © 2018 Anne Rowthorn.

Betty Lynn Schwab, "From the Ocean Comes All Life," in United Church of Canada, *Celebrate God's Presence: A Book of Services for the United Church of Canada*, ed. Karen J. Verveda (Etobicoke, Ontario: United Church Publishing House, 2000), 618, alt. Used by permission of Betty Lynn Schwab.

"Song of the Three Young Men," in Episcopal Church, *Book of Common Prayer* (New York: Church Publishing Inc., 1986), 89.

"O God, how . . . ," in Anglican Church of Canada, *Occasional Celebrations of the Anglican Church of Canada* (Toronto: Anglican Book Centre, 1992), 167–68, alt. © 1992 General Synod of the Anglican Church in Canada. Used by permission.

Thor Heyerdahl, "If Man Is to Survive, the Ocean Is Not Dispensable," in *Speaking of Earth: Environmental Speeches that Moved the World*, ed. Alon Tal (New Brunswick, NJ: Rutgers University Press, 2006), 30, 32, and 33. Used by permission of the Kon-Tiki Museum.

"As I hold this . . . ," in "Ocean Sunday," Australia Version 1, *Season of Creation*, accessed May 12, 2016, https://seasonofcreation.com/wp-content/uploads/2010/04/liturgy-ocean-sunday-1.doc, alt. © Season of Creation, developed by Norm Habel and the Uniting Church in Australia, Synod of Victoria and Tasmania, 2004, seasonofcreation.com, used with permission.

"God, our Creator . . . ," in "Ocean Sunday," Australia Version 1, *Season of Creation*, accessed May 12, 2016, https://seasonofcreation.com/wp-content/uploads/2010/04/liturgy-ocean-sunday-1.doc, alt. © Season of Creation, developed by Norm Habel and the Uniting Church in Australia, Synod of Victoria and Tasmania, 2004, seasonofcreation.com, used with permission.

Words by Andrew Pratt, "In the Beginning God Played with the Planets" © 1999 Stainer & Bell, Ltd. (admin. Hope Publishing Company, Carol Stream, IL 60188). All rights reserved. Used by permission.

9. SKY

On deserts and plains and on the rolling oceans, the sky is everywhere the eye can see. For millennia human beings have read the skies and marked their days and seasons by movements in the celestial canopy. Sailors discerned approaching storms; farmers found guidance for planting; philosophers sought wisdom. Kings and shepherds followed a bright star to Bethlehem where they beheld a baby who would become the Savior of the world.

The heavens are telling the glory of God;
    and the firmament proclaims God's handiwork. *(Psalm 19:1)*

PRAYERS OF PRAISE AND THANKSGIVING

Creator God, who divided heaven from earth by a firmament so that living things might flourish by your word and holy breath: We give thanks for the atmosphere and its cycles of renewal by plants and animals of the planet. Teach us to cherish the air we breathe as your gift to all life, worthy to be kept clean and healthful for the good of all. We pray in the name of Jesus, whom even the winds and seas obeyed. **Amen.** *(The Episcopal Church)*

God, our Creator, as we look into the skies we celebrate the wonders of the worlds that surround us. Help us to see your presence in the evening sky, your spirit in the wind, your mercy in the falling rain. Teach us to hear the good news from the sky, celebrating the glory of God on Earth. Rejoice with us as we behold the dawn, revealing the mysteries of the skies above and Earth below. In the name of Christ who unites heaven and Earth. **Amen.** *(Season of Creation)*

9. Sky

PSALM 97:1-2, 4-6, 10-12

YHWH [Yahweh] reigns! Let the earth rejoice;
   let the many coastlands be glad!
Clouds and thick darkness surround you, YHWH;
   righteousness and justice are the foundations of your judgment seat.
Your lightning bolts light up the world;
   the earth sees and trembles.
The mountains melt like wax at your sight,
   at the sight of the God of all the earth.
The heavens proclaim your justice,
   and all the peoples see your glory.
YHWH, you love those who hate evil;
   preserve the lives of your faithful ones
   and deliver them from the hands of the wicked.
Light dawns for the just,
   and joy for the upright in heart.
Rejoice in YHWH, you just,
   and give praise to God's holy name!

SCRIPTURE   ECCLESIASTICUS (SIRACH) 43:1-12

The pride of the higher realms is the clear vault of the sky,
   as glorious to behold as the sight of the heavens.
The sun, when it appears, proclaims as it rises
   what a marvelous instrument it is, the work of the Most High.
At noon it parches the land,
   and who can withstand its burning heat?
A man tending a furnace works in burning heat,
   but three times as hot is the sun scorching the mountains;
it breathes out fiery vapors,
   and its bright rays blind the eyes.
Great is the Lord who made it;
   at his orders it hurries on its course.
It is the moon that marks the changing seasons,
   governing the times, their everlasting sign.
From the moon comes the sign for festal days,
   a light that wanes when it completes its course.

The new moon, as its name suggests, renews itself;
> how marvelous it is in this change,
a beacon to the hosts on high,
> shining in the vault of the heavens!
The glory of the stars is the beauty of heaven,
> a glittering array in the heights of the Lord.
On the orders of the Holy One they stand in their appointed places;
> they never relax in their watches.
Look at the rainbow, and praise him who made it;
> it is exceedingly beautiful in its brightness.
It encircles the sky with its glorious arc;
> the hands of the Most High have stretched it out.

LITANY

We invite the skies to worship with us:
the subtle orange skies at dawn and the bold red skies at sunset.

We join the heavens in praising God:
proclaiming God's glory across the globe and hailing God's name with the evening stars.

We join with the atmosphere in worship:
the air, the moisture, the oxygen, the wind and all the expressions of God's Spirit.

We call the clouds to celebrate with storms:
to carry the life-giving drops of rain, that give hope and healing to Earth.

We invite the winds to join our petitions:
to carry our prayers to God above and breathe our hopes to Christ in person.

We celebrate the song of the skies!
Sing, skies! Sing! *(Season of Creation)*

9. Sky

REFLECTION   THOMAS BERRY

Our most urgent need at the present time is for a reorientation of the human venture toward an intimate experience of the world around us. If we would go back to our primary experience of any natural phenomena—on seeing the stars scattered across the heavens at night, on looking out over the ocean at dawn, of seeing the colors of the oaks and maples and poplars in autumn, on hearing a mockingbird sing in the evening, or breathing the fragrance of the honeysuckle while journeying through a southern lowland—we would recognize that our immediate response to any of these experiences is a moment akin to ecstasy. There is wonder and reverence and inner fulfillment in some overwhelming mystery. We experience a vast new dimension to our own existence.

Historian of religions Thomas Berry (1914–2009) would often recall his childhood experience of coming upon a flower-filled meadow on the outskirts of his new home in Greensboro, N.C. "The field was covered with white lilies rising above the thick grass," he said. "A magic moment, this experience gave to my life something that seems to explain my thinking at a more profound level than almost any other experience I can remember." He was eleven years old! Years later he reflected, "It was a wonder world that I have carried in my unconscious and that has evolved all my thinking."

PRAYERS OF CONFESSION AND INTERCESSION

We remember and confess that we have filled our atmosphere with pollutants, toxins, fumes and carbon dioxide, creating a greenhouse in the air above us, with a global warming that changes the weather and upsets the current balance of nature. We have been thoughtless and greedy, ready to pollute rather than preserve, to abuse the atmosphere rather than believe the air is indeed the breath of God for us. We have choked the air with ugly gases, polluted the very breath of God. We are sorry. We are sorry. **Amen.** *(Season of Creation)*

God, our Creator, as we view the atmosphere, we have a sense of wonder. Help us to sense your presence in every wind, breeze and breath we take. Teach us to recognize that to care for the atmosphere is to celebrate the very life we, and all of this planet, receive directly from you. In the name of Christ who reconciles and renews all things in creation. **Amen.** *(Season of Creation)*

HYMN — HERMAN C. STUEMPFLE, JR.

1. Sing praise to God, you heavens!
   Sing praise, each shining light!
   Sing, planets in your orbits;
   sing, stars all burning bright!
   Sing praise, you winds and tempests,
   you driving rain and snow!
   Sing, clouds that race and billow
   and shadow earth below!

2. Sing praise, O earth, sing praises!
   Sing praises, hill and plain,
   you mountains thrusting skyward,
   you valleys ripe with grain!
   Sing praise, each fragrant flower;
   your fairest hues display.
   Sing praise, you trees of autumn
   in glowing glad array!

3. Sing praises, all you creatures
   in whom God takes delight:
   you whales that roam the oceans,
   you eagles in your flight!
   Sing praise, you sheep on hillsides,
   you cattle in the stall!
   Though wordless, sing your praises
   to God who made you all!

4. Sing praises now, God's people;
   your gift of speech employ
   to praise the Lord, your Maker,
   with thankfulness and joy!
   Sing with the whole creation;
   a cosmic chorus raise:
   "To God alone be glory
   and everlasting praise!"

Tune: WIE LIEBLICH IST DER MAIEN, 7.6.7.6.D.

> Sing to the Lord with thanksgiving;
>   make melody to our God on the lyre.
> He covers the heavens with clouds,
>   prepares rain for the earth,
>   makes grass grow on the hills. *(Psalm 147:7-8)*

SOURCES

Psalm 19:1 from *The New Testament and Psalms: An Inclusive Version* (New York: Oxford University Press, 1995), an adaptation of the New Revised Standard Version Bible, copyright © 1989 National Council of the Churches of Christ in the United States of America. Used by permission. All rights reserved.

"A Rogation Day Procession and Liturgy: For the Air, Winds, and All That Flies," in Standing Commission on Liturgy and Music, "Liturgical Materials Honoring God in Creation and Various Rites and Prayers for Animals," in *Report to the 77th General Convention* (Episcopal Church, July 5-12, 2012), 323–34, alt.

"God, our Creator . . . ," in "Sky Sunday," Australian Version 1, *Season of Creation*, accessed May 12, 2016, https://seasonofcreation.com/wp-content/uploads/2010/04/liturgy-sky-sunday-1.doc, alt. © Season of Creation, developed by Norm Habel and the Uniting Church in Australia, Synod of Victoria and Tasmania, 2004, seasonofcreation.com, used with permission.

Psalm 97:1-2, 4-6, 10-12 from *The Inclusive Bible* (Landham, MD: Rowman & Littlefield, 2007). A Sheed & Ward Book published by Rowman & Littlefield Publishers, Inc. All rights reserved. Used by permission.

"We invite the skies . . . ," in "Sky Sunday," Australian Version 1, *Season of Creation*, accessed May 12, 2016, https://seasonofcreation.com/wp-content/uploads/2010/04/liturgy-sky-sunday-1.doc, alt. © Season of Creation, developed by Norm Habel and the Uniting Church in Australia, Synod of Victoria and Tasmania, 2004, seasonofcreation.com, used with permission.

Thomas Berry, "An Ecologically Sensitive Spirituality," in *The Sacred Universe: Earth, Spirituality, and Religion in the Twenty-First Century*, ed. Mary Evelyn Tucker (New York: Columbia University Press, 2009), 132. Used by permission.

"As we hold these . . . ," in "Atmosphere Sunday," *Season of Creation*, accessed April 14, 2017, https://seasonofcreation.com/wp-content/uploads/2010/08/Atmosphere-Sunday.doc, alt. © Season of Creation, developed by Norm Habel and the Uniting Church in Australia, Synod of Victoria and Tasmania, 2004, seasonofcreation.com, used with permission.

"God, our Creator . . . ," in "Atmosphere Sunday," *Season of Creation*, accessed April 14, 2017, https://seasonofcreation.com/wp-content/uploads/2010/08/Atmosphere-Sunday.doc, alt. © Season of Creation, developed by Norm Habel and the Uniting Church in Australia, Synod of Victoria and Tasmania, 2004, seasonofcreation.com, used with permission.

Words by Herman C. Stuempfle, Jr., "Sing Praise to God, You Heavens!" © 2006, GIA Publications, Inc. Used by permission.

10. WILDERNESS

Wilderness, such as Christ and the prophets went out into; harshly and beautifully colored, broken and worn until its bones are exposed, its great sky without a smudge of taint from Technocracy. . . . Save a piece of country like that intact, and it does not matter in the slightest that only a few people every year will go into it. That is precisely its value. . . . Those who haven't the strength or youth to go into it and live can simply sit and look. . . . They can simply contemplate the idea, take pleasure in the fact that such a timeless and uncontrolled part of earth is still there. (Wallace Stegner)

The wilderness and the dry land shall be glad,
    the desert shall rejoice and blossom;
like the crocus it shall blossom abundantly,
    and rejoice with joy and singing. *(Isaiah 35:1-2a)*

PRAYERS OF PRAISE AND THANKSGIVING

We thank you, God, for this land, our place of belonging. We thank you for the sight of towering mountain peaks, rolling countryside, checkered plains, multi-hued bush. We thank you for the sound of birds, rushing mountain streams, gurgling braided rivers, waves pounding the shore, the silence of solitary places. We thank you for the smell of rain-soaked forests, scents of city gardens, fresh frosted air, earth itself. We thank you for the touch of soft moist moss, sharp mountain rock, smooth coastal stones, crisp leaves and snow, tender hands of friends and lovers, the heart-beat of all that lives. **Amen.** *(Bill Wallace)*

Gichi Manidoo, Great Spirit God, we give you thanks for another day on this earth.

We give you thanks for this day to enjoy the compassionate goodness of you, our Creator. We acknowledge with one mind our respect and gratefulness for all the sacred cycles of life. Bind us together in the circle of compassion to embrace all living creatures and one another and the land on which we dwell. **Amen.** *(The Episcopal Church)*

PSALM 96:1-3, 9-12

O sing to the Lord a new song;
> sing to the Lord, all the earth.

Sing to the Lord, bless his name;
> **tell of his salvation from day to day.**

Declare his glory among the nations,
> his marvelous works among all the peoples. . . .

Worship the Lord in holy splendor;
> **tremble before him, all the earth.**

Say among the nations, "The Lord is King!
> The world is firmly established; it shall never be moved.
> He will judge the peoples with equity."

Let the heavens be glad, and let the earth rejoice;
> let the sea roar, and all that fills it;
> let the field exult, and everything in it.

Then shall all the trees of the forest sing for joy.

SCRIPTURE   ISAIAH 41:18-20 AND MATTHEW 4:1-4

1. I will open rivers on the bare heights,
    and fountains in the midst of the valleys;
I will make the wilderness a pool of water,
    and the dry land springs of water.
I will put in the wilderness the cedar,
    the acacia, the myrtle, and the olive;
I will set in the desert the cypress,
    the plane and the pine together,
so that all may see and know,
    all may consider and understand,
that the hand of the Lord has done this,
    the Holy One of Israel has created it.

2. Jesus was led up by the Spirit into the wilderness to be tempted by the devil. He fasted forty days and forty nights, and afterwards he was famished. The tempter came and said to him, "If you are the Son of God, command these stones to become loaves of bread." But he answered, "It is written,

> 'One does not live by bread alone,
>> but by every word that comes from the mouth of God.'"

LITANY

Creating God of the Universe, have mercy,
Creating God, have mercy.

On your earth, as it changes,
Creating God, have mercy.

On the soil, that it may be built up and be fruitful,
Creating God, have mercy.

On the minerals below ground that nourish life,
Creating God, have mercy.

On your volcanoes and lava flows,
Creating God, have mercy.

On your hills and great mountains, on your valleys, cliffs, and caves,
Creating God, have mercy.

On your deserts and their hardy creatures,
Creating God, have mercy.

On your forests of many kinds, on your trees and shrubs and vines,
Creating God, have mercy.

On your grasslands and plains, on your tundras and their plants,
Creating God, have mercy.

On your ferns and your fungi, on the spore-bearing plants and the seed-bearing plants,
Creating God, have mercy. *(The Episcopal Church)*

10. Wilderness

REFLECTIONS EDWARD ABBEY AND STEPHEN TRIMBLE

1. The love of wilderness is more than a hunger for what is always beyond reach; it is also an expression of loyalty to the earth, the earth which bore us and sustains us. The only home we shall ever know, the only paradise we ever need, . . . the paradise of which I write is the here and now, the actual, tangible, dogmatically real earth on which we stand. . . . Wilderness is not a luxury but a necessity of the human spirit, and as vital to our lives as water and good bread. A civilization which destroys what little remains of the wild, the spare, the original, is cutting itself off from its origins and betraying the principle of civilization itself.

This selection is taken from Desert Solitaire, *a collection of essays that Edward Abbey (1927–1989) wrote as a summer park ranger at Arches National Monument in southern Utah. Abbey was an iconoclastic author and passionate defender of the southwestern American wilderness. His writings have inspired a generation of activists to protect natural environments against development.*

2. We need not see a wilderness to know it's worth saving; the idea of such a refuge creates our geography of hope. To experience such remoteness firsthand surely would change us forever, but the trip isn't mandatory. When we grind away our joy and strength in Pittsburgh, in Peoria, in Watts, or in West Palm Beach, we can close our eyes and picture this place.

The thunder of caribou hooves runs through our dreams, coursing like the blood of life that we share. Wolf eyes return our gaze, we feel the tread of a polar bear on ice. We see the wildflowered sweep of the tundra and feel the sweet exhilaration of twenty-four-hour summer sun, of boundless space. Eiderdown from a nesting snow goose slips into the wind. The fierceness of musk oxen circling their young surrounds us.

Though I haven't stepped across the boundary of the Arctic National Wildlife Refuge, I have been there. I have been journeying on the words and paintings and photographs and music of artists inspired by the Arctic wild. I have been there, in spirit, whenever I have made pilgrimages to other wild places. I have been there, with fox and falcon, in my dreams.

The ecologist, writer, and photographer Stephen Trimble (b. 1950) has served as a park ranger in Colorado and Utah and now teaches writing at the University of Utah.

PRAYERS OF CONFESSION AND INTERCESSION

Yesteryear was a time when the rivers flowed without poison, wind blew untainted air, sun shown brightly through not-hazed sky, everything was safe to eat, simplicity was the rule, technology had no say. But now I hear your cry—all is not as you created, we have made a different time. Forgive us for not using our minds to remember the Seventh Generation not yet born. Creator, we come before you with humble spirit. Open hearts to see what we have done. Give us wisdom to undo what we have done. Give us hope that we may one day live where rivers flow pure, winds blow free, the sun shines brightly, and our bodies are nourished. Give us courage to change. Give us courage to return to our homelands, and remember those yet to come. **Amen.** *(Ginny Doctor)*

O God, your voice can split the heavens, part the waters, divide night from day. It can flash forth fire, shake the wilderness, thunder over the storm. Yet your word so often heard among us is not in the tempest, but in the silence. Speak to us, O God, and let us listen, that we might detect the whisper of a wing, the rustle of a feather. Listen to us, that we might glimpse the dove and hear the voice that Jesus heard, saying, "You are my beloved; with you I am well pleased." Speak to us again, O Lord, for when you speak, it is done, and behold, it is very good. **Amen.** *(Phyllis Cole and Everett Tilson)*

10. Wilderness

HYMN   DANIEL C. DAMON

1. Pray for the wilderness, vanishing fast,
   pray for the rain forest, open and vast;
   pray for the waterfalls, pray for the trees,
   pray for the planet brought down by degrees.

2. Learn from the elephant, eagle and whale,
   learn from the dragon fly, spider and snail;
   learn from the people in neighboring lands,
   learn from the children who play in their sands.

3. Work for the justice created things need,
   work for the health of each plant and its seed;
   work for the creatures abuse has betrayed,
   work for the garden God's wisdom once made.

4. Trust that God's Christ overcame nails and wood,
   trust that earth's people will turn to the good;
   trust that creation forever will grow,
   trust that God's goodness to us overflows.

5. Pray for the atmosphere, pray for the sea,
   learn from the river, the rock and the tree;
   work till shalom in full harmony rings,
   trust the connection of all living things.

Tune: WILDERNESS (Lee Yu San), 10.10.10.10. Words © 1991 Hope Publishing

In the wilderness justice will come to live and integrity in the fertile land; integrity will bring peace and justice give lasting security. *(Isaiah 32:16-17)*

SOURCES

Wallace Stegner, "Coda: Wilderness Letter," in *The Sound of Mountain Water: The Changing American West*, by Wallace Stegner (New York: Vintage, 2017), 153. Used by permission of Penguin Random House. Copyright © 1960, 1988 by Wallace Stegner. Used by permission of Brandt & Hochman Literary Agents, Inc. All rights reserved.

Bill Wallace, "Prayer of Thanksgiving," in *Singing the Circle, Book 1: Sacred Earth, Holy Darkness: Hymns, Poems and Reflections for Aotearoa* (Christchurch, New Zealand: W. L. Wallace, 1990), 47, alt.

"Gichi Manidoo . . . ," in *Native American/Alaska Native and Native Hawaiian Liturgies* (76th General Convention of the Episcopal Church, Anaheim, CA, July 2009), alt.

"A Litany for the Planet," in Standing Commission on Liturgy and Music, "Liturgical Materials Honoring God in Creation and Various Rites and Prayers for Animals," in *Report to the 77th General Convention* (Episcopal Church, July 5–12, 2012), 327–29, alt.

Edward Abbey, *Desert Solitaire: A Season in the Wilderness* (New York: Ballantine, 1971), 209 and 211. Reprinted by permission of Don Congdon Associates, Inc. © 1968 by Edward Abbey, renewed 1996 by Clarke C. Abbey.

Stephen Trimble, "Covenant," in *Arctic Refuge: A Circle of Testimony*, comp. Hank Lentfer and Carolyn Servid (Minneapolis: Milkweed Editions, 2001), 90–92, alt. Copyright © Stephen Trimble | www.stephentrimble.net. Used by permission.

Ginny Doctor, "Prayer for the Homelands," in *Women's Uncommon Prayers: Our Lives Revealed, Nurtured, Celebrated*, by Elizabeth Rankin Geitz, Ann Smith, and Marjorie A. Burke (Harrisburg, PA: Morehouse, 2000), 231–32, alt. *Women's Uncommon Prayers: Our Lives Revealed, Nurtured, Celebrated* © 2000 the Morehouse Publishing. Used by permission of Church Publishing Incorporated, New York, NY.

Phyllis Cole and Everett Tilson, "Your Voice Can Split the Heavens," in *Litanies and Other Prayers for the Revised Common Lectionary: Year B* (Nashville: Abingdon Press, 1993), 33. © 2003 Abingdon Press. Used by permission. All rights reserved.

Words by Daniel Charles Damon, "Pray for the Wilderness" © 1991 Hope Publishing Company, Carol Stream, IL 60188. All rights reserved. Used by permission.

Isaiah 32:16-17 from *The Jerusalem Bible*, ed. Alexander Jones (Garden City, NY: Doubleday, 1966). © 1996 by Darton, Longman & Todd, Ltd. and Doubleday, a division of Penguin Random House LLC. Reprinted by permission.

11. MOUNTAINS

Mountains are mysterious, ethereal, enchanting, captivating, mystical, and places of insight and temptation. They can also be challenging and dangerous, especially when the weather suddenly and adversely changes. Mountains attract poets, dreamers, loners, adventurers, and prophets. They both compel and repel, and therein lies their attraction.

Before the mountains were brought forth,
> or ever you had formed the earth and the world,
> from everlasting to everlasting you are God. *(Psalm 90:2)*

PRAYERS OF PRAISE AND THANKSGIVING

Many and great are your works, O God, Maker of earth and sky; Your hands set the heavens with stars, Your fingers spread the mountains and plains. Lo, at your word the waters are formed; and the deep seas obey your voice. *(Joseph Renville)*

Mighty and majestic God, we thank you for the great mountain ranges you have created, the high places of the earth where you have revealed yourself to your people. On Mount Sinai you gave the Commandments to Moses; on a high mountain top Jesus resisted the temptations of the devil; on the Mount of Transfiguration you charged the disciples to listen to your beloved Son; on the mountainside Jesus identified those who are truly blessed in God's sight. Grant that we also may encounter you amid the awesome beauty of the mountains where we may be inspired by their majesty and humbled by your glory which they reflect; through Jesus Christ our Lord. **Amen.** *(Jeffery Rowthorn)*

We give you thanks, most gracious God, for the beauty of earth and sky and sea; for the richness of mountains, plains, and rivers; for the songs of birds and the loveliness of flowers. We praise you for these good gifts, and pray that we may safeguard them for posterity. Grant that we may continue to grow in our grateful enjoyment of your abundant creation, to the honor and glory of your name, now and forever. **Amen.** *(The Episcopal Church)*

PSALM 121

I lift up my eyes to the hills—
>from where will my help come?

My help comes from the Lord,
>**who made heaven and earth.**

He will not let your foot be moved;
>he who keeps you will not slumber.

He who keeps Israel
>**will neither slumber nor sleep.**

The Lord is your keeper;
>the Lord is your shade at your right hand.

The sun shall not strike you by day,
>**nor the moon by night.**

The Lord will keep you from all evil;
>he will keep your life.

The Lord will keep
>**your going out and your coming in**
>**from this time forth and forevermore.**

SCRIPTURE   ISAIAH 2:2-3A AND EXODUS 19:16-19

1. In days to come
>the mountain of the Lord's house

shall be established as the highest of the mountains,
>and shall be raised above the hills;

all the nations shall stream to it.
>Many peoples shall come and say,

"Come, let us go up to the mountain of the Lord,
>to the house of the God of Jacob;

that he may teach us his ways
>and that we may walk in his paths."

2. On the morning of the third day there was thunder and lightning, as well as a thick cloud on the mountain, and a blast of a trumpet so loud that all the people who were in the camp trembled. Moses brought the people out of the camp to meet God. They took their stand at the foot of the mountain. Now Mount Sinai was wrapped in smoke, because the LORD had descended upon it in fire; the smoke went up like the smoke of a kiln, while the whole mountain shook violently. As the blast of the trumpet grew louder and louder, Moses would speak and God would answer him in thunder.

LITANY

Let us give thanks for the East, for the ancient mountains and valleys and streams without end, for the green Atlantic from the reaches of Maine to the Florida Keys, for larch and hemlock, for black bear and mountain trout, for cardinals and eastern bluebirds, for heat in the hayfields of late August:
We bless you, O God, for the East.

Let us give thanks for the West, for soaring mountains and searing deserts, for waters roaring into the Pacific Ocean, for Columbia River salmon, snow buntings and western meadowlarks, for ponderosa and Jeffrey pine, for the mists of the Oregon coast and for the Olympic peninsula:
We bless you, O God, for the West.

Let us give thanks for the North, for the bright band of prairie and wheat fields stretching across the land, for the jay hawk and the loon, the northern pike and the walleye, for the badlands of the Dakotas, the lakes of Minnesota and the lofty mountains of Wyoming:
We bless you, O God, for the North

Let us give thanks for the South, for the broad Mississippi delta and the great Smokey Mountains, for the bayous of Louisiana, for magnolia trees, for the kiskadee and egret, for catfish and parrotfish and for the cotton and the colors on the sands and strands of the southland:
We bless you, O God, for the South. *(Gabriel Rochelle)*

REFLECTION   ROBERT O'ROURKE

Long ago nature's music played along
    the slopes of our sacred Chuska Mountains;
        their bright melodies lingered deep in the valleys.

My people, the Dineh, took solace in
   wind whispers,
      coyote songs,
         the silence of rocks and
            high-soaring eagles.
Today I return to this place where my ancestors
   gathered medicine herbs.
I stop to listen for the old melodies
   running softly through the trees,
      for the beating heart of Mother Earth,
         the rhythm of sparkling waters.
The sonorous sounds are no more!
   What remain are
      lamentations of blasted boulders,
         clanking of chain saws,
            crashing trees,
               rocks crumbling into dust.
My spirit yearns for the long-ago, lost harmonies—
   the musing of insects,
      rustle of leaves,
         the voice of the hawk.

Stooping down, I choose one tormented rock;
   holding it gently toward the sky;
      together we pray to the GOD-OF-ALL-THINGS
         for the return of earth song,
            the murmur of grass,
               butterfly wings and
                  the gentle silence of rocks
                     at peace.

Robert O'Rourke (1926–2018) was a poet, wood-carver, and environmental activist living in Colorado. This modern-day St. Francis said, "My poem was written during a trip to the Navajo Nation with my son, David. We crossed the Chuska Mountains on a rough, rugged road before we came to a place called Canyon de Chelly. All along the route trees were bulldozed, rocks dynamited, the earth broken and scarred. It seemed to me that even the rocks cried out in pain. Wildlife must have been panicked by the blasting and desolation of their homes and habitat. It was enough to make us depressed and heart-broken."

PRAYERS OF CONFESSION AND INTERCESSION

Great Spirit, still brooding over the world—as we hear the cries of the earth, we see the sorrow of land raped, plundered, and mountain tops removed, in our greed for its varied resources. As we hear the cry of the waters, and see the sorrow of stream and ocean polluted by poisons we release into them; as we hear the cry of animals, and see the sorrow of bird, fish, and beast needlessly suffering and dying to serve our profit or sport or vanity—teach us in your love: sensitivity towards our feeling for creation; appreciation for the connectedness of all things; respect for the shalom of the universe. Creator of life, we turn from our arrogant ways to seek you again. Redeem us. Redeem your world. Heal its wounds and dry its tears. May our response to you bear fruit in a fresh sense of responsibility towards everything you have made. **Amen.** *(Kate Compston)*

Gracious God, we thank you for the rich texture of our land—for your hollows, rivers, tree-covered mountains and rolling hills. We bring before you those who, for reasons of injustice, cannot share in the riches and bounty you provide in these hills. Send your spirit to nourish, strengthen and guide us to be helpful companions with those who thirst for righteousness and peace. Where can we find a way? With whom can we make a difference? We seek your guidance. All this we ask through Jesus on whom your spirit rested in all power to proclaim release for the captives, recovery of sight for the blind, and freedom for the oppressed. And in all that is before us, help us to remember that this is the year of the Lord's favor. **Amen.** *(Scott Allen)*

HYMN — JOHN THORNBURG

1. God the sculptor of the mountains,
   God the miller of the sand.
   God the jeweler of the heavens,
   God the potter of the land:
   you are womb of all creation,
   we are formless; shape us now.

2. God the nuisance to the Pharaoh,
   God the cleaver of the sea,
   God the pillar of the darkness,
   God the beacon of the free:
   you are gate of all deliverance,
   we are aimless; lead us now.

3. God the unexpected infant,
   God the calm, determined youth,
   God the table-turning prophet,
   God the resurrected Truth:
   you are present every moment,
   we are searching; meet us now.

4. God the dresser of the vineyard,
   God the planter of the wheat,
   God the reaper of the harvest,
   God the source of all we eat:
   you are host at every table,
   we are hungry; feed us now.

Tune: REGENT SQUARE, 8.7. 8.7. 8.7.

Shout, O depths of the earth;
break forth into singing, O mountains,
O forest, and every tree in it! *(Isaiah 44:23b)*

SOURCES

Joseph Renville, "Many and Great, O God," (1842), trans. Philip Frazier (1929). Public domain.

Jeffery Rowthorn, "Mighty and Majestic God" © 2017 Jeffery Rowthorn.

"For the Beauty of the Earth," in Episcopal Church, *Book of Common Prayer* (New York: Church Publishing, 1979), 840.

Gabriel Rochelle, "Litany for the Four Directions," in *Let All Creation Praise*, accessed November 17, 2015, http://www.letallcreationpraise.org/liturgy/litanies, alt. Used by permission.

Robert O'Rourke, "Rock Ritual XX: Lamentation of the Rocks," in *Fellowship in Prayer* (Princeton, NJ: Fellowship in Prayer, 1995).

Robert O'Rourke, letter to Anne Rowthorn, June 15, 1999.

Kate Compston, "New Responsibility," in *Dare to Dream: A Prayer and Worship Anthology from around the World*, ed. Geoffrey Duncan (London: HarperCollins, 1995), 30–31, alt. Used by permission.

Scott Allen, "A Prayer for Appalachia." Used by permission.

Words by John Thornburg, "God the Sculptor of the Mountains" © 1993 John Thornburg. Used by permission.

12. TREES AND FORESTS

Covering a third of the earth's land surface, forests are essential to life and home to a multitude of species. Trees harness the energy of the sun and through photosynthesis they release life-giving oxygen into the air. In the Bible, the tree of life is first mentioned in Genesis 2:9 and at the end, in Revelation 22:2, "The leaves of the tree are for the healing of the nations."

Sing for joy, O heavens. Shout out, O earth below! Break out in song, O mountains, all you forests, and all you trees. *(Isaiah 44:23a)*

PRAYER OF PRAISE AND THANKSGIVING

Glory to you, great God of the universe, for this joyous and bright morning. The delicious purple of the dawn changes softly to daffodil yellow and white; while the sunbeams pouring through the mountain passes between the peaks give a margin of gold to each of them. The spires of the fir trees in the hollows catch the glow, and the grove is filled with light. The birds begin to stir, seeking sunny branches on the edge of the meadow after the cold night, and looking for their breakfasts, every one of them as fresh as a lily and as charmingly arrayed. Innumerable insects begin to dance; the deer withdraw from the open glades and ridge-tops to their leafy hiding-places in the chaparral. The flowers open and straighten their petals as the dew vanishes, every pulse beats high, every cell of life rejoices; the very rocks seem to tingle with life. We offer you, great God, our unending thanks and praise for creating, sustaining and brooding over everything great and small. **Amen.** *(Inspired by John Muir)*

12. Trees and Forests

PSALM 148:1-13A

Praise the Lord!
Praise the Lord from the heavens;
    praise him in the heights!
Praise him, all his angels;
    praise him, all his host!

Praise him, sun and moon;
    praise him, all you shining stars!
Praise him, you highest heavens,
    and you waters above the heavens!

Let them praise the name of the Lord,
    for he commanded and they were created.
He established them for ever and ever;
    he fixed their bounds, which cannot be passed.

Praise the Lord from the earth,
    you sea monsters and all deeps,
fire and hail, snow and frost,
    stormy wind fulfilling his command!

Mountains and all hills,
    fruit trees and all cedars!
Wild animals and all cattle,
    creeping things and flying birds!

Kings of the earth and all peoples,
    princes and all rulers of the earth!
Young men and women alike,
    old and young together!

Let them praise the name of the Lord.

READINGS   DEUTERONOMY 8:7-8A
                         AND THE DEAD SEA SCROLLS

1. The Lord your God is bringing you into a good land, a land with flowing streams, with springs and underground waters welling up in valleys and hills, a land of wheat and barley, of vines and fig trees and pomegranates, a land of olive trees and honey.

2. I will praise you, O God, for you have put me by a source of streams on the dry ground, by the budding springs on the parched land, by the waters that irrigate your luxuriant garden—a grove of pine together with fir and box elder—which you planted for your glory. These are the Trees of Life, set beside a secret spring, concealed among all the well-watered trees.

One day the Trees of Life will put forth a shoot which will become the Everlasting Plant, for it will take root and extend roots towards the stream. And the plant will open its stem to the living waters. It will become an everlasting source [of blessing]. All the wild creatures will graze among its fallen leaves; all the wayfarers will pass by its stem; all the winged birds will nest in its boughs.

But now the Well-Watered Trees tower over it, for they grow as soon as they are planted; but their roots do not extend towards the stream. And the trees will one day put forth the holy shoot of the Plant of Truth—these trees are hidden away; their secret is sealed, it is not valued, it is not known. For you, O God, have hedged in its fruit on every side with the mystery of angels, creatures of might, and of holy spirits, with a whirling, flashing fire. *(The Dead Sea Scrolls)*

LITANY

As a tree in the forest becomes tall reaching for the light,
May we grow above the shadows of sin, fear and doubt.

As it gives shelter and shade to its friends of fur and feather,
So may we help those brothers and sisters that are smaller and weaker than ourselves.

The tree sends down roots deep into the soil that it may be nourished by Mother Earth.
May we be as firmly grounded by the love of Christ and sustained by his grace.

If a tree falls and decays, it provides nourishment for new plants and gives its place in the sun for others.
Our Lord and Savior died to make new life and a new place for us.

When a tree in the forest is cut down, its wood is used for shelter and fuel.
Jesus taught that only when life is surrendered, when love is poured out, can we build His Kingdom and reflect the warmth of His spirit. Amen.
(Milton Vahey)

12. Trees and Forests

REFLECTION   ALEXANDER VON HUMBOLDT

The beasts of the forest retire to the thickets; the birds hide themselves beneath the foliage of the trees, or in the crevices of the rocks. Yet, amid the apparent silence, when we lend an attentive ear to the most feeble sounds transmitted by the air, we hear a dull vibration, a continual murmur, a hum of insects, that fill all the lower strata of the air. Nothing is better fitted to make man feel the extent and the power of organic life. Myriads of insects creep upon the soil, and flutter around the plants parched by the ardor of the sun. A confused noise issues from every bush, from the decayed trunks of trees, from the clefts of the rock, and from the ground undermined by the lizards and millipedes. There are so many voices proclaiming to us that all nature breathes; and that, under a thousand different forms, life is diffused throughout the cracked and dusty soil, as well as in the bosom of the waters, and in the air that circulates around us.

Two centuries before James Lovelock formulated the Gaia Hypothesis, the Prussian scientist and explorer Alexander von Humboldt (1769–1859) described the concept of nature as an interrelated web of life in which all matter is connected, and from which nothing can be removed without unraveling the whole fabric. Influenced by his friend and mentor, the poet Goethe, he saw the natural world not only from a scientific perspective but also with a lyrical sense that enlarges the human spirit. Von Humboldt's many books and papers were to influence Darwin, Thoreau, and Muir.

PRAYERS OF CONFESSION AND INTERCESSION

O God, you gave us a garden of Eden and we chose to wander in deserts of our own making. You gave us the Light of the world and we chose to do our night-crawling. Forgive us our squandering, our wandering, our lack of commitment. Forget not your covenant with us, O God, and choose us still to tell your good news, to give all that we have that we might be one in your shalom. In Jesus' name we pray. **Amen.** *(Anne Weems)*

O God, the only source of life and energy and wealth, defend our planet Earth. Teach us to conserve and not to squander the riches of nature, to use aright the heritage of former generations, and to plan for the welfare of our children's children. Renew our wonder, awaken our concern, and make us better stewards and more careful tenants of the world you lend us as our home. Hear us, O Lord, our Creator and Redeemer, in the name of Christ. **Amen.** *(Timothy Dudley-Smith)*

God's Good Earth

HYMN WALTER FARQUHARSON

1. For beauty of meadows, for grandeur of trees,
   for flowers of woodlands, for creatures of seas,
   for all you created and gave us to share,
   we praise you, Creator, extolling your care.

2. As stewards of beauty received at your hand,
   as creatures who hear your most urgent command,
   we turn from our wasteful destruction of life,
   confessing our failures, confessing our strife.

3. Teach us once again to be gard'ners in peace;
   all nature around us is ours but on lease;
   your name we would hallow in all that we do,
   fulfilling our calling, creating with you.

   Tune: ST. DENIO, 11.11.11.11.
   Words © 1971 Walter Farquharson (admin. Hope Publishing)

For you shall go out in joy,
    and be led back in peace;
the mountains and the hills before you
    shall break forth into song,
        and all the trees of the field shall clap their hands. *(Isaiah 55:12)*

SOURCES

Isaiah 44:23a from *The Inclusive Bible* (Landham, MD: Rowman & Littlefield, 2007). A Sheed & Ward Book published by Rowman & Littlefield Publishers, Inc. All rights reserved. Used by permission.

John Muir, *The Mountains of California* (New York: Century, 1894), 179, alt. Public domain.

"Parable of the Trees," from the section "Poems from the Dead Sea Scrolls" from *The Penguin Book of Hebrew Verse*, ed. T. Carmi (New York: Viking Press, 1981), 187–88. Copyright © T. Carmi, 1981. Reproduced by permission of Penguin Books Ltd.

Milton Vahey, "Psalm of the Woodlands," in United Methodist Church (US), *United Methodist Book of Worship* (Nashville: United Methodist Publishing House, 1992), no. 508.

Alexander von Humboldt, *Personal Narrative: Voyage to the Equinoctial Regions of the New Continent* (London: Longman, 1825), 4:505–506. Public domain.

Anne Weems, "Forgive Us," in *Searching for Shalom: Resources for Creative Worship* (Louisville: Westminster John Knox, 1991), 62, alt. Used by permission.

Timothy Dudley-Smith, "O God, the only source . . . ," in *Chalice Worship*, ed. Colbert S. Cartwright and O. I. Cricket Harrison (St. Louis: Chalice, 1997), 165. Used by permission.

Words by Walter Farquharson, "For Beauty of Meadows (Prairies)" © 1971 Walter Farquharson (admin. Hope Publishing Company, Carol Stream, IL 60188). All rights reserved. Used by permission.

13. DESERTS

In the stark wide-open beauty of the desert, the sun shines and the wind blows. Everything is visible as far as the eye can see and life is stripped to the bare essentials. Jesus, Mohammad, the Desert Fathers, Charles de Foucauld, and the Little Brothers of Jesus took to the desert for insight and enlightenment. Indigenous people the world over still do.

In those days John the Baptist appeared in the wilderness of Judea, proclaiming, "Repent, for the kingdom of heaven has come near." This is the one of whom the prophet Isaiah spoke when he said,
"The voice of one crying out in the wilderness:
'Prepare the way of the Lord,
make his paths straight.'" *(Matthew 3:1-3)*

PRAYER OF PRAISE AND THANKSGIVING

Creator God, your presence is as the wind, the breath and sustainer of life. We are grateful for being a part of your beautiful creation; rugged mountains, rolling plains, and uncultivated desert. We thank you for the birds of the air, animals, and fish of the sea; for purity of water and air and healing medicines that remind us of the need for holy virtue in life, physical and spiritual. In your holy mystery, you have revealed that we are God's children, a wonderful mosaic of humanity with different cultures and heritages. We have a work yet to do, to work for truth and equity. We pray that we might always be found faithful, reflecting your love. Cause light to overcome the darkness of this world. Be present, O God, through your Son Jesus, in whose name we pray. **Amen.** *(Cecil Corbett)*

13. Deserts

CANTICLE   JOB 38:4-7, 25-27, 37A

"Where were you when I laid the foundation of the earth?
    Tell me, if you have understanding.
Who determined its measurements—surely you know!
    Or who stretched the line upon it?
On what were its bases sunk,
    or who laid its cornerstone
when the morning stars sang together
    and all the heavenly beings shouted for joy? . . .

"Who has cut a channel for the torrents of rain,
    and a way for the thunderbolt,
to bring rain on a land where no one lives,
    on the desert, which is empty of human life,
to satisfy the waste and desolate land,
    and to make the ground put forth grass? . . .

"Who has the wisdom to number the clouds?
    Or who can tilt the waterskins of the heavens . . . ?"

SCRIPTURE   ISAIAH 35:1-10

The wilderness and the dry land shall be glad,
    the desert shall rejoice and blossom;
like the crocus it shall blossom abundantly,
    and rejoice with joy and singing.
The glory of Lebanon shall be given to it,
    the majesty of Carmel and Sharon.
They shall see the glory of the Lord,
    the majesty of our God.

Strengthen the weak hands,
    and make firm the feeble knees.
Say to those who are of a fearful heart,
    "Be strong, do not fear!
Here is your God.
    He will come with vengeance,
with terrible recompense.
    He will come and save you."

Then the eyes of the blind shall be opened,
    and the ears of the deaf unstopped;

then the lame shall leap like a deer,
    and the tongue of the speechless sing for joy.
For waters shall break forth in the wilderness,
    and streams in the desert;
the burning sand shall become a pool,
    and the thirsty ground springs of water;
the haunt of jackals shall become a swamp,
    the grass shall become reeds and rushes.

A highway shall be there,
    and it shall be called the Holy Way;
the unclean shall not travel on it,
    but it shall be for God's people;
    no traveler, not even fools, shall go astray.
No lion shall be there,
    nor shall any ravenous beast come up on it;
they shall not be found there,
    but the redeemed shall walk there.
And the ransomed of the Lord shall return,
    and come to Zion with singing;
everlasting joy shall be upon their heads;
    they shall obtain joy and gladness,
    and sorrow and sighing shall flee away.

LITANY

For the gift of our lives and the life of this world, we give you thanks and recommit our lives to you anew this day. Lord, hear our prayer. Señor, escúchanos.
Señor, escúchanos.

Help us to learn from this good land and the beauty of creation all around us.
Señor, escúchanos.

In this land of endless sky, teach us the boundlessness of your beauty and love.
Señor, escúchanos.

In this land of little rain, teach us to share and to bless what you have given us.
Señor, escúchanos.

In this land of brilliant sunrise and golden sunset, teach us to use each day to bless the lives of others.
Señor, escúchanos. *(Talitha Arnold)*

13. Deserts

REFLECTION   EDWARD ABBEY

The desert is a vast world, an oceanic world, as deep in its way and complex and various as the sea. . . . The wind will not stop. Gusts of sand swirl before me, stinging my face. But there is still so much to see and marvel at, the world very much alive in the bright light and wind, exultant with the fever of spring, the delight of morning. . . . It seems to me that the strangeness and wonder of existence are emphasized here in the desert by the comparative scarcity of the flora and fauna: life not crowded upon life as in other places but scattered abroad in sparseness and simplicity, with a generous gift of space for each herb and bush and tree, each stem of grass, so that the living organism stands out bold and brave and vivid against the lifeless sand and barren rock. The extreme clarity of the desert light is equaled by the extreme individuation of desert life-forms. . . . In the evening the wind stops. A low gray ceiling of clouds hangs over the desert from horizon to horizon, silent and still. One small opening remains in the west. The sun peers through as it goes down.

Environmentalist, novelist, and nonfiction writer Edward Abbey (1927–1989) developed an immense affection for the desert while serving as a seasonal ranger in Arches National Monument, a vast expanse of 33,000 acres near Moab, Utah, where, "I am the sole inhabitant, observer and custodian. This is the most beautiful place on earth."

PRAYERS OF CONFESSION AND INTERCESSION

Creator of all, you entrusted the earth to the human race, yet we disrupt its peace with violence and corrupt its purity with our greed. Prevent your people from ravaging creation, that coming generations may inherit lands brimming with life. God of mercy, hear our prayer. **Amen.** *(Presbyterian Church, USA)*

Through the wide horizon of the open desert, open our eyes, O God, to the stark beauty all around us; clarify our vision that it may become your vision. Show us new possibilities; reveal the power of your presence. Strengthen our faith that we may know the wonders of your glory. **Amen.** *(Anne Rowthorn)*

Almighty God, Giver of life and strength, creator of rain and sky, dust and earth, preserver of people and plants and animals: as our cattle leave their enclosures, as we work on a dry and weary land, we look to you for heavenly showers; quench our thirst, strengthen our herds, raise our crops and refresh our land; through Jesus Christ, the water of life. **Amen.** *(Anglican Church in Kenya)*

HYMN   JANE PARKER HUBER

1. When, in awe of God's creation,
   we view earth from outer space,
   this mysterious, floating marble,
   strewn with clouds and bathed in grace!
   how can we not pause in wonder,
   seeing earth as one and whole,
   then, confessing our divisions,
   make earth's healing our prime goal.

2. Blue and tan, with lace clouds swirling,
   flung in space and circling there,
   habitat for myriad creatures
   meant for land and sea and air!
   Must we draw our lines of hatred
   marking land and class and race?
   God, forgive us, we entreat you,
   for all pride of self and place.

3. Living now, this is the picture
   we no longer can deny,
   for we see no angry boundaries
   when our view is from the sky:
   rivers, deserts, forests, snowfields,
   oceans, lakes and mountains too,
   but no fences built for barring
   you from me or me from you.

4. Now we face the unknown future,
   challenged by the work at hand.
   Still the God of all creation
   summons us with one command:
   "Love each other!" Will we do it?
   "Love each other!" Wars must cease!
   "Love each other!" Justice follows.
   "Love each other!" There is peace!

   Tune: HYFRYDOL, 8.7.8.7. D.

May God go with us as we depart into the desert, there to meet the temptations of the soul. May the Spirit lead us to an oasis where waters run deep and clouds rise high and where the voice of heaven whispers in the cool of the trees. *(Phyllis Cole and Everett Tilson)*

SOURCES

Cecil Corbett, "Gratitude for Creation," in *A Book of Reformed Prayers*, ed. Howard L. Rice and Lamar Williamson Jr. (Louisville, KY: Westminster John Knox, 1998), 159. Used by permission of Cecil Corbett.

Talitha Arnold, "For the Gift of Our Lives and the Life of This World." Used by permission.

Edward Abbey, "The Desert Is a Vast World," in *Desert Solitaire: A Season in the Wilderness* (New York: Ballantine, 1971), x, 31, and 47. Reprinted by permission of Don Congdon Associates, Inc. © 1968 by Edward Abbey, renewed 1996 by Clarke C. Abbey.

"Prayers of the People: B," in Presbyterian Church (USA), *Book of Common Worship* (Louisville, KY: Westminster John Knox, 1993), 103. Reprinted by permission from *Book of Common Worship*, © 1993 Westminster John Knox Press.

Anne Rowthorn, "Through the Wide Horizon of the Open Desert" © 2017 Anne Rowthorn.

"Prayer for Rain," in Anglican Church in Kenya, *Our Modern Services* (Nairobi, Kenya: Uzima Press, 2003), 293.

Jane Parker Huber, "When, in Awe of God's Creation," in *Singing in Celebration: Hymns for Special Occasions* (Louisville, KY: Westminster John Knox Press, 1996), no. 2. Used by permission.

Phyllis Cole and Everett Tilson, "May God Go with You," from *Litanies and Other Prayers for the Revised Common Lectionary: Year B* (Nashville: Abingdon Press, 1993), 35, alt. © 2003 Abingdon Press. Used by permission. All rights reserved.

14. UNIVERSE

The celestial tapestry of bright stars, bursting supernovas, spinning planets, shimmering northern lights, galaxies beyond galaxies dazzle our imagination. Can our minds conceive of this vastness? Are our hearts large enough to cherish all of God's majestic creation with humility and awe?

Long ago you laid the foundation of the earth,
> and the heavens are the work of your hands. *(Psalm 102:25)*

PRAYERS OF PRAISE AND THANKSGIVING

God of the galaxies, yet accessible to every human heart; Mind behind the universe, yet one whom we can call our Father; Infinite, yet within our reach; Awesome and majestic, yet compassionate and tender; Above and beyond us, yet here beside us: We praise your name, through Jesus Christ our Lord. **Amen.** *(John Platts)*

God, our Creator, as we reflect on the mysteries of the cosmos, we celebrate the wondrous design of the universe and the Wisdom that guides its course. Help us to discern how we are connected with living members of the cosmic community. Teach us to sense the presence of the cosmic Christ, whose presence fills and reconciles all forces in creation. **Amen.** *(Season of Creation)*

Praise to you, Lord Jesus Christ, who in your self-emptying love gathered up and reconciled all creation to the Father. Innumerable galaxies of the heavens worship you. Creatures that grace the earth rejoice with you. All those in the deepest seas bow to you in adoration. As with them we give you praise; grant that we may cherish the earth, our home, and live in harmony with this good creation, for you live and reign with the Father and the Holy Spirit, one God, now and forever. **Amen.** *(Evangelical Lutheran Church in America)*

PSALM 147:7-9, 12-18

Sing to the Lord with thanksgiving;
    make melody to our God on the lyre.
He covers the heavens with clouds,
    prepares rain for the earth,
    makes grass grow on the hills.
He gives to the animals their food,
    and to the young ravens when they cry. . . .

Praise the Lord, O Jerusalem!
    Praise your God, O Zion!
For he strengthens the bars of your gates;
    he blesses your children within you.
He grants peace within your borders;
    he fills you with the finest of wheat.
He sends out his command to the earth;
    his word runs swiftly.
He gives snow like wool;
    he scatters frost like ashes.
He hurls down hail like crumbs—
    who can stand before his cold?
He sends out his word, and melts them;
    he makes his wind blow, and the waters flow.

SCRIPTURE   JOB 9:4-10 AND COLOSSIANS 1:15-17, 19-20A

1. God is wise of heart and supremely powerful; who has challenged God and survived? God moves mountains before they know what is happening, and throws them down when angry; the Almighty shakes the earth and moves it from place to place, making its support columns tremble. God commands, and the sun doesn't rise and the stars don't shine their light. God stretches out the heavens, and treads on the waves of the seas. God made the Bear and Orion, the Pleiades and the constellations of the south. God's deeds are beyond understanding; God's wonders are numberless.

2. Christ is the image of the unseen God and the firstborn of all creation, for in Christ were created all things in heaven and on earth: everything visible and invisible: thrones, dominions, sovereignties, powers—all things were created through Christ and for Christ. Before anything was created, Christ existed, and all things hold together in Christ. God wanted all perfection to be found in Christ, and all things to be reconciled to God through Christ—everything in heaven and everything on earth.

LITANY

Our God is the God of all,
The God of heaven and earth.

The God of sea, of river, of sun and moon and stars;
The God of the lofty mountains and the lowly valleys.

God dwells around heaven and earth,
and the seas, and all that is part of them.

God inspires all,
God quickens all.

God dominates all,
God sustains all.

God lights the light of the sun,
God furnishes the light of the night.

God made springs in dry land.
God is the God of heaven and earth,

of sun, moon and stars.
God above in heaven, and under heaven. *(Attributed to Saint Patrick)*

REFLECTION   ANNE ROWTHORN

The cosmic gong is struck
    and the universe is called into being.
Light and dark, day and night,
    sea, soil, seasons,
Waters, walruses, and wallabies,
    bears, butterflies, bats and bees,
    seeds, sunflowers, sycamores and sequoia,
    fruits, flowers, fields and ferns,

Frozen earth and howling winds,
    sleet, snow and driving rains,
    frost and hail and Arctic chill,
    boiling deserts and blistering heat,
Stars and planets and galaxies
    dancing across the northern sky,
    Southern Cross and Milky Way,
Dense forests and towering pines,
    wide deserts and treeless tundra,
    tides and waves, mighty rivers and pounding waterfalls,
The human family in all its colors and cultures,
    men and women, babies and children,
    all in perfect harmony with all creation,
    singing one unbroken song
    fifteen billion years long.
Will greed and lust, powers and principalities, and fatal faceless forces
    reach out through ages and eons and
    still the cosmic gong?

Anne Rowthorn, with her husband, Jeffery, is co-compiler of this book. "The Cosmic Gong" was written for Karatana, a religious community.

PRAYERS OF CONFESSION AND INTERCESSION

We confess, dear Lord, as creatures privileged to live in companionship with your creation, that we have abused your gift through arrogance, ignorance, and greed. We confess risking permanent damage to your handiwork; we confess impoverishing creation's ability to bring you praise. We confess that we are often unaware of how deeply we have hurt your good earth and its marvelous gifts. For our wrongs, we ask forgiveness. May we increasingly love your creation as we increasingly come to love you. **Amen.** *(North American Conference on Christianity and Ecology)*

God, maker of marvels, you weave the planet and all its creatures together in kinship; your unifying love is revealed in the interdependence of relationships in the complex world that you have made. Save us from the illusion that humankind is separate and alone, and join us in communion with all inhabitants of the universe; through Jesus Christ, our Redeemer, who topples the dividing walls by the power of your Holy Spirit, and who lives and reigns with you, for ever and ever. **Amen.** *(The Episcopal Church)*

HYMN   HERMAN STUEMPFLE, JR.

1. Stars and planets flung in orbit,
   galaxies that swirl through space,
   powers hid within the atom,
   cells that form an infant's face:
   these, O God, in silence praise you;
   by your wisdom they are made.

2. Skies adorned with sunset splendor,
   silent peaks in calm repose,
   golden fields awaiting harvest,
   foaming surf and fragrant rose:
   earth, its bounty clothed with beauty,
   echoes all creation's praise.

3. Life in wondrous, wild profusion,
   seed and fruit, each flower and tree,
   beast and fish and swarming insect,
   soaring bird, rejoicing, free:
   these, your creatures, join in chorus,
   praising you in wordless song.

4. Humankind, earth's deepest mystery,
   born of dust but touched by grace,
   torn apart by tongue and color,
   yet a single, striving race:
   we, in whom you trace your image,
   add our words to nature's song.

Tune: LAUDA ANIMA, 8.7.8.7.8.7.
Words © 1989 The Hymn Society (admin. Hope Publishing)

Christ, whose glory fills the skies, fill you with radiance and scatter the darkness from your path. Christ, the Sun of Righteousness, gladden your eyes and warm your heart. Christ, the Dayspring from on high, draw near to guide your feet into the way of peace. **Amen.** *(Michael Perham)*

SOURCES

John Platts, "God of the galaxies . . . ," in *Oceans of Prayer*, comp. Maureen Edwards and Jan S. Pickard (Nutfield, UK: National Christian Education Council, UK, 1991), 13. © 1991 National Christian Education Council. Used by permission.

"God, our Creator . . . ," in "Cosmos Sunday," Australian Version 1, *Season of Creation*, accessed May 12, 2016, https://seasonofcreation.com/wp-content/uploads/2010/04/liturgy-cosmos-sunday-1.pdf, alt. © Season of Creation, developed by Norm Habel and the Uniting Church in Australia, Synod of Victoria and Tasmania, 2004, seasonofcreation.com, used with permission.

"Creation's Praise," in Evangelical Lutheran Church in America, *Evangelical Lutheran Worship*, Leaders Desk ed. (Minneapolis: Augsburg Fortress, 2006), 152. Used by permission.

Job 9:4-10 from *The Inclusive Bible* (Landham, MD: Rowman & Littlefield, 2007). A Sheed & Ward Book published by Rowman & Littlefield Publishers, Inc. All rights reserved. Used by permission.

Colossians 1:15-17, 19-20a from *The Inclusive Bible* (Landham, MD: Rowman & Littlefield, 2007). A Sheed & Ward Book published by Rowman & Littlefield Publishers, Inc. All rights reserved. Used by permission.

St. Patrick, in John Bagnell Bury, *The Life of St. Patrick and His Place in History* (London: Macmillan, 1905), 139, alt. Public domain.

Anne Rowthorn, "The Cosmic Gong" © 2011 Anne Rowthorn.

North American Conference on Christianity and Ecology, "For the marvelous grace . . . ," in *Earth Prayers from Around the World: 365 Prayers, Poems, and Invocations Honoring Earth*, ed. Elizabeth Roberts and Elias Amidon (New York: HarperCollins, 1991), 228–31, alt.

"The Kinship and Unity of All Creation in Christ," in Standing Commission on Liturgy and Music, "Liturgical Materials Honoring God in Creation and Various Rites and Prayers for Animals," in *Report to the 77th General Convention* (Episcopal Church, July 5–12, 2012), 320.

Words by Herman G. Steumpfle, Jr., "Stars and Planets Flung in Orbit" © 1989 The Hymn Society (admin. Hope Publishing Company, Carol Stream, IL 60188). All rights reserved. Used by permission.

Michael Perham, "Christ, whose glory . . . ," in *Enriching the Christian Year*, ed. Michael Perham (Collegeville, MN: Liturgical Press, 1993), 80. Adaptation of a hymn by Charles Wesley.

The Diversity of God's Creatures

15. GOD'S GIFT OF DIVERSITY

Diversity is about the variety and richness of life on earth, from the genetic variations within and between species and the diversity of entire ecosystems. Open God's gift of diversity and marvel at the myriad of ways species interact with each other and with the environment.

Then people will come from east and west, from north and south, and will eat in the kingdom of God. *(Luke 13:29)*

For my house shall be called a house of prayer
    for all peoples. *(Isaiah 56:7b)*

PRAYERS OF PRAISE AND THANKSGIVING

Gracious God, we praise you for the beauty and infinite diversity of your Creation. Everything you have made testifies to your glory and teaches us how to live in love. The vast expanse of the desert teaches us resilience, making us grateful for every drop of rain and every cactus flower. The rain forests, teeming with cacophonous life, teach us the riotous joys and risks of community. The struggles in urban, suburban, and rural landscapes show us what is at stake for the widow, orphan, and stranger; the challenges in our own families teach us the radical need to love others as ourselves. The glinting of sun on marsh grass, the tumbling of fox kits at play, the joyous howl of the wolf for its pack: all these show us that we need one another. Teach us, holy God, to love across lines of difference. Teach us to persist in love through every color and texture of embodiment and need, through every moment of hope and struggle, that we may know you more deeply, God of all Creation, and make you known. In the holy Name of Jesus we pray. **Amen.** *(Carolyn J. Sharp)*

PSALM 126

When the Lord restored the fortunes of Zion,
    we were like those who dream.
Then our mouth was filled with laughter,
    and our tongue with shouts of joy;
then it was said among the nations,
    "The Lord has done great things for them."
The Lord has done great things for us,
    and we rejoiced.

Restore our fortunes, O Lord,
    like the watercourses in the Negeb.
May those who sow in tears
    reap with shouts of joy.
Those who go out weeping,
    bearing the seed for sowing,
shall come home with shouts of joy,
    carrying their sheaves.

SCRIPTURE   ACTS 17:21-28A

Now all the Athenians and the foreigners living there would spend their time in nothing but telling or hearing something new.

    Then Paul stood in front of the Areopagus and said, "Athenians, I see how extremely religious you are in every way. For as I went through the city and looked carefully at the objects of your worship, I found among them an altar with the inscription, 'To an unknown god.' What therefore you worship as unknown, this I proclaim to you. The God who made the world and everything in it, he who is Lord of heaven and earth, does not live in shrines made by human hands, nor is he served by human hands, as though he needed anything, since he himself gives to all mortals life and breath and all things. From one ancestor he made all nations to inhabit the whole earth, and he allotted the times of their existence and the boundaries of the places where they would live, so that they would search for God and perhaps grope for him and find him—though indeed he is not far from each one of us. For 'In him we live and move and have our being'; as even some of your own poets have said,

    'For we too are his offspring.' "

LITANY

Peoples from every corner of creation,
Celebrate with all creatures on Earth!

Young and old across the planet,
Rejoice in the day that God has made!

Indigenous peoples of every land,
Help us sense the spirit deep in each land!

Black and white and brown and grey,
Celebrate with us the colors of creation!

All humanity on Planet Earth,
Praise God for our planet home.

Sing, peoples, sing!
Sing, creation, sing! *(Season of Creation)*

REFLECTIONS   LAO-TZU AND POPE FRANCIS

1. Every being in the universe
is an expression of the Tao.
It springs into existence,
unconscious, perfect, free,
takes on a physical body,
lets circumstances complete it.
That is why every being
spontaneously honors the Tao.
The Tao gives birth to all beings,
nourishes them, maintains them,
cares for them, comforts them, protects them,
takes them back to itself,
caring without possessing,
acting without expecting,
guiding without interfering.
That is why love of the Tao
is in the very nature of things.

Nothing is known about Lao-Tzu (ca. 571 B.C.E.) except that he left behind him a book of eighty-one chapters, which for the last 2,000 years have been called Tao Te Ching. *This modest little book bred Taoism and deeply influenced Buddhism;*

it led to Zen meditation and inspired Chinese poetry and landscape painting. It continues to serve as a guide for persons in search of the meaning of existence.

2. A sense of deep communion with the rest of nature cannot be real if our hearts lack tenderness, compassion and concern for our fellow human beings. It is clearly inconsistent to combat trafficking in endangered species while remaining completely indifferent to human trafficking, unconcerned about the poor, or undertaking to destroy another human being deemed unwanted. Everything is connected. Concern for the environment thus needs to be joined to a sincere love for our fellow human beings and an unwavering commitment to resolving the problems of society.

Pope Francis was named Jorge Mario Bergoglio when he was born in Buenos Aires in 1936, the first of five children of parents who had immigrated to Argentina from Italy. His father was an accountant and his mother a homemaker. He has always been a humble person, continuously reaching out to those around him, especially the poor. He became Pope in 2013. The encyclical Laudato Si', *from which this reflection and others in this book are drawn, is a seminal treatise on care for the earth, our common home.*

PRAYERS OF CONFESSION AND INTERCESSION

Living God, from the beginning you have been teaching us what goodness is and how human beings should live together: with integrity and justice, each one a refuge for the others. Forgive our hard-heartedness, our lack of imagination, our inability to read the value of each person and to bring out the best in everyone we meet. God, forgive us: we have made such a chaos of the earth. Forgive our babel sounds, our lust for power, religious strife, separating us from one another and sapping all life's joys. Teach us humility, keep our hope alive, sustain our love for all humanity, until conflict is stifled and we stand together in your silence which is filled with eternal praise. **Amen.** *(Alan Gaunt)*

O God, who created all peoples in your image, we thank you for the wonderful diversity of races and cultures in this world. Enrich our lives by ever-widening circles of fellowship, and show us your presence in those who differ most from us, until our knowledge of your love is made perfect in our love for all your children; through Jesus Christ our Lord. **Amen.** *(The Episcopal Church)*

15. God's Gift of Diversity

HYMN — O.I. CRICKET HARRISON

1. Restless Weaver, ever spinning
   threads of justice and shalom;
   dreaming patterns of creation
   where all creatures find a home;
   gathering up life's varied fibers—
   every texture, every hue:
   grant us your creative vision.
   With us weave your world anew.

2. Where earth's fragile web is raveling,
   help us mend each broken strand.
   Bless our urgent, bold endeavors
   cleansing water, air and land.
   Through the Spirit's inspiration—
   offering health where once was pain—
   strengthen us to be the stewards
   of your world knit whole again.

3. When our violent lust for power
   ends in lives abused and torn,
   from compassion's sturdy fabric
   fashion hope and trust reborn.
   Where injustice rules as tyrant,
   give us courage, God, to dare
   live our dreams of transformation.
   Make our lives incarnate prayer.

4. Restless Weaver, still conceiving
   new life—now and yet to be—
   binding all our vast creation
   in one living tapestry:
   you have called us to be weavers;
   let your love guide all we do.
   With your reign of peace our pattern,
   we will weave your world anew.

Tune: BEACH SPRING, 8.7.8.7.D.

May people live in peace, and may the Gospel of mercy become the source of good to all. May there be mutual love in the world encompassing all.
(Benediction from the Jain tradition)

SOURCES

Prayer by Carolyn J. Sharp © 2017 Carolyn J. Sharp. Used by permission.

"Peoples from every . . . ," in "Humanity Sunday," Australian Version 1, *Season of Creation*, accessed May 12, 2016, https://seasonofcreation.com/wp-content/uploads/2010/04/liturgy-humanity-sunday-1.doc, alt. © Season of Creation, developed by Norm Habel and the Uniting Church in Australia, Synod of Victoria and Tasmania, 2004, seasonofcreation.com, used with permission.

Lao-tzu, #15 ["Every being in the universe . . . "], from *Tao Te Ching: New English Version, with Foreword and Notes*, trans. Stephen Mitchell (New York: Perennial Classics, 2000), 51. Translation copyright © 1988 by Stephen Mitchell. Reprinted by permission of HarperCollins Publishers.

Pope Francis, *Laudato Si'*, accessed December 1, 2017, Vatican.va, 91. © Libreria Editrice Vaticana. Used by permission.

Alan Gaunt, "Living God, from the beginning . . ." and "God, forgive us . . . " in *New Prayers for Worship*, by Alan Gaunt (Leeds, UK. John Paul the Preacher's Press, 1972), p. 12 and p. 15 of section 3, "Confession and Forgiveness." Used by permission.

"For the Diversity of Races and Cultures," in Episcopal Church, *Book of Common Prayer* (New York: Church Publishing, 1986), 840.

Words by O. I. Cricket Harrison, "Restless Weaver, Ever Spinning" © 1995 Chalice Press. Used by permission of Chalice Press.

"May people live in peace . . . ," from Shri Jugal Kishor Mukhtyarji, "He who has subdued . . . ," in *World Prayers Project*, alt. Used courtesy of *The World Prayers Project*, www.worldprayers.org.

16. BIODIVERSITY

The rich interconnected varieties of plant and animal life on earth have a purpose in the web of life and benefit all. The humble earthworm breaks down organic matter that enriches the soil, enabling fruits and vegetables to flourish; insects and birds pollinate crops; microorganisms break down nutrients and metals and purify water. All of life is bound together in ways both known and yet to be discovered.

Let everything that breathes praise the Lord!
Praise the Lord! *(Psalm 150:6)*

PRAYERS OF PRAISE AND THANKSGIVING

We praise you, our Creator, for the grandeur and mystery of the universe. Its stretching back in time and its reaching out in space are beyond imagining. We praise you for the miracle of life on earth, the mysterious creation of living beings, the eternal cycle of life and death, the ceaseless emergence of new out of old. We praise you for the infinity of different creatures, each unique in its own way, each fitting into its own niche and all dependent on one another. We praise you, our Creator. **Amen.** *(Alan Litherland)*

Gracious God, you reveal your goodness in the beauty and diversity of creation: in the circle dance of earth and air and water; in a universe rich in processes that support growth and coherence, distinctiveness and community; and above all in the gift of Jesus Christ, who emptied himself to serve your world. And so we offer thanks and praise to you, one God in three persons: the Author and Source of all, Christ the Incarnate Word, and the Holy Spirit, one God, now and forever. **Amen.** *(The Episcopal Church)*

PSALM 98

O sing to the Lord a new song,
> for he has done marvelous things.

His right hand and his holy arm
> **have gotten him victory.**

The Lord has made known his victory;
> he has revealed his vindication in the sight of the nations.

He has remembered his steadfast love and faithfulness
> **to the house of Israel.**

All the ends of the earth have seen
> the victory of our God.

Make a joyful noise to the Lord, all the earth;
> **break forth into joyous song and sing praises.**

Sing praises to the Lord with the lyre,
> with the lyre and the sound of melody.

With trumpets and the sound of the horn
> **make a joyful noise before the King, the Lord.**

Let the sea roar, and all that fills it;
> the world and those who live in it.

Let the floods clap their hands;
> **let the hills sing together for joy**

at the presence of the Lord, for he is coming
> to judge the earth.

He will judge the world with righteousness,
> **and the peoples with equity.**

SCRIPTURE   GENESIS 1:11-12, 21-22, 24-25, 27, 29-31A

God said, "Let the earth put forth vegetation: plants yielding seed, and fruit trees of every kind on earth that bear fruit with the seed in it." And it was so. The earth brought forth vegetation: plants yielding seed of every kind, and trees of every kind bearing fruit with the seed in it. And God saw that it was good. . . . So God created the great sea monsters and every living creature that moves, of every kind, with which the waters swarm, and every winged bird of every kind. And God saw that it was good. God blessed them, saying, "Be fruitful and multiply and fill the waters in the seas, and let birds multiply on the earth." . . .

And God said, "Let the earth bring forth living creatures of every kind: cattle and creeping things and wild animals of the earth of every kind." And it was so. God made the wild animals of the earth of every kind, and the cattle of every kind, and everything that creeps upon the ground of every kind. And God saw that it was good. . . .

So God created humankind in his image,
    in the image of God he created them;
    male and female he created them. . . .

God said, "See, I have given you every plant yielding seed that is upon the face of all the earth, and every tree with seed in its fruit; you shall have them for food. And to every beast of the earth, and to every bird of the air, and to everything that creeps on the earth, everything that has the breath of life, I have given every green plant for food." And it was so. God saw everything that he had made, and indeed, it was very good.

LITANY

Loving God, we thank you that we live in a world with fish, birds and animals and you trust us to look after them.

Whales that sing beneath the waves, jellyfish and crabs, sticklebacks and sharks, leaping dolphins and porpoise schools, rainbow trout and octopus, halibut and piranha, carp and cod and cuttlefish. Living God, these are your creatures . . .
and we have named them.

Thrushes singing, swallows skimming, herons fishing, buzzards hovering, ospreys diving, penguins shuffling, pigeons pecking. Gracious God, these are your creatures . . .
and we have named them.

Elephants and cockroaches, gorillas and gerbils, badgers and hedgehogs, cows, pigs and sheep, kangaroos and koala bears, lions and lemurs, crocodiles and great apes. Amazing God, these are your creatures . . .
and we have named them.

Loving God, we pray for the unity of the whole breathing world, that we and all other creatures may live together in harmony and peace, in the name of Jesus.
Amen. *(Anthony G. Burnham)*

REFLECTION   ECUMENICAL PATRIARCH BARTHOLOMEW I

People of all faith traditions praise the Divine, for they seek to understand their relationship to the cosmos. The entire universe participates in the celebration of life, which St. Maximos the Confessor described as a "cosmic liturgy." We see this cosmic liturgy in the symbiosis of life's rich biological complexes. These complex relationships draw attention to themselves in humanity's self-conscious awareness of the cosmos. As human beings, created "in the image and likeness of God" (Genesis 1:26), we are called to recognize this interdependence between our environment and ourselves. In the bread and the wine of the Eucharist, as priests standing before the altar of the world, we offer Creation back to the Creator in relationship to Him and to each other.

We celebrate the beauty of creation and consecrate the life of the world, returning it to God with thanks. Thus it is that we offer the fullness of creation at the Eucharist, and receive it back as a blessing, as the living presence of God.

Ecumenical Patriarch Bartholomew I (b. 1940), Patriarch of Constantinople, is the spiritual leader of 300 million Orthodox Christians around the world. He has been active in interfaith dialogue seeking common ground between the Orthodox, Roman Catholics, Jews, and Muslims. For his outspoken calls to Christians to embrace their environmental responsibility and to care for God's good earth, he has earned the title "The Green Patriarch."

PRAYERS OF CONFESSION AND INTERCESSION

God of all creation, you love us into being, yet we often flee our rightful place in your creation. We confess that we exploit the gifts you place around us, and dominate the riches of the natural order. Forgive our greedy grasping. We confess our part in the devastation of our planet home, mirrored in the violence of cities, and the brokenness of hearts. Forgive and restore us, O God. Nurturing God, remind us of other ways to live and of a place called home, where creation reflects your goodness and each thing lives in balance with all others. Come and find us, set us right again, and take us home. **Amen.** *(Janet Cawley)*

Holy God, your mercy is over all your works, and in the web of life each creature has its role and place. We praise you for ocelot and owl, cactus and kelp, lichen and whale; we honor you for whirlwind and lava, tide and topsoil, cliff and marsh. Give us hearts and minds eager to care for your planet, humility to recognize all creatures as your beloved ones, justice to share the resources of the earth with all its inhabitants, and love not limited by our ignorance. This we pray in the name of Jesus, who unifies what is far off and what is near, and in whom, by grace and the working of your Holy Spirit, all things hold together. **Amen.** *(The Episcopal Church)*

HYMN   CECIL FRANCES ALEXANDER

Refrain:
All things bright and beautiful,
all creatures great and small,
all things wise and wonderful,
the Lord God made them all.

1. Each little flower that opens,
   each little bird that sings,
   he made their glowing colors,
   he made their tiny wings. *Refrain.*

2. The purple-headed mountain,
   the river running by,
   the sunset, and the morning
   that brightens up the sky. *Refrain.*

3. The cold wind in the winter,
   the pleasant summer sun,
   the ripe fruits in the garden,
   he made them every one. *Refrain.*

4. He gave us eyes to see them,
   and lips that we might tell
   how great is God Almighty,
   who has made all things well. *Refrain.*

Tune: ROYAL OAK, 7.6.7.6. and Refrain

Blessing and honor and thanksgiving and praise, more than we can utter, more than we can conceive, be to you, O most adorable Trinity, Father, Son and Holy Spirit, by all angels, all people, all creatures, for ever and ever. **Amen.** *(Thomas Ken)*

SOURCES

Alan Litherland, "Creation," in *Harvest for the World: A Worship Anthology on Sharing in the Work of Creation*, ed. Geoffrey Duncan (Cleveland: Pilgrim Press, 2003), 6–7. © Alan Litherland.

"Reading God's Goodness in the Diversity of Life," in Standing Commission on Liturgy and Music, "Liturgical Materials Honoring God in Creation and Various Rites and Prayers for Animals," in *Report to the 77th General Convention* (Episcopal Church, July 5–12, 2012), 320.

Anthony G. Burnham, "One World," first published 1990, revised March 2018. © 2018 Anthony G. Burnham. Used by permission.

Ecumenical Patriarch Bartholomew I, "Remarks as Prepared for Delivery Address of His All Holiness Ecumenical Patriarch Bartholomew at the Environmental Symposium Saint Barbara Greek Orthodox Church, Santa Barbara, California, 8 November 1997," Ecumenical Patriarchate, accessed March 15, 2018, https://www.patriarchate.org/-/remarks-as-prepared-for-delivery-address-of-his-all-holiness-ecumenical-patriarch-b-a-r-t-h-o-l-o-m-e-w-at-the-environmental-symposium-saint-barbara-g.

Janet Cawley, "God of all creation . . . ," in United Church of Canada, *Celebrate God's Presence: A Book of Services for The United Church of Canada*, ed. Karen J. Verveda (Etobicoke, Ontario: United Church Publishing House, 2000), 32. Used by permission.

"The Justice of God and the Dignity of All Creatures," in Standing Commission on Liturgy and Music, "Liturgical Materials Honoring God in Creation and Various Rites and Prayers for Animals," in *Report to the 77th General Convention* (Episcopal Church, July 5–12, 2012), 319.

Words by Cecil Frances Alexander, "All Things Bright and Beautiful" (1848). Public domain.

Thomas Ken, *A Manual of Prayers for the Use of the Scholars of Winchester College* (London, 1675), 57, alt. Public domain.

17. THE ONE HUMAN FAMILY

The carbon, nitrogen, and oxygen in our bodies, and in the bodies of all animals, and in earth itself were created in the previous generation of stars. The astronomer Carl Sagan said, "We are a way for the universe to know itself. Some part of our bodies knows this is where we come from. We're star stuff!" We are one human family intimately related to all that lives on earth.

There was a great multitude that no one could count, from every nation, from all tribes and peoples and languages, standing before the throne and before the Lamb, robed in white, with palm branches in their hands. They cried out in a loud voice, saying,

"Salvation belongs to our God who is seated on the throne, and to the Lamb!" *(Revelation 7:9-10)*

PRAYERS OF PRAISE AND THANKSGIVING

All humankind is one vast family, this world, our home. We sleep beneath one roof, the starry sky. We warm ourselves before one hearth, the blazing sun. Upon one soil we stand, and breathe one air, and drink one water, and walk the night beneath one luminescent moon. The children of one God are we, brothers and sisters of one blood, members in one worldwide family of God. Come, let us worship God. **Amen.** *(Cathedral of St. Paul the Apostle, Los Angeles)*

God, our Father and our Mother, Creator and Sustainer of the universe, we thank you for the wondrous ways in which you have revealed your love to us through the teaching of the sages of India, the wise of the East; through the enlightened words of the Buddha and the disciplined words of the prophet Mohammed, and through the light of the gospel of Jesus Christ. We pray that you will pour your love into our hearts, that with open minds we may accept all peoples of the world as brothers and sisters, and serve them in humility, so that all humankind may find the joy of true freedom in you. **Amen.** *(Rajah Jacob)*

CANTICLE   ISAIAH 60:1-5, 11A, 18, 20-21, 22A

Arise, shine; for your light has come,
    and the glory of the Lord has risen upon you.
For darkness shall cover the earth,
    and thick darkness the peoples;
but the Lord will arise upon you,
    and his glory will appear over you.
Nations shall come to your light,
    and kings to the brightness of your dawn.

Lift up your eyes and look around;
    they all gather together, they come to you;
Your sons shall come from far away,
    and your daughters shall be carried on their nurses' arms.
Then you shall see and be radiant;
    your heart shall thrill and rejoice,
because the abundance of the sea shall be brought to you,
    the wealth of the nations shall come to you. . . .
Your gates shall always be open;
day and night they shall not be shut. . . .

Violence shall no more be heard in your land,
    devastation or destruction within your borders;
you shall call your walls Salvation,
    and your gates Praise. . . .

Your sun shall no more go down,
    or your moon withdraw itself;
for the Lord will be your everlasting light,
    and your days of mourning shall be ended.
Your people shall all be righteous;
    they shall possess the land for ever.
They are the shoot that I planted, the work of my hands,
    so that I might be glorified. . . .

The least of them shall become a clan,
    and the smallest one a mighty nation.

17. The One Human Family

SCRIPTURE   EXODUS 3:2-5, 7-8A

There the angel of the Lord appeared to him in a flame of fire out of a bush; he looked, and the bush was blazing, yet it was not consumed. Then Moses said, "I must turn aside and look at this great sight, and see why the bush is not burned up." When the Lord saw that he had turned aside to see, God called to him out of the bush, "Moses, Moses!" And he said, "Here I am." Then he said, "Come no closer! Remove the sandals from your feet, for the place on which you are standing is holy ground." . . . Then the Lord said, "I have observed the misery of my people who are in Egypt; I have heard their cry on account of their taskmasters. Indeed, I know their sufferings, and I have come down to deliver them from the Egyptians, and to bring them up out of that land to a good and broad land, a land flowing with milk and honey."

LITANY

Like the seed grows into new bud by meeting with the earth,
you and I will become new people by meeting each other.
**Like the heaven creates a new day by meeting with the earth,
you and I will become a new creation by meeting each other.**

Everyone holds God's love by meeting each other.
**They meet again and again in love and hope,
you and I will create a new day by meeting each other.**

We believe in the love of God with endless hope,
you and I will become new people by meeting each other.
**Our lands and our nations are the country of God,
you and I will become new people by meeting each other.**

East and West will create peace by meeting each other,
North and South will embrace love by meeting each other,
you and I will become new people by meeting each other. *(Women Church, Seoul, Korea)*

REFLECTION   THE DALAI LAMA

No matter what part of the world we come from, we are all basically the same human beings. We have the same basic human needs and concerns. All of us human beings want freedom and the right to determine our own destiny as individuals and as peoples. As a Buddhist monk, my concern extends to all members of the human family and, indeed, to all sentient beings who suffer. I believe all suffering is caused by ignorance. People inflict pain on others in the selfish pursuit of their happiness or satisfaction. Yet true happiness comes from a sense of inner peace and contentment, which in turn must be achieved through the cultivation of altruism, of love and compassion and elimination of ignorance, selfishness and greed. Both science and the teachings of the Buddha tell us of the fundamental unity of all things. This understanding is crucial if we are to take positive and decisive action on the pressing global concern with the environment. I believe all religions pursue the same goals, that of cultivating human goodness and bringing happiness to all human beings. Though the means might appear different, the ends are the same.

Nobel Prize winner Tenzin Gyatso, the fourteenth Dalai Lama (b. 1935 in Tibet) works tirelessly for the liberation of Tibet, from which he has been exiled since 1959. Since then he has traveled to over sixty countries, teaching Buddhism's message of compassion toward all as a way of experiencing deep happiness. He collaborates with other world religious leaders, seeking common ground in fulfilling our universal responsibility to care for the earth.

PRAYERS OF CONFESSION AND INTERCESSION

O God, you made us in your own image and redeemed us through Jesus your Son: Look with compassion on the whole human family; take away the arrogance and hatred which infect our hearts; break down the walls that separate us; unite us in bonds of love; and work through our struggle and confusion to accomplish your purposes on earth; that, in your good time, all nations and races may serve you in harmony around your heavenly throne; through Jesus Christ our Lord. **Amen.** *(The Episcopal Church)*

O God, you are the hope of all the ends of the earth, the God of the spirits of all flesh. Hear our humble intercession for all races and families on earth, that you will turn all hearts to yourself. Remove from our minds hatred, prejudice, and contempt for those who are not of our own race or color, class or creed, that, departing from everything that estranges and divides, we may by you be brought into unity of spirit, in the bond of peace. **Amen.** *(Church of Scotland)*

17. The One Human Family

HYMN   JEFFERY ROWTHORN

1. As conflicts rage and lives are lost,
   in war we trust, whate'er the cost;
   yet here, amid the dust, we pray:
   "Have mercy, Lord, grant peace today."

2. Come, Man of Sorrows, weeping still
   to see such readiness to kill,
   each heart from rage and fear release
   to find in you fresh hope and peace.

3. Come, Risen Christ, throw open wide
   the doors we bolt from scorn and pride,
   and bless us with humility
   to live at peace, one family.

4. Come, Lord of All, and help us see
   the havoc done to land and sea;
   let our indulgent greed give way
   to making peace with earth this day.

5. Come, Prince of Peace, our hatreds stem
   and build your new Jerusalem
   where spire and minaret and dome
   proclaim to all: Salaam! Shalom!

Tune: BRESLAU, L.M., 8.8.8.8.
Words © 2003 Hope Publishing

Praise the LORD, all you nations!
    Extol him, all you peoples!
For great is his steadfast love toward us,
    and the faithfulness of the LORD endures forever.
Praise the LORD! *(Psalm 117:1-2)*

SOURCES

"All humankind is one vast family . . . ," in *Human Rites*, ed. Hannah Ward and Jennifer Wild (London: Mowbray Publishing, 1995), p. 243, alt. Attributed to the Book of Remembrance of the Cathedral of St. Paul the Apostle, Los Angeles, California. © 1995, *Human Rites*, Mowbray, used by permission of Bloomsbury Publishing Plc.

Rajah Jacob, "God, our Father . . . ," in *Oceans of Prayer*, comp. Maureen Edwards and Jan S. Pickard (Nutfield, UK: National Christian Education Council, U.K., 1991), 57. Originally from *Healing the Earth* (Uniting Church in Australia, 1990). Used by permission of the Uniting Church in Australia.

"New Meeting," trans. Sook Ja Chung, in *Dissident Daughters: Feminist Liturgies in Global Context*, ed. Theresa Berger (Louisville, KY: Westminster John Knox, 2001), 95. Translated from *Our Hymns*, Women Church Resources, No. 8 (Seoul: Women Church, 1995). Used by permission of Westminster John Knox Press.

Tenzin Gyatso [Dalai Lama], "Acceptance," in *Nobel Lectures Including Presentation and Acceptance Speeches and Laureates' Biographies: Peace, 1981–1990*, ed. Tore Frängsmyr and Irwin Abrams (Singapore: World Scientific, 1997), 247–49. © The Nobel Foundation. Used by permission.

"For the Human Family," in Episcopal Church, *Book of Common Prayer* (New York: Church Publishing, 1986), 815.

"O God, who art [you are] . . . ," in *Prayers for the Christian Year*, by General Assembly of the Church of Scotland (London: Oxford University Press, 1935), 103, alt. Used by permission of the Church of Scotland.

Words by Jeffery Rowthorn, "As Conflicts Rage and Lives Are Lost" © 2003 Hope Publishing Company, Carol Stream, IL 60188. All rights reserved. Used by permission.

18. CHILDREN

Emerging from the birth canal, the baby's first cry announces, "I am!" "I am here!" As the years pass, this tiny bundle will bring joy, wonder, laughter, hope, and yes, heartbreak. This child, and every child, is the Creator's promise that the human family on earth will continue, to the next generation and the next.

"Truly I tell you, unless you change and become like children, you will never enter the kingdom of heaven." *(Matthew 18:3)*

PRAYERS OF PRAISE AND THANKSGIVING

God of wonder, God of joy, we thank you for your precious gift of children. Through their eyes, we see your hopes and dreams for all humanity; through their love we feel your love; through their idealism we envision a world of justice and liberation for every person on earth; through their generous hearts we reach out to all who need and seek you; through their courage we act courageously. We thank you for all children and we pray that you will protect and guide them in all their ways. We pray especially for children who are endangered, abused, or used; for all who are living in poverty and despair; and for all whose hopes and dreams are being crushed. Give them comfort and strength to hold fast to you, feeling your love for them in the depth of their hearts; and may we follow the example of our Lord and Savior Jesus Christ who said, "Let the children come to me." (Matt. 19:14). **Amen.** *(Anne Rowthorn)*

Holy God, from whom every family on earth takes its name, we thank you. Strengthen parents to be responsible and loving that their children may know security and joy. Lead children to honor parents by compassion and forgiveness. May all people discover your parental care by the respect and love given them by others. God of mercy, hear our prayer. **Amen.** *(Presbyterian Church, USA)*

CANTICLE   ISAIAH 11:6-9

The wolf shall live with the lamb,
>   the leopard shall lie down with the kid,
> **the calf and the lion and the fatling together,**
>   **and a little child shall lead them.**
> The cow and the bear shall graze,
>   their young shall lie down together;
>   **and the lion shall eat straw like the ox.**
> The nursing child shall play over the hole of the asp,
>   and the weaned child shall put its hand on the adder's den.
> **They will not hurt or destroy**
>   **on all my holy mountain;**
> for the earth will be full of the knowledge of the Lord
>   as the waters cover the sea.

SCRIPTURE   MARK 9:33-37; 10:13-16

They came to Capernaum; and when he was in the house he asked them, "What were you arguing about on the way?" But they were silent, for on the way they had argued with one another who was the greatest. He sat down, called the twelve, and said to them, "Whoever wants to be first must be last of all and servant of all." Then he took a little child and put it among them; and taking it in his arms, he said to them, "Whoever welcomes one such child in my name welcomes me, and whoever welcomes me welcomes not me but the one who sent me." . . . People were bringing little children to him in order that he might touch them; and the disciples spoke sternly to them. But when Jesus saw this, he was indignant and said to them, "Let the little children come to me; do not stop them; for it is to such as these that the kingdom of God belongs. Truly I tell you, whoever does not receive the kingdom of God as a little child will never enter it." And he took them up in his arms, laid his hands on them, and blessed them.

LITANY

We pray for all children growing up in our world . . .
Pause.
We pray for children growing up in places of danger where there is fighting and fear (especially—) . . . *Name them.*

We pray for children who are in trouble, who are bullied or abused, who are hungry . . .
Pause.
We pray for children who are ill, for children whose life is a struggle, for children who are in pain . . .
Pause.

We pray for children whose names we know and we ask God to help them.
Pause.
Jesus, you called the children to you and you blessed them. We ask you to bless the children we have prayed for today and to help us all to grow in love. Amen. *(Ruth Burgess)*

REFLECTION   ANTÓNIO GUTERRES

Dear young people, the future of our planet . . . the future peace of our world . . . is in your hands. I am sorry to say that we adults are letting you down. Millions of girls and boys like you are in danger, and we are letting them down. They are fleeing deadly conflicts. They are going hungry or without the medicine they need. They are separated from their parents or making long, dangerous journeys to safety. They are displaced and living in refugee camps far from home. Many are being bullied online or in school. Or suffer from discrimination because of their religion, the color of their skin, or their ethnicity. And so often, they are victims of violence or exploitation at the hands of adults. All this is completely unacceptable. As a global community, we cannot continue failing all the children.

Every child has a right to a safe, healthy, peaceful childhood and to develop to their full potential. Today's children are tomorrow's leaders . . . Tomorrow's presidents and prime ministers . . . Tomorrow's teachers and innovators . . . Tomorrow's mothers and fathers . . .

How can we work together to best support and protect you—the children of the world? And how can we benefit from your vision and your suggestions? How can we shape a more sustainable future that will give every child, in every society, every opportunity not merely to survive, but to thrive?

Whenever I meet children—including and especially those living in the poorest, most desperate situations, suffering terrible hardships—they never fail to inspire me with their smiles, their laughter, their vision and their hope. In a world that can so often seem to be a hopeless place, we need children's hope, more than ever. The future of the world is in children's hands. But we can never forget that children's futures are in our hands.

There is no greater responsibility. No more important job. And no better pathway to a better, healthier, more peaceful world for every person . . . every family . . . and every child.

Secretary-General of the United Nations António Guterres (b. 1949) was prime minister of Portugal and then United Nations high commissioner for refugees. This Reflection is taken from a speech to the children of the world on World Children's Day, November 20, 2017.

PRAYERS OF CONFESSION AND INTERCESSION

I saw a child today, Lord, who will not die tonight, harried into hunger's grave. He was bright and full of life because his father has a job and feeds him, but somewhere, everywhere, ten thousand life-lamps will go out and not be lit tomorrow. Lord, teach me my sin. **Amen.** *(Anonymous African Christian)*

Jesus, you saw the world through the eyes of a child. Save us from the pride that would refuse your command to live like you in simplicity and joy. **Amen.** *(Anglican Church of New Zealand)*

God of all good gifts, your Son gathered children into his arms and blessed them. Help us to understand our young people as they grow in years and in knowledge of your world. Give us compassion when they face temptations and experience failures. Teach us to encourage their search for truth and value in their lives. Help us to appreciate their ideals and sympathize with their frustrations; that with them we may look for a better world than either we or they have known; through Jesus Christ our Lord. **Amen.** *(Evangelical Lutheran Church in America)*

18. Children

HYMN   SHIRLEY ERENA MURRAY

1. There is no child so small,
   no scrap of life so precious
   who is not born like Jesus,
   whose cry is like us all.

2. There is no child unfed,
   left hungry now at Christmas
   but God will ask for justice,
   for shelter and for bread.

3. There is no child so lost,
   no refugee so nameless
   that God will leave us blameless,
   who share no care or cost.

4. There is no child so cheap,
   in warfare or destruction,
   that love cannot take action
   when God is made to weep.

5. There is not one of us
   who could not be more giving,
   and in the gift more loving,
   to light a star for peace.

Tune: LEAST CHILD, 6.7.7.6.
Words © 2008 Hope Publishing

> Speak out for those who cannot speak,
>   for the rights of all the destitute.
> Speak out, judge righteously,
>   defend the rights of the poor and needy. *(Proverbs 31:8-9)*

SOURCES

Anne Rowthorn, "God of Wonder, God of Joy" © 2016 Anne Rowthorn.

"Prayers of the People: B," in Presbyterian Church (USA), *Book of Common Worship* (Louisville, KY: Westminster John Knox, 1993), 105, alt. Reprinted by permission from *Book of Common Worship*, © 1993 Westminster John Knox Press.

Ruth Burgess, "We pray for all . . . ," in *Holy Ground: Liturgies and Worship Resources for an Engaged Spirituality*, ed. Neil Paynter and Helen Boothroyd (Glasgow: Wild Goose, 2005), 139. © Contributors, *Holy Ground* (2005), Wild Goose Publications, Glasgow. Used by permission.

António Guterres, speech marking United Nations World Children's Day, November 20, 2017, United Nations, accessed February 3, 2018, http://www.un.org/en/events/childrenday/messages.shtml. © 2017 United Nations. Reprinted with the permission of the United Nations.

"I saw a child . . . ," in *With All God's People: The New Ecumenical Prayer Cycle*, ed. John Carden (Geneva: WCC Publications, 1989), 178. From prayer of an African Christian in "Prayers for the Harvest Leaflet 1986," Christian Aid, London, UK.

"Jesus, your ways [you saw] . . . ," in Church of the Province of New Zealand, *A New Zealand Prayer Book: He Karakia Mihinare o Aotearoa* (Auckland, New Zealand: William Collins, 1989), 563. © 1989 The Provincial Secretary, The Church of the Province of New Zealand, Box 2148, Rotorua. Used by permission.

"Young Persons," in Evangelical Lutheran Church in America, *Evangelical Lutheran Worship*, Leaders Desk ed. (Minneapolis: Augsburg Fortress, 2006), 152. Adapted from prayer by Massey H. Shepherd Jr. in *Give Us Grace: An Anthology of Anglican Prayers*, 406. Used by permission.

Words by Shirley Erena Murray, "There Is No Child So Small (Carol of the Least Child)" © 2008 Hope Publishing Company, Carol Stream, IL 60188. All rights reserved. Used by permission.

19. THE WISDOM OF INDIGENOUS CULTURES

The United Nations counts 370 million indigenous people living in 70 nations worldwide. Though richly varied in traditions, they share certain core beliefs: a religious attachment to the land many consider sacred; an intimate knowledge of and respect for the Earth; the necessity of living in harmony with the forces of nature and with all living creatures; a sense of sharing and hospitality.

When we hear the warbling of the mountain thrush in the blossoms or the voice of the frog in the water, we know that every living being has a song. *(Ki no Tsurayuki)*

PRAYERS OF PRAISE AND THANKSGIVING

Ho! Grandfather, Grandmother, you have made everything and are in everything, you sustain everything, guide everything, provide everything, and protect everything because everything belongs to you. We are weak, poor and lowly, nevertheless help us to care in appreciation and gratitude to you for everything. We love the stars, the sun, and the moon, and we thank you for our beautiful mother, the earth, whose many gifts nourish the fish, the fowl, and the animals too. **Amen.** *(Vine Deloria)*

O great and kind Spirit, you have always been and before you nothing has been. There is no one to pray to but you. The star nations all over the heavens are yours, and yours are the grasses of the earth. You are older than all need, older than all pain and prayer. O great and kind Spirit, all over the world, the faces of the living ones are alike. With tenderness they have come out of the earth from which you give us food. Look on your people. With children in their arms, they face the wind and walk the red road to the day of quiet.

O great and kind Spirit, fill us with light. Give us strength to understand and eyes to see deeply. Teach us to walk softly on earth as relatives to all that live. Help us! Without you, we are nothing.

Make our spirits one with yours, Great Spirit. Help us to know, like the soaring eagle, the heights of knowledge. From the Four Directions, fill us with the four virtues of fortitude, generosity, respect and wisdom, so that we will help our people walk in the path of understanding and peace. Finally, great and kind Spirit, help us always to return our thanks to you. **Amen.** *(A prayer in the Lakota tradition)*

PSALM 104:1, 2B-5, 10-13

Bless the Lord, O my soul.
    O Lord my God, you are very great.
    You are clothed with honor and majesty. . . .
You stretch out the heavens like a tent,
    you set the beams of your chambers on the waters,
you make the clouds your chariot,
    you ride on the wings of the wind,
you make the winds your messengers,
    fire and flame your ministers.

You set the earth on its foundations,
    so that it shall never be shaken. . . .
You make springs gush forth in the valleys;
    they flow between the hills,
giving drink to every wild animal;
    the wild asses quench their thirst.
By the streams the birds of the air have their habitation;
    they sing among the branches.
From your lofty abode you water the mountains;
    the earth is satisfied with the fruit of your work.

READINGS   HYMN TO THE EARTH, ATHARVA-VEDA, AND JOB 28:24-28A

1. O Mother, with your oceans, rivers and other bodies of water, you give us land to grow grains on which our survival depends. Please give us as much milk, fruits, water and cereals as we need to eat and drink. O Mother, bearing folk who speak different languages, and follow different religions, treating

them all as residents of the same house, please pour, like a cow who never fails, a thousand streams of treasure to enrich us. May you, our motherland, on whom grow wheat, rice and barley, on whom are born five races of humanity, be nourished by the cloud, and loved by the rain.

2. "For he looks to the ends of the earth,
   and sees everything under the heavens.
When he gave to the wind its weight,
   and apportioned out the waters by measure;
when he made a decree for the rain,
   and a way for the thunderbolt;
then he saw it and declared it;
   he established it, and searched it out.
And he said to humankind,
'Truly, the fear of the Lord, that is wisdom.'"

LITANY

Creator, we long for wholeness in our families, for honest, open communication to say what we need to say in safety and without fear.

We give thanks for the knowledge you give in all traditions of the world. Help us to honor the gifts of all traditions.
Teach us to know how to love and live.

We give thanks for new life, for youth, represented by the eastern direction. We give thanks for new learning, for the sun which rises to begin each new day, and for the teachings of the peoples of the east.
Teach us to know how to love and live.

We give thanks for the people of the south, for the growth of the summertime in our lives, the learnings of our adult lives, to be kind and accept ourselves. Teach us as parents to love and respect our children, to care for the elders and those who cannot care for themselves.
Teach us to know how to love and live.

We give thanks for the west, for the gifts of aboriginal peoples of the world, for understandings of care of the earth, for teachings about rocks, leaves and trees, for the knowledge we have in our own teachings, all of these given by our Creator. Help us to use our understandings to bring joy and new life to our communities.
Teach us to know how to love and live.

We give thanks for the people of the north and for the elders in our families and communities. Help us to receive gifts of wisdom from all peoples. Help us to grow our roots deeper through life's journey, that we may grow in kindness to ourselves and each other.
Teach us to know how to love and live. *(United Church of Canada and Anglican Church of Canada)*

REFLECTION   VINE DELORIA, JR.

American society could save itself by listening to tribal people. The land-use philosophy of Indians is so utterly simple that it seems stupid to repeat it: man must live with other forms of life on the land and not destroy it. Interest in the survival of humanity as a species must take precedence over economic interests. In addition to cleaning up streams and rivers and cutting down on air pollution, a total change in land use should be instituted. . . . Increase in oxygen-producing plants and organisms should be made first priority. Vast land areas should be reforested and bays should be returned to their natural state. Erosion and destruction of topsoil by wind reduces effectiveness of conservation efforts. To survive, white society must return the land to the Indians in the sense that it restores the land to the condition it was in before the white man came.

Vine Deloria, Jr. (1933–2005), championed the rights of indigenous Americans. Nephew of anthropologist Ella Deloria and son of Vine Deloria, beloved Episcopal priest and archdeacon of South Dakota, Vine Deloria, Jr., aroused the consciousness of the nation with the publication of his book Custer Died for Your Sins *in 1969. He worked to demythologize the ways white Americans thought of Native Americans; not romantic figures of the hunt and vision quest, but living persons who have been robbed of ancestral lands, abused, and made victims of genocide.*

PRAYERS OF CONFESSION AND INTERCESSION

Grandfather, look at our brokenness. Now we must put the sanctity of life as the most sacred principle of power, and renounce the awesome might of materialism. We know that in all creation only the human family has strayed from the Sacred Way. We know that we are the ones who are divided and we are the ones who must come back together to worship and walk in the Sacred Way. Grandfather, Sacred One, teach us love, compassion and honor that we may heal the earth and heal each other. **Amen.** *(Arthur Solomon)*

Creator God, you have called us to be keepers of your Earth. Through greed we have established an economy that destroys the web of life. We have changed our climate and we drown in despair. Let oceans of justice flow. May we learn to sustain and renew the life of our Mother Earth. We stand with indigenous people worldwide who are demanding restoration of their ancestral lands. We pray for our leaders, custodians of Mother Earth, that they may negotiate with wisdom and fairness. May they act with compassion and courage; and lead us into the path of justice for the sake of our children and our children's children. **Amen.** *(Desmond Tutu)*

HYMN   JEFFERY ROWTHORN

1. The whole creation is a song
   of praise to God millennia long;
   each star, each wave, each cell and seed
   gives thanks for God's creating deed.

2. Transcending time, encircling space,
   this song resounds in every place;
   each nation, language, creed and race
   reveals God's providential grace.

3. From Bethlehem to Calvary
   one voice sang out to set us free,
   so earth below joins heaven above
   to tell of God's redeeming love.

4. Now let us sing with gratitude,
   for Christ is raised and hope renewed,
   and for earth's sake be bold and dare
   to mirror God's unfailing care.

Tune: O WALY WALY, L.M., 8.8.8.8
Words © 1993 Hope Publishing

Overshadow us now with your beauty and your joy, that our world may know a sabbath of wholeness and peace, today and forever. *(Brothers of Weston Priory)*

SOURCES

Ki no Tsurayuki, "Kanajo: The Japanese Preface," trans. Laurel Rasplica Rodd, in *Kokinshū: A Collection of Poems Ancient and Modern*, trans. Laurel Rasplica Rodd and Mary Catherine Henkenius (Boston: Cheng & Tsui, 1996), 35, alt. Used by permission.

Vine Deloria, "Ho! Grandfather, Grandmother . . . ," in *Worship Resources*, comp. Juanita J. Helphrey (Minneapolis: Council for American Indian Ministry, United Church of Christ, 1991), 9, alt.

Adapted by Talitha Arnold from "My spirit is one . . . ," in United Church of Christ, *The New Century Hymnal* (Cleveland: Pilgrim Press, 1995), no. 851. Used by permission of Talitha Arnold.

Atharva-Veda XII, "Hymn to the Earth," in *Hymns from the Vedas: Original Text and English Translation*, trans. Abinash Chandra Bose (Bombay: Asia Publishing House, 1966), 363–79, alt.

"A Four Directions Prayer," in *The Dancing Sun*, vol. 7, alt. © United Church of Canada and Anglican Church of Canada. Used with permission of United Church Publishing House and Anglican Church of Canada.

Vine Deloria Jr., *We Talk, You Listen: New Tribes, New Turf*, Bison Books ed. (Lincoln: University of Nebraska Press, 2007), 189–90, 194. Reproduced from *We Talk, You Listen: New Tribes, New Turf* by Vine Deloria Jr. by permission of the University of Nebraska Press. Copyright © 1970 by Vine Deloria Jr.

Arthur Solomon, "Grandfather Look at Our Brokenness," in *Songs for the People: Teachings on the Natural Way: Poems and Essays of Arthur Solomon, A Nishnawbe Spiritual Teacher*, ed. Michael Posluns (Toronto: NC Press, 1990), 159, alt. © 1990 Arthur Solomon. Used by permission of S. Eva Solomon, CSJ.

Desmond Tutu, "Climate Prayer" (prayer, United Nations Climate Summit, New York, NY, September 23, 2014), alt.

Words by Jeffery Rowthorn, "The Whole Creation Is a Song" © 1993 Hope Publishing Company, Carol Stream, IL 60188. All rights reserved. Used by permission.

The Brothers of Weston Priory, "Prayer of Blessing 1," in *Hear the Song of Your People: Morning and Evening Prayer at Weston Priory* (Weston, VT: The Brothers of Weston Priory, 1998). © 1998 The Benedictine Foundation of the State of Vermont, Inc. Weston Priory, Weston, Vermont. Used by permission.

20. ANIMALS

Snakes, spiders, slugs and sharks, bats and rats, mosquitoes and maggots, hyenas, alligators, crocodiles, and jellyfish; seals and snow leopards, horses and buffalo, polar bears and panda bears, otters and owls, penguins, parrots, cats of the forest and cats of the home, dogs and dolphins—whether we are attracted or repelled by them, every living creature on earth has its purpose and place in the web of life.

You make springs gush forth in the valleys;
    they flow between the hills,
giving drink to every wild animal;
    the wild asses quench their thirst. *(Psalm 104:10-11)*

PRAYERS OF PRAISE AND THANKSGIVING

Father, we praise you with all your creatures. They came forth from your all-powerful hand; they are yours, filled with your presence and your tender love. Praise be to you! Awaken our praise and thankfulness for every being that you have made. Give us the grace to feel profoundly joined to everything that is. God of love, show us our place in this world as channels of your love for all the creatures of this earth, for not one of them is forgotten in your sight. Praise be to you! **Amen.** *(Pope Francis)*

The animals of God's creation inhabit the skies, the earth, and the sea. They share in the fortunes of our existence and are an important part of human life. In the story of the great flood, the animals were saved from the waters, and afterwards were made a part of the covenant with Noah. A giant fish saved Jonah; ravens brought bread to Elijah. Animals were included in the repentance of Nineveh; and animals share in Christ's redemption of all creation. We therefore gather to ask God's blessing on these animals. As we do so, let us praise the Creator and give thanks to God for the animals in all our lives. **Amen.** *(United Methodist Church)*

CANTICLE   JOB 12:7-10, PSALM 147:9, PSALM 148:9-10, PSALM 150:6

"Ask the animals, and they will teach you;
    the birds of the air, and they will tell you;
ask the plants of the earth, and they will teach you;
    and the fish of the sea will declare to you.
Who among all these does not know
    that the hand of the LORD has done this?
In his hand is the life of every living thing
    and the breath of every human being." . . .
He gives to the animals their food,
    and to the young ravens when they cry. . . .
Mountains and all hills,
    fruit trees and all cedars!
Wild animals and all cattle,
    creeping things and flying birds!
Let everything that breathes praise the LORD!
Praise the LORD!

SCRIPTURE   JOB 38:41; 39:1-6, 9-12, 19-20A, 26-29

Who provides for the raven its prey,
    when its young ones cry to God,
    and wander about for lack of food? . . .
"Do you know when the mountain goats give birth?
    Do you observe the calving of the deer?
Can you number the months that they fulfill,
    and do you know the time when they give birth,
when they crouch to give birth to their offspring,
    and are delivered of their young?
Their young ones become strong, they grow up in the open;
    they go forth, and do not return to them.

"Who has let the wild ass go free?
    Who has loosed the bonds of the swift ass,
to which I have given the steppe for its home,
    the salt land for its dwelling-place? . . .
"Is the wild ox willing to serve you?
    Will it spend the night at your crib?

Can you tie it in the furrow with ropes,
> or will it harrow the valleys after you?
Will you depend on it because its strength is great,
> and will you hand over your labor to it?
Do you have faith in it that it will return,
> and bring your grain to your threshing-floor? . . .
"Do you give the horse its might?
Do you clothe its neck with mane?
> Do you make it leap like the locust? . . .
"Is it by your wisdom that the hawk soars,
> and spreads its wings towards the south?
Is it at your command that the eagle mounts up
> and makes its nest on high?
It lives on the rock and makes its home
> in the fastness of the rocky crag.
From there it spies the prey;
> its eyes see it from far away."

LITANY

God created us and all animals, sharing the spirit of life with us and all creatures; therefore let us praise God, saying:
O God, how wonderful are the works of your hands.

We thank you, God, for the gift of life: for the beauty and wonder of creation, and for our own life which comes from you.
O God, how wonderful are the works of your hands.

We thank you for the richness and variety of animal life: for fish and birds, insects, reptiles, and mammals.
O God, how wonderful are the works of your hands.

We thank you for animals of the farm: cattle and goats, pigs, sheep and chickens.
O God, how wonderful are the works of your hands.

We thank you for animals of the forest: wolves and foxes, deer, wild sheep, bears and badgers, elk and mountain lions.
O God, how wonderful are the works of your hands.

We thank you for the animals who give us faithful companionship, joy when we are happy, and comfort when we are sad.
O God, how wonderful are the works of your hands.

We thank you for animals who are our partners in daily life and work: seeing eye dogs, rescue, service and police dogs, animals that pull plows, wagons and sleighs.
O God, how wonderful are the works of your hands. *(Anglican Church in Canada)*

REFLECTION   JOHN MUIR

The world, we are told, was made especially for man, a presumption not supported by all the facts. They have precise dogmatic insight of the intentions of the Creator, and it is hardly possible to be guilty of irreverence in speaking of *their* God any more than of heathen idols. How about those man-eating animals—lions, tigers, alligators—which smack their lips over raw man? Or about those myriads of noxious insects that destroy labor and drink his blood? It never seems to occur to these far-seeing teachers that Nature's object in making animals and plants might possibly be first of all the happiness of each one of them, not the creation of all for the happiness of one. Why should man value himself as more than a small part of the one great unit of creation? And what creature of all that the Lord has taken the pains to make is not essential to the completeness of that unit—the cosmos? The universe would be incomplete without man; but it would also be incomplete without the smallest trans-microscopic creature that dwells beyond our conceited eyes and knowledge. From the dust of the earth, from the common elementary fund, the Creator has made *homo sapiens*. From the same material he has made every creature. They are earth-born companions and our fellow mortals.

Throughout all his writings, the great naturalist John Muir (1838–1914) refers to animals as "people" and as "our fellow mortals," as in this selection. He maintained that every life is of value for its own sake, not for its usefulness to human beings, and that every being—whether plant or animal—has its unique place in the cosmos.

PRAYERS OF CONFESSION AND INTERCESSION

God, our Creator, help us to love all creatures as kin to us, all animals as partners on Earth, all birds as messengers of praise, all minute beings as expressions of your mysterious design and all frogs as voices of hope. We are sorry for all the times we have hurt or neglected animals. We are sorry for all the times we have used poisons that have killed animals. We are sorry for all the times we have destroyed the homes of animals in forests, oceans, deserts and fields. We are sorry we have polluted the air that birds fly through. We repent and pledge to honor the place of animals in the circle of life. **Amen.** *(Season of Creation)*

Hear our humble prayer, O God, for our friends the animals, especially the animals who are suffering; for any that are hunted or lost or deserted or frightened or hungry; for all who must be put to death. We entreat for them all your mercy and pity, and for those who deal with them we ask a heart of compassion, gentle hands, and kind words. Make us ourselves to be true friends to animals, and so to share the blessings of the Merciful One. **Amen.** *(Albert Schweitzer)*

O God who has made the earth and every creature that dwells therein, help us, we pray, to treat with compassion the living creatures entrusted to our care, that they may not suffer neglect, nor be cruelly treated. Bless all who serve in their behalf, and help us in our care for them to have a deeper understanding of your love for all creation; through Jesus Christ our Lord. **Amen.** *(Anglican Church in Kenya)*

HYMN — CAROLYN WINFREY GILLETTE

1. O God, your creatures fill the earth
    with wonder and delight,
   and every living thing has worth and
    beauty in your sight.
   So playful dolphins dance and swim;
    your sheep bow down and graze.
   Your songbirds share a morning
    hymn to offer you their praise.

2. You made the pets we welcome in—
    they're wondrous blessings, too.
   With paws and whiskers, wings and
    fins, they offer praise to you.
   O Lord, you call us to embrace these
    creatures in our care.
   May we show kindness, love and
    grace to all pets everywhere.

3. You made the creatures on each farm;
    you know the things they need.
   May they grow healthy, safe from
    harm, and safe from human greed.
   Just as a shepherd loves the sheep,
    you know their joy, their pain.
   Lord, bless the animals we keep; may
    all farms be humane.

4. Your creatures live in every land; they
    fill the sky and sea.
   O Lord, you give us your command
    to love them tenderly.
   We're called to have dominion here—
    to care for them always.
   By loving creatures you hold dear, we
    offer you our praise.

Tune: ELLACOMBE, 8.6.8.6.D.

> O Lord, how manifold are your works!
> In wisdom you have made them all;
>   the earth is full of your creatures. *(Psalm 104:24)*

SOURCES

Pope Francis, "A Christian Prayer in Union with Creation," in *Laudato Si'*, accessed December 1, 2017, Vatican.va. © Libreria Editrice Vaticana. Used by permission.

"The animals of God's creation . . . ," in United Church of Canada, *Celebrate God's Presence: A Book of Services for the United Church of Canada*, ed. Karen J. Verveda (Etobicoke, Ontario: United Church Publishing House, 2000), 624. Altered from *The United Methodist Book of Worship* (Nashville: United Methodist Publishing House, 1992), 608–609. Used with permission of the United Church of Canada and United Methodist Publishing House. © 1992 The United Methodist Publishing House. Used by permission. All rights reserved.

"We thank you, God . . . ," in Anglican Church of Canada, *Occasional Celebrations of the Anglican Church of Canada* (Toronto: Anglican Book Centre, 1992), 160–61, alt. © 1992 General Synod of the Anglican Church in Canada. Used by permission.

John Muir, *A Thousand Mile Walk to the Gulf* (Boston: Houghton Mifflin, 1916), 136, 138–39. Public domain.

"God, our Creator . . . ," in "Blessing of the Animals: St Francis Sunday," *Season of Creation*, accessed October 18, 2017, https://seasonofcreation.com/wp-content/uploads/2010/04/liturgy-blessing-of-animals-sunday-1.doc, alt. © Season of Creation, developed by Norm Habel and the Uniting Church in Australia, Synod of Victoria and Tasmania, 2004, seasonofcreation.com, used with permission.

Attributed to Albert Schweitzer. Source unknown.

"For Animals," in Anglican Church in Kenya, *Our Modern Services* (Nairobi, Kenya: Uzima Press, 2003), 296, alt.

Carolyn Winfrey Gillette, "O God, Your Creatures Fill the Earth" © 2011 by Carolyn Winfrey Gillette. All rights reserved. www.carolynshymns.com. Used by permission.

The Human Community and Its Needs

21. A GOOD SOCIETY

Public schools, libraries, parks, access to medical care, housing, healthy food, freedom to worship and speak out freely—these are legal provisions of a good society. Habits of the heart also contribute to a good society—caring, helping, respecting, and encouraging, especially children, the elderly, and those on the margins. A good society makes good people better.

Thus says YHWH: "Do what is right! Work for justice! For my liberation is about to come, and my justice is about to be revealed." *(Isaiah 56:1)*

PRAYERS OF PRAISE AND THANKSGIVING

Eternal God of all people and races, may all your children learn to live together in peace and friendship. Let the day come when oppression, discrimination, and prejudice will be forgotten, and all the world filled with your spirit. May that day come soon, O Lord; the day foretold by our prophets and sages, the day for which we long, when all humanity will recognize that it is one family. **Amen.** *(Central Conference of American Rabbis)*

Blessed are you, Sovereign God, conqueror of death; your light invades the places of darkness, restores sight and joy to the blind, and summons those enslaved by death to walk free in hope. For us Jesus poured out his life like water, and lay bound in the dusk of death. In his rising a new world is created, where light, goodness, and joy spring forth. The rule of sin is broken forever; love and truth drive out hatred and folly; a new humanity is clothed with your love and sings with hope of beauty to come. Joy to those who walk in darkness, Destroyer of death, Hope of resurrection; blessed are you, Sovereign God, Light of the World. **Amen.** *(Michael Vasey)*

CANTICLE   ISAIAH 65:17, 21-25

For I am about to create new heavens
    and a new earth;
the former things shall not be remembered
or come to mind. . . .
They shall build houses and inhabit them;
    they shall plant vineyards and eat their fruit.
They shall not build and another inhabit;
they shall not plant and another eat;
for like the days of a tree shall the days of my people be,
    and my chosen shall long enjoy the work of their hands.
They shall not labor in vain,
    or bear children for calamity;
for they shall be offspring blessed by the Lord—
    and their descendants as well.
Before they call I will answer,
    while they are yet speaking I will hear.
The wolf and the lamb shall feed together,
    the lion shall eat straw like the ox. . . .
    They shall not hurt or destroy
    on all my holy mountain,
    says the Lord.

SCRIPTURE   GALATIANS 5:16-18, 22-23; 6:2, 9-10A

Live by the Spirit, I say, and do not gratify the desires of the flesh. For what the flesh desires is opposed to the Spirit, and what the Spirit desires is opposed to the flesh; for these are opposed to each other, to prevent you from doing what you want. But if you are led by the Spirit, you are not subject to the law. . . . The fruit of the Spirit is love, joy, peace, patience, kindness, generosity, faithfulness, gentleness, and self-control. There is no law against such things. . . . Bear one another's burdens, and in this way you will fulfill the law of Christ. . . . So let us not grow weary in doing what is right, for we will reap at harvest time, if we do not give up. So then, whenever we have an opportunity, let us work for the good of all, and especially for those of the family of faith.

LITANY

Christ of peace, Prince of peace, Giver of peace—we pray for peace.
We have had enough of hatred
   which aims a gun at another and pulls the trigger.

We have had enough of resentment
   which destroys by malice or slander.
We have had enough of greed
   which by force or trickery takes what is not rightfully theirs.

We have had enough of fear
   which makes children hide lest evil strikes them.
We have had enough of anger
   which explodes to shatter joy.

We have had enough of jealousy
   which denigrates the grace it envies.
We have had enough of memories
   which embitter and feed the evil of our souls.

We have had enough of ancient divisions
   which old people enshrine and which children imbibe with their mothers' milk.
We have had enough of power
   which usurps the rights of others, and manipulates for its own ends.

We have had enough of injustices
   which refuse to be righted.
We have had enough!

Child of peace
   Prince of peace
      Giver of peace—we pray for peace—and let it begin with us! *(E. Body)*

REFLECTION   JEFFREY SACHS

The American economy increasingly serves only a narrow part of society, and America's national politics has failed to put the country back on track through honest, open, and transparent problem-solving. Too many of America's elites—among the super-rich, the CEOs, and many of my colleagues in academia—have abandoned a commitment to social responsibility. They chase wealth and power, the rest of society be damned.

We need to re-conceive the idea of a good society and to find a creative path toward it. Most important, we need to be ready to pay the price of civilization through multiple acts of good citizenship: bearing our fair share of taxes, educating ourselves deeply about society's needs, acting as vigilant stewards for future generations, and remembering that compassion is the glue that holds society together.

The economist Jeffrey D. Sachs (b. 1954) is the director of the Earth Institute at Columbia University and served as special advisor to United Nations Secretary-General Ban Ki-moon for the Millennium Development Goals, eight development goals approved by all UN member states to ameliorate poverty, enhance universal education and health care, improve gender equality, and promote environmental sustainability.

PRAYERS OF CONFESSION AND INTERCESSION

Look with pity, O God of compassion, on the people in this land who live with injustice, terror, disease and death as constant companions. Have mercy upon us. Help us to eliminate our cruelty to these our neighbors. Strengthen those who spend their lives establishing equal protection of the law and equal opportunities for all. Grant that every one of us may enjoy a fair portion of the riches of this land; through Jesus Christ our Lord. **Amen.** *(The Episcopal Church)*

Generous God, you created this world for all to share—Unclench our hands to let go of the greed which robs the poor. Unclog our ears to hear the agony of all who cry for justice. Unbind our hearts to recognize those who are oppressed by debt. Open our lips to proclaim Jubilee in our own time and place. May our care be thorough and our solidarity active. May this community of hope be a sign of hope, for now is the favorable time. **Amen.** *(People of Saint Michael's Parish, Liverpool, England)*

21. A Good Society

HYMN   MARTIN WILLETT

1. Go, be justice to God's people;
   teach the hardened heart to learn.
   Break the bread of true communion,
   pour the cup of true concern.
   Feed the hungry, house the homeless,
   catch the tyrants in their lies;
   be the Lord's anointed servant
   so God's justice never dies.

2. Go, be healing to God's people;
   seek and share the saving call.
   Be the touch of Christ for others,
   be the voice of Christ for all.
   Lives are broken all around you,
   and Christ has no hands but yours;
   hold in them the ones who suffer
   so Christ's healing love endures.

3. Go, be mercy to God's people
   in forgiveness freely shown;
   find the stranger, call her kindred,
   find the exile, call him home.
   Age to age God's mercy welcomes
   with a love that will not cease;
   go, be Christ-light to God's people,
   be an instrument of peace.

Tune: NETTLETON, 8.7.8.7.D.

And now, my friends, all that is true, all that is noble, all that is just and pure, all that is lovely and gracious, whatever is excellent and admirable—fill all your thoughts with these things. *(Philippians 4:8)*

SOURCES

Isaiah 56:1 from *The Inclusive Bible* (Landham, MD: Rowman & Littlefield, 2007). A Sheed & Ward Book published by Rowman & Littlefield Publishers, Inc. All rights reserved. Used by permission.

"Eternal God of all peoples . . . ," in *Gates of Prayer: The New Union Prayerbook* (New York: Central Conference of American Rabbis, 1975), 690, alt. © 1975, by Central Conference of American Rabbis, under the copyright protection of the Central Conference of American Rabbis and reprinted for use by permission of the CCAR. All rights reserved.

Michael Vasey, "Blessed are you . . . ," from *Enriching the Christian Year*, ed. Michael Perham (Collegeville, MN: Liturgical Press, 1993), 44.

E. Body, "Anzac Dawn," in *Seeing Christ in Others*, ed. Geoffrey Duncan, new enl. ed. (Norwich: Canterbury Press, 2002), 242–43. © E. Body.

Jeffrey D. Sachs, *The Price of Civilization: Reawakening American Virtue and Prosperity* (New York: Random House, 2011), 4–5. Used by permission of Penguin Random House and Wylie Agency. Excerpt from *The Price of Civilization* by Jeffery Sachs. Copyright © 2011, 2012 Jeffrey Sachs, used by permission of The Wylie Agency LLC.

"For the Oppressed," in Episcopal Church, *Book of Common Prayer* (New York: Church Publishing, 1979), 826.

"Generous God, you created . . . ," in *The Westminster Collection of Christian Prayers*, ed. Dorothy M. Stewart (Louisville, KY: John Knox, 2002), 144. Attributed to the people of Saint Michael's Parish, Liverpool, England.

Words by Martin Willett, "Go, Be Justice." Copyright © 2001, World Library Publications, wlpmusic.com. All rights reserved. Used with permission.

Philippians 4:8 from *The New English Bible*, copyright © Cambridge University Press and Oxford University Press 1961, 1970. All rights reserved.

22. FARMS

For two million years humans subsisted by gathering and hunting. About ten thousand years ago, the greatest transition in the human journey on earth began with the invention of farming. Farming enabled settled communities and the rise of cities. The first cultivated crops—corn, wheat, and rice—continue to make up half the world's food consumption.

The Lord will send rain to water the seeds you have planted—your fields will produce more crops than you need, and your cattle will graze in open pastures. *(Isaiah 30:23)*

PRAYERS OF PRAISE AND THANKSGIVING

Holy God, you brought us into this life as into an enchanted paradise. We have seen the sky, like a deep blue cup ringing with birds in the azure heights. We have listened to the soothing murmur of the forest and the sweet-sounding music of the waters. We have tasted fragrant fruit of fine flavor and sweet-scented honey. How pleasant is our stay with you on earth: it is a joy to be your guest. Glory to you for the feast-day of life. Glory to you for the perfume of lilies and roses. Glory to you for each different taste of berry and fruit. Glory to you for the sparkling silver of early morning dew. Glory to you for each smiling, peaceful awakening. Glory to you, O Holy God, from age to age. **Amen.** *(Metropolitan Tryphon)*

O God, creator and source of life, we thank you for the gifts given from your abundance and through the work of human hands, by which we are blessed with nourishing food. Pour your blessings on all farms and on the multitude of fruits, grains and vegetables nourished by their soils. Pour your blessings on those who work the land in love and reverence, that the earth may yield its abundance and that we your children may be fed. This we ask through Jesus Christ our Lord. **Amen.** *(Community of the Sisters of the Church)*

CANTICLE   2 CORINTHIANS 9:6B-11A

The one who sows bountifully will also reap bountifully.

Each of you must give as you have made up your mind, not reluctantly or under compulsion, for God loves a cheerful giver.

And God is able to provide you with every blessing in abundance,

**so that by always having enough of everything,
you may share abundantly in every good work.**

As it is written,
'He scatters abroad, he gives to the poor;
his righteousness endures for ever.'

**He who supplies seed to the sower and bread for food
will supply and multiply your seed for sowing and increase the harvest of your righteousness.**

You will be enriched in every way for your great generosity.

SCRIPTURE   DEUTERONOMY 8:7-10, 17-19

The LORD your God is bringing you into a good land, a land with flowing streams, with springs and underground waters welling up in valleys and hills, a land of wheat and barley, of vines and fig trees and pomegranates, a land of olive trees and honey, a land where you may eat bread without scarcity, where you will lack nothing, a land whose stones are iron and from whose hills you may mine copper. You shall eat your fill and bless the LORD your God for the good land that he has given you. . . . Do not say to yourself, "My power and the might of my own hand have gotten me this wealth." But remember the LORD your God, for it is he who gives you power to get wealth, so that he may confirm his covenant that he swore to your ancestors, as he is doing today. If you do forget the LORD your God and follow other gods to serve and worship them, I solemnly warn you today that you shall surely perish.

LITANY

God of place and history, we pray for the broken and torn fabric of the earth as it yearns for healing.

Jesus, who walked with farmers and fisher-folk and sat in village kitchens, walk with us now.

We hold before you those who have the privilege and responsibility of working the land, and those who struggle to make a living.

Jesus, who walked with farmers and fisher-folk and sat in village kitchens, walk with us now.

We hold before you those whose relationship with the earth is ruptured through conflict, poverty, stunted opportunities, and environmental degradation.

Jesus, who walked with farmers and fisher-folk and sat in village kitchens, walk with us now.

We hold before you rural communities where people feel isolated, marginalized and powerless in the face of distant economic and political forces; and we remember especially those who have lost hope.

Jesus, who walked with farmers and fisher-folk and sat in village kitchens, walk with us now.

We hold before you those whose policies affect the land, the earth and all of our lives; and we pray for those in positions of power, in particular that the leaders of wealthy nations will have the courage and vision to make hard decisions.

Jesus, who walked with farmers and fishers-folk and sat in village kitchens, walk with us now.

God of the sheltering wings, hear these prayers today and fill us with your Spirit; that we may live in peace with the earth and with each other; and that your Kingdom may come. **Amen.** *(Christian Maclean)*

REFLECTION   WENDELL BERRY

Agrarian farmers see, accept, and live within their limits. They understand and agree to the proposition "this much and no more." Everything that happens on an agrarian farm is determined or conditioned by the understanding that there is only so much land, so much water in the cistern, so much hay in the barn, so much corn in the crib, so much firewood in the shed, so much food in the cellar or freezer, so much strength in the back and arms—and no more. This is the understanding that induces thrift, family coherence, neighborliness, local economies. Within accepted limits, these become necessities. The agrarian sense of abundance comes from the experienced possibility of frugality and renewal within limits.

This is exactly opposite to the industrial idea that abundance comes from the violation of limits by personal mobility, extractive machinery, long-distance transport, and scientific or technological breakthroughs. If we use up the good possibilities in this place, we will import goods from some other place, or we will go to some other place. If nature releases her wealth too slowly, we will take it by force. If we make the world too toxic for honeybees, some compound brain will invent tiny robots that will fly about pollinating flowers and making honey.

In our time it is useless and probably wrong to suppose that a great many urban people ought to go out into the countryside and become homesteaders or farmers. But it is not useless or wrong to suppose that urban people have agricultural responsibilities that they should try to meet. And in fact this is happening. The agrarian population among us is growing, and by no means is it made up merely of some farmers and some country people. It includes urban gardeners, urban consumers who are buying food from local farmers, consumers who have grown doubtful of the healthfulness, the trustworthiness, and the dependability of the corporate food system.

The eminent poet, essayist, and cultural critic Wendell Berry (b. 1934) is also a Kentucky farmer. This selection was written to mark the twenty-fifth anniversary of the publication of his classic book The Unsettling of America: Culture and Agriculture. *Since then half the farms in the United States have disappeared, topsoil has continued to erode, monoculture and the use of chemicals and bioengineering of crops have increased. Large-scale industrial farms are now almost 100 percent dependent upon fossil fuels.*

PRAYERS OF CONFESSION AND INTERCESSION

Gracious God, we have taken the fruits of your creation and your merciful abundance for granted. We have uttered prayers of thanksgiving without true gratitude. Meanwhile, we have failed to recognize the suffering of the earth and of the people who have produced our food. Ignoring our connection to the rest of your creation as we reap nourishment, we move further away from your vision of your beloved community. Forgive us, O God, and transform us. Open us to the richness and beauty in connecting our food—at the Lord's Table and at our individual tables—to all the natural and human resources who have brought it to those tables. Help us to give thanks not just for our food but for all those who have brought it before us and to work that they also might flourish. Encourage us to work for justice for all, so that all may give you thanks and be fed. In Christ Jesus we pray. **Amen.** *(Carol Devine and Rebecca Barnes)*

Blessed are you, God of planting and harvest, birthing and growth. Through the gifts of creation, you care for all. Bless us and our families, O God, as each new season of seeding and growth begins. Increase in us an awareness of our interdependence with all creation. Bless the land, bless our tilling, seeding, and harvest; bless the growth of our flocks and herds, that we might see in them your hand, and praise you. **Amen.** *(Author unknown)*

HYMN   MATTHIAS CLAUDIUS, TR. JANE MONTGOMERY CAMPBELL

1. We plow the fields and scatter
   the good seed on the land,
   but it is fed and watered
   by God's almighty hand;
   God sends the snow in winter,
   the warmth to swell the grain,
   the breezes and the sunshine,
   and soft refreshing rain.

Refrain:
   All good gifts around us
   are sent from heaven above,
   then thank the Lord, O thank the Lord
   for all his love.

2. God only is the Maker
   of all things near and far;
   God paints the wayside flower,
   and lights the evening star;
   the winds and waves obey him,
   by him the birds are fed;
   much more to us, his children,
   God gives our daily bread. *Refrain.*

3. We thank thee, then, O Father,
   for all things bright and good,
   the seed time and the harvest,
   our life, our health, our food;
   the gifts we have to offer
   are what thy love imparts,
   but chiefly thou desirest
   our humble, thankful hearts. *Refrain.*

   Tune: WIR PFLÜGEN, 7.6.7.6.D.

Be a gardener for creation. Dig, toil, and sweat, and turn the earth upside down, seek the deepness, and water the plants in time. Continue this labor, and make sweet floods to run, and noble and abundant fruits to spring. Then take this food, drink, and beauty, and carry it to God as your true worship. **Amen.** *(Julian of Norwich)*

SOURCES

Isaiah 30:23 from *Contemporary English Version* (New York: American Bible Society, 1995). © 1995 American Bible Society.

Metropolitan Tryphon [Prince Boris Petrovich Turkestanov], Ikos 2 of "An Akathist in Praise of God's Creation," in *SYNDESMOS Orthodoxy and Ecology Resource Book*, Annex 1, *Orthodox Services for the Creation*, ed. Alexander Belopopsky and Dmitri Oikonomou (Bialystok, Poland: Orthdruk Orthodox Printing House, 1996), 20–25, alt.

Community of the Sisters of the Church, "Prayer in the Vegetable Garden," in *Harvest for the World: A Worship Anthology on Sharing in the Work of Creation*, ed. Geoffrey Duncan (Cleveland: Pilgrim Press, 2003), 41, alt. © Community of the Sisters of the Church.

Christian Maclean, "God of place . . .," in "A Rural Liturgy," in *Holy Ground: Liturgies and Worship Resources for an Engaged Spirituality*, ed. Neil Paynter and Helen Boothroyd (Glasgow: Wild Goose, 2005), 114–15, alt. © Contributors, *Holy Ground* (2005), Wild Goose Publications, Glasgow. Used by permission.

Wendell Berry, "The Agrarian Standard," *Orion Magazine*, July 1, 2002, https://orionmagazine.org/article/the-agrarian-standard/. Used by permission.

Carol Devine and Rebecca Barnes, "Gracious God, we have taken . . .," in *Have You Anything Here to Eat? Sustainable Food in a Changing Climate*, Creation Justice Ministries Earth Day Sunday resource 2015, p. 3, *Creation Justice Ministries*, www.creationjustice.org/educational-resources. Used by permission.

"Blessed are you . . .," in United Church of Canada, *Celebrate God's Presence: A Book of Services for the United Church of Canada*, ed. Karen J. Verveda (Etobicoke, Ontario: United Church Publishing House, 2000), 616. Author unknown.

Words by Matthias Claudius, "We Plow the Fields and Scatter" (1782), trans. Jane Montgomery Campbell (1861), alt. Public domain.

Julian of Norwich, "There is a treasure . . .," in *Meditations with Julian of Norwich*, ed. Brendan Doyle (Santa Fe, NM: Bear & Co., 1983), 84, alt. Inner Traditions International and Bear & Company, © 1983. All rights reserved. http://www.Innertraditions.com. Reprinted with permission of publisher.

23. AGRICULTURE WITH A HUMAN FACE

A quiet revolution is spreading across the land. Agriculture is becoming more local and organic with urban farms, community gardens, community-supported agriculture, rooftop gardens, church gardens, school gardens, local orchards, and farmers markets. Urban deserts are blooming. Long may it continue until more and more of God's people are fed and satisfied.

[God] commanded the skies above,
    and opened the doors of heaven;
he rained down on them manna to eat,
    and gave them the grain of heaven.
Mortals ate the bread of angels;
    he sent them food in abundance. *(Psalm 78:23-25)*

PRAYERS OF PRAISE AND THANKSGIVING

We give thanks for the creative power that pours forth its bounty in grass and grain. The earth and all its fullness are yours, O God. You are the seed within the seed, giving it life and sustaining all your creatures. Spring and summer and autumn your radiant power makes the earth yield its fruit. For this we give you praise and pledge that more than words shall show our thankfulness. We shall cherish the good earth you have placed in our keeping; we shall share with others the food we have gathered; and we shall work to make this a world where only good is sown that our harvest may generate contentment and peace. **Amen.** *(Central Conference of American Rabbis)*

We give you thanks, O God of abundant life, for bread and friendship and hope. With these gifts of your grace we are nourished. With these signs of your presence we are able to be faithful. Continue to nourish us, inspire us, and call us, that we might help make your reign more of a reality in our day. **Amen.** *(Pat Kozak and Janet Schaffran)*

Almighty God; you give seed for us to sow, and bread for us to eat; make us thankful for what we have received; make us rich to do those generous things which supply your people's needs; so all the world may give you thanks and glory. **Amen.** *(Anglican Church of New Zealand)*

CANTICLES   ISAIAH 32:16-18, 20

Then justice will dwell in the wilderness,
   and righteousness abide in the fruitful field.
The effect of righteousness will be peace,
and the result of righteousness, quietness and trust forever.
My people will abide in a peaceful habitation,
   in secure dwellings, and in quiet resting places. . . .

Happy will you be who sow beside every stream,
   who let the ox and the donkey range freely.

JOB 12:7-10

Go and ask the cattle, ask the birds of the air to inform you,

or tell the creatures that crawl to teach you,
   and the fishes of the sea to give you instruction.

Who cannot learn from all these
   that the Lord's own hand has done this?

In God's hand are the souls of all that live,
   the spirits of all humankind.

SCRIPTURE   LEVITICUS 25:8-12 AND DEUTERONOMY 24:19-21

1. You shall count off seven weeks of years, seven times seven years, so that the period of seven weeks of years gives forty-nine years. Then you shall have the trumpet sounded loud; on the tenth day of the seventh month—on the

day of atonement—you shall have the trumpet sounded throughout all your land. And you shall hallow the fiftieth year and you shall proclaim liberty throughout the land to all its inhabitants. It shall be a jubilee for you: you shall return, every one of you, to your property and every one of you to your family. That fiftieth year shall be a jubilee for you: you shall not sow, or reap the after-growth, or harvest the unpruned vines. For it is a jubilee; it shall be holy to you: you shall eat only what the field itself produces.

2. When you reap your harvest in your field and forget a sheaf in the field, you shall not go back to get it; it shall be left for the alien, the orphan, and the widow, so that the LORD your God may bless you in all your undertakings. When you beat your olive trees, do not strip what is left; it shall be for the alien, the orphan, and the widow. When you gather the grapes of your vineyard, do not glean what is left; it shall be for the alien, the orphan, and the widow.

LITANY

God of seed-time and harvest—
have mercy on us and hear our prayer:
For children who go to bed hungry at night, and for parents who cannot find food for them,
Lord, hear our prayer.
For communities hungry because of flood, fire or drought, and for governments who struggle to provide for them,
Lord, hear our prayer.
For farmers sowing seed and raising livestock to feed the world, and for their care for the land that provides their livelihood,
Lord, hear our prayer.
For subsistence farmers vulnerable to climate changes, and for market gardeners vulnerable to price variations,
Lord, hear our prayer.
For those who are committed to organic farming practices,
Lord, hear our prayer.
For the wellbeing and ethical treatment of livestock, and for those who raise, transport and slaughter animals for food,
Lord, hear our prayer.
For soup kitchens, food banks and aid agencies, and for the donors, volunteers and staff who help to feed the hungry,
Lord, hear our prayer.

For remote communities where fresh food is expensive and in short supply,
Lord, hear our prayer.
For policy-makers and planners in land use and food production, and for community educators in diet and nutrition,
Lord, hear our prayer.
Gather us around the table of your love.
Gather us in to your heavenly feast where all who hunger and thirst for justice will be satisfied. *(The Anglican Church of Australia)*

REFLECTIONS   WES JACKSON AND BILL MCKIBBEN

1. For the artistic farmer, the tool is not the brush but rather the pitchfork, the hoe, the rake, the shovel, the pruning shears, a team of horses, even a diesel tractor if it is run on vegetable oil. Whether in China, Peru, Africa, Sicily, or among the Hopi of the Southwest, the agricultural artist prefers wisdom over cleverness. The realities of industrialization are all around us. What we must think about, therefore, is an agriculture with a human face. We must give standing to the new pioneers, the home-comers bent on the most important work for the century—a massive salvage operation to save the vulnerable but necessary pieces of nature and culture, and to keep the good and artful examples before us. It is time for a new breed of artists to enter front and center, for the point of art, after all, is to connect. This is the home-comer I have in mind: the scientist, the accountant who converses with nature, a true artist devoted to the building of agriculture and culture to match the scenery presented to those first European eyes.

It is no accident that E. F. Schumacher, the author of Small Is Beautiful: Economics as if People Mattered *would want to visit the Land Institute in Kansas in 1977, a year after its founding, for his philosophy of small, local, and organic is shared by Wes Jackson (b. 1936), founder of the Land Institute.*

2. I've reclined under a palm tree in Bangladesh where a hundred species of fruit and vegetable grew in a single acre: the farm featured guava, lemon, pomegranate, cocoanut, betel nut, mango, jackfruit, apple, lychee, chestnut, date, fig, and bamboo trees, as well as squash, okra, eggplant, zucchini, blackberry, bay leaf, cardamom, cinnamon, and sugarcane plants, not to mention dozens of herbs, far more flowers, and a flock of ducklings. A chicken coop produced not just eggs and meat but waste that fed a fish pond, which in turn produced thousands of pounds of protein annually, and a healthy crop of water hyacinths that were harvested to feed a small herd of cows, whose

dung in turn fired a biogas cooking system. The guy who was showing me around summed it up like this: "food is everywhere, and in twelve hours it will double." In the new world we're creating, it's like having small banks instead of one big one.

Bill McKibben (b. 1960) acknowledged that he had already been published in "all the right places"; he had written The End of Nature *and had been speaking and writing about climate change for years. Still, he didn't think he was doing enough. It was on his trip to Bangladesh, from which this selection is taken, where he came down with dengue fever and saw many people dying, that he became an environmental activist. "Something snapped. Nothing concrete had come of my work or anyone else's; Washington had done absolutely nothing to slow down climate change."*

PRAYERS OF CONFESSION AND INTERCESSION

God of compassion and infinite mercy, we need your companionship, and we are in desperate need of your mercy: because our compassion fails and our mercy is severely rationed. Our fellow human beings—our neighbors—are treated unjustly while we live on the products of their labor. Our fellow human beings die of hunger while we have, and eat, more than enough. Forgive our helplessness and carelessness. Forgive us the hurt we do not feel for those who suffer cruelty and oppression; for the sorrow we fail to share with those whose lives are cut short, through human violence or natural disaster. By your compassion, increase ours; by your mercy, make us merciful; make us feel the compassion of Christ, who has died for us and gives us the power to proclaim, in word and deed, the mercy of Christ for those who crucify him. **Amen.** *(Alan Gaunt)*

Almighty God, we thank you for making the earth fruitful, so that it might produce what is needed for life: Bless those who work in the fields; give us seasonable weather; and grant that we may all share the fruits of the earth, rejoicing in your goodness; through Jesus Christ our Lord. **Amen.** *(The Episcopal Church)*

HYMN   BRIAN WREN

1. Praise God for the harvest of orchard and field,
   praise God for the people who gather their yield,
   the long hours of labor, the skills of a team,
   the patience of science, the power of machine.

2. Praise God for the harvest that comes from afar,
   from market and harbor, the sea and the shore:
   foods packed and transported, and gathered and grown
   by God-given neighbors, unseen and unknown.

3. Praise God for the harvest that's quarried and mined,
   selected and smelted, or shaped and refined:
   for oil and iron, for copper and coal,
   praise God who in love has provided them all.

4. Praise God for the harvest of science and skill,
   the urge to discover, create, and fulfill:
   for plans and inventions that promise to gain
   a future more hopeful, a world more humane.

5. Praise God for the harvest of mercy and love
   from leaders and peoples who struggle and serve
   with patience and kindness, that all may be led
   to freedom and justice, and all may be fed.

Tune: STOWEY, 11.11.11.11.
Words © 1974, rev. 1996 Hope Publishing

Holy is the soil we walk on, holy everything that grows, holy all beneath the surface, holy every stream that flows. *(Edmund Banyard)*

SOURCES

"On this day we give thanks . . . ," in *Gates of Prayer: The New Union Prayerbook* (New York: Central Conference of American Rabbis, 1975), 469. © 1975, by Central Conference of American Rabbis, under the copyright protection of the Central Conference of American Rabbis and reprinted for use by permission of the CCAR. All rights reserved.

Pat Kozak and Janet Schaffran, "We give you thanks . . ." in *More Than Words*, by Pat Kozak and Janet Schaffran (New York: Meyer, Stone, and Company, 1988), 40–41. Used by permission of Pat Kozak and Janet Schaffran.

"An Offering Prayer," in Church of the Province of New Zealand, *A New Zealand Prayer Book: He Karakia Mihinare o Aotearoa* (Auckland, New Zealand: William Collins, 1989), 141. © 1989 The Provincial Secretary, The Church of the Province of New Zealand, Box 2148, Rotorua. Used by permission.

Scripture quotation taken from the New English Bible, copyright © Cambridge University Press and Oxford University Press 1961, 1970. All rights reserved.

Anglican Church of Australia, "Litany: Food Theme," *Anglican Communion*, accessed February 2, 2018, http://acen.anglicancommunion.org/media/612521/Litany-Food-Theme.pdf, alt. © Anglican Church of Australia. Used by permission of the Anglican Consultative Council.

Wes Jackson, *Nature as Measure: The Selected Essays of Wes Jackson* (Berkeley: Counterpoint Press, 2011), 95. © 2011 by Wes Jackson. Reprinted by permission of Counterpoint Press.

Bill McKibben, *Eaarth* (New York: Henry Holt, 2010), 170. © 2010 Bill McKibben. Used by permission of the author.

Alan Gaunt, "Harvest Prayer of Confession," in *Harvest for the World: A Worship Anthology on Sharing in the Work of Creation*, ed. Geoffrey Duncan (Cleveland: Pilgrim Press, 2003), 88–89, alt. Used by permission.

"For Agriculture," in Episcopal Church, *Book of Common Prayer* (New York: Church Publishing, 1986), 824.

Words by Brian Wren, "Praise God for the Harvest" © 1974, rev. 1996 Hope Publishing Company, Carol Stream, IL 60188. All rights reserved. Used by permission.

Edmund Banyard, "Holy is the soil . . . ," in *Dare to Dream: A Prayer and Worship Anthology from around the World*, ed. Geoffrey Duncan (London: HarperCollins, 1995), 4. © Edmund Banyard. Used by permission.

24. WATER

That water is a human right was enshrined by the United Nations in 2010: "The human right to water entitles everyone to safe, acceptable, physically accessible and affordable water for personal and domestic uses." Yet 1.1 billion people lack access to clean water and some 2 million people, mostly children, die of water-borne diseases every year.

The Lord said to Moses, "Go on ahead of the people, and take some of the elders of Israel with you; take in your hand the staff with which you struck the Nile, and go. I will be standing there in front of you on the rock at Horeb. Strike the rock, and water will come out of it, so that the people may drink." Moses did so, in the sight of the elders of Israel. *(Exodus 17:5-6)*

PRAYERS OF PRAISE AND THANKSGIVING

God, whose Spirit moved over the deep at its creation, and whose Son Jesus entered the waters of baptism and hallowed them for ever: We thank you for the gift of water—the waters on the surface of the earth, the waters beneath the ground, the water in our atmosphere, and the water in our bodies—and for all that dwells in the waters. Make us mindful of the care of all the planet's waters, that they may richly sustain life for us and for those who will come after us; through Jesus Christ, who is the source of living water. **Amen.** *(The Episcopal Church)*

O Supreme Power, in the beginning you ordered the waters to gather in one place and become pools for the irrigation of your creation. Bless, O Lord, the waters of this land by your grace and mercy. Remove from them all impurities that cause illness and harm and make them a source of help and health for all, so that your name may be glorified forever. **Amen.** *(Syrian Orthodox Church)*

24. Water

CANTICLE   REVELATION 7:16-17; 21:1A, 3-5

They will hunger no more, and thirst no more;
> the sun will not strike them,
> nor any scorching heat;

for the Lamb at the center of the throne will be their shepherd,
> **and he will guide them to springs of the water of life,**

and God will wipe away every tear from their eyes." . . .
Then I saw a new heaven and a new earth; . . .
And I heard a loud voice from the throne saying,
> "See, the home of God is among mortals.
> He will dwell with them;
> **they will be his peoples,**
> **and God himself will be with them;**
> **he will wipe every tear from their eyes.**
> Death will be no more;
> mourning and crying and pain will be no more,
> for the first things have passed away."

And the one who was seated on the throne said, "See, I am making all things new." Also he said, "Write this, for these words are trustworthy and true."

SCRIPTURE   EZEKIEL 47:7-9, 12

I saw on the bank of the river a great many trees on the one side and on the other. He said to me, "This water flows toward the eastern region and goes down into the Arabah; and when it enters the sea, the sea of stagnant waters, the water will become fresh. Wherever the river goes, every living creature that swarms will live, and there will be very many fish, once these waters reach there. It will become fresh; and everything will live where the river goes. . . . On the banks, on both sides of the river, there will grow all kinds of trees for food. Their leaves will not wither nor their fruit fail, but they will bear fresh fruit every month, because the water for them flows from the sanctuary. Their fruit will be for food, and their leaves for healing."

LITANY

Rejoice in the Lord, for he has refreshed the parched earth. Where there was nothing but brown, hard, dead land, now the soft earth is covered with fresh green. Where death was in power, new life has come forth, awakening hope throughout the land—
We praise you, O God.

For the clouds which protect us from the sun, for the thunder, at which the earth trembles, for the lightning which splits the sky—
We praise you, O God.

Rejoice for the rain that falls by night, and soaks at once into the dry ground, causing half-dried-up roots to swell, and the deep cracks in the earth to close. Rejoice for the cool nights, the budding flowers, the shooting trees, and the tender, green grass—
We praise you, O God.

Rejoice for the great drops that fall at midday; rejoice for the small streams, singing on their way from the hills down into the valleys, to make the rivers swell and fill the reservoirs, and supply the cities and irrigation channels with water—
We praise you, O God.

Rejoice over the new activity in the villages, where neighbors take their hoes and baskets and hurry to the fields, to test the fruitfulness of the earth by planting seeds of hope and expectation. Rejoice for those who have already prepared their seedbeds, and are now hurrying to try the strength of carefully chosen seeds—
We praise you, O God.

For the ground, for rain, seeds and tools, for strength in arms and backs, for the will to work and for creative minds—
We praise you, O God. *(Praise of Creation from Africa)*

REFLECTION   ECUMENICAL PATRIARCH BARTHOLOMEW I

Responding to the environmental crisis is a matter of truthfulness to God, humanity, and the created order. It is not too far-fetched to speak of environmental damage as being a contemporary heresy or natural terrorism. We have repeatedly condemned this behavior as nothing less than sinful. For beings to cause species to become extinct and to destroy the biological diversity of God's creation; for humans to degrade the integrity of the earth by causing changes in its climate, by stripping the Earth of its natural forests, or by destroying its wetlands; for humans to injure other humans with disease by contaminating the earth's waters, its land, its air, and its life with poisonous substances—all these are sins before God, humanity and the world. We have tended to restrict the notion of sin to the individual sense of guilt or the social sense of wrongdoing. Yet sin also contains a cosmic dimension, and repentance from environmental sin demands a radical transformation of the way we perceive the natural world and a tangible change in the way we choose to live.

The Ecumenical Patriarch, Bartholomew I (b. 1940) is the spiritual leader of the Eastern Orthodox Church. He has been informally named the "Green Patriarch" because of his bold efforts in speaking about care for the earth as a religious responsibility.

PRAYERS OF CONFESSION AND INTERCESSION

O God of the running waters, we pray for our world where waterways are clogged with trash, where streams that were once clean now carry poisonous chemicals and bacteria, where water has dried up. Hear the cries of those without clean water. We pray for those who have the power to bring water where people need it, especially for governments that set policy and decide where to dig wells and build irrigation systems. May they listen to the people and acknowledge their continuing roles in maintaining water systems while seeking better ways of sharing water with all who depend on it. **Amen.** *(Evangelical Lutheran Church in Canada)*

O God, pour out on us the water of life that we may quench our thirst and draw strength from you. Help us to stand alongside those who struggle daily for clean water so that all may be refreshed and renewed by your love. **Amen.** *(Christian Aid)*

HYMN   HERMAN STUEMPFLE, JR.

1. The thirsty cry for water, Lord;
   the hungry plead for bread.
   And many long to rise again
   where hope, cast down, lies dead.

2. The cup of water poured in love
   the pangs of thirst will still.
   The bread of earth you bid us share
   the famished child can fill.

3. But help us also hear the cry
   of hungering, thirsting hearts
   for living water, bread of life
   your grace alone imparts.

4. And come to us, O risen Christ,
   our restless souls relieve;
   and satisfy our starving hearts
   that we may rise and live.

Tune: DETROIT, C.M., 8.6.8.6.

Deep peace of the Running Wave to you. Deep peace of the Flowing Air to you. Deep peace of the Quiet Earth to you. Deep peace of the Shining Stars to you. Deep peace of the Son of Peace to you. *(A Celtic blessing, Fiona MacLeod)*

SOURCES

Exodus 17:5-6 from *The Inclusive Bible* (Landham, MD: Rowman & Littlefield, 2007). A Sheed & Ward Book published by Rowman & Littlefield Publishers, Inc. All rights reserved. Used by permission.

"A Rogation Day Procession and Liturgy: For Waters and Those Whose Work Depends on Them," in Standing Commission on Liturgy and Music, "Liturgical Materials Honoring God in Creation and Various Rites and Prayers for Animals," in *Report to the 77th General Convention* (Episcopal Church, July 5–12, 2012), 333, alt.

Syrian Orthodox Church, "Blessing of Springs and Wells," in *Harvest for the World: A Worship Anthology on Sharing in the Work of Creation*, ed. Geoffrey Duncan (Cleveland: Pilgrim Press, 2003), 255, alt.

"We Belong to the Earth," trans. Elizabeth Burtzlaff, a service celebrating the Second European Ecumenical Assembly in Graz, Austria, 1997, in *Sinfonia Oecumenica: Worship with the Churches of the World*, ed. Beatrice Aebi et al. (Gütersloh, Germany: Gütersloher Verlagshaus, 1999), 844 and 856, alt.

Patriarch Bartholomew I, "The Orthodox Church and the Environmental Crisis: Spiritual Insights and Personal Reflections," in *Holy Ground: A Gathering of Voices on Caring for Creation*, ed. Lyndsay Moseley et al. (San Francisco: Sierra Club Books, 2008), 37–38. © by the Sierra Club and individual authors as credited. Reprinted by permission of Counterpoint Press.

Evangelical Lutheran Church in Canada, "Prayer of the Day," in *Right to Water: Liturgy*, 1, *Evangelical Lutheran Church in Canada*, accessed November 16, 2017, http://elcic.ca/Youth/documents/WaterAssemblyLiturgy_PRINT.pdf, alt. Used by permission.

"The Water of Life," in *Holy Ground: Liturgies and Worship Resources for an Engaged Spirituality* (Glasgow: Wild Goose, 2005), 71. © Christian Aid.

Words by Herman Stuempfle, Jr., "The Thirsty Cry for Water, Lord" © 1997, GIA Publications, Inc. Used by permission.

Fiona MacLeod [William Sharp], *The Dominion of Dreams: Under the Dark Star* (New York: Duffield & Co., 1910), 423–24. Public domain.

25. CITIES

Until 200 years ago, most of the world's population lived in towns and small rural communities. By 2007, trends had shifted with more than half the world's population now living in cities. The greatest urban growth has been in Asia, which is now home to nine of the world's ten largest cities. The social and environmental consequences have been immense.

Unless God builds the house, those who build it labor in vain. Unless God guards the city, the guard keeps watch in vain. *(Psalm 127:1-2)*

PRAYERS OF PRAISE AND THANKSGIVING

God of our daily lives, we thank you for the people of the cities of this world, working and without work; homeless and well-housed; fulfilled and frustrated; confused and cluttered with material goods, or scraping a living from others' leavings; angrily scrawling on walls, or reading the writing on the wall; lonely or living in community; finding their own space and respecting the space of others. We pray for our sisters and brothers, mourning and celebrating. May we share their suffering and hope. **Amen.** *(Jan S. Pickard)*

This is the place and this the time; here and now God waits to break into our experience: to change our minds, to change our lives, to change our ways; to make us see the world and the whole of life in a new light; to fill us with hope, joy and certainty for the future. This is the place, as are all places; this is the time, as are all times. Here and now, let us praise God. **Amen.** *(Alan Gaunt)*

25. Cities

CANTICLE   ISAIAH 61:1-4

The spirit of the Lord God is upon me,
    because the Lord has anointed me;
he has sent me to bring good news to the oppressed,
to bind up the brokenhearted,
to proclaim liberty to the captives,
    and release to the prisoners;
to proclaim the year of the Lord's favor,
    and the day of vengeance of our God;
    to comfort all who mourn;
to provide for those who mourn in Zion—
    to give them a garland instead of ashes,
the oil of gladness instead of mourning,
    the mantle of praise instead of a faint spirit.
They will be called oaks of righteousness,
    the planting of the Lord, to display his glory.
They shall build up the ancient ruins,
    they shall raise up the former devastations;
they shall repair the ruined cities,
    the devastations of many generations.

SCRIPTURE   JEREMIAH 29:1, 4-14

These are the words of the letter that the prophet Jeremiah sent from Jerusalem to the remaining elders among the exiles, and to the priests, the prophets, and all the people, whom Nebuchadnezzar had taken into exile from Jerusalem to Babylon. . . . Thus says the Lord of hosts, the God of Israel, to all the exiles whom I have sent into exile from Jerusalem to Babylon: Build houses and live in them; plant gardens and eat what they produce. Take wives and have sons and daughters; take wives for your sons, and give your daughters in marriage, that they may bear sons and daughters; multiply there, and do not decrease. But seek the welfare of the city where I have sent you into exile, and pray to the Lord on its behalf, for in its welfare you will find your welfare. For thus says the Lord of hosts, the God of Israel: Do not let the prophets and the diviners who are among you deceive you, and do not listen to the dreams that they dream, for it is a lie that they are prophesying to you in my name; I did not send them, says the Lord. For thus says the Lord: Only when Babylon's seventy years are completed will I visit you, and I will fulfill to you my promise and bring you back to this place. For surely I know the plans I have for you, says the Lord, plans for your welfare and not for harm, to give you a future with hope. Then when you call upon me and come and pray to me, I will hear you. When you search for me, you will find me; if you seek me with all your heart, I will let you find me, says the LORD, and I will restore your fortunes and gather you from all the nations and all the places where I have driven you, says the LORD, and I will bring you back to the place from which I sent you into exile.

LITANY

Creating God of the Universe, have mercy on this *city/town,* and all who live here,
Creating God, have mercy.

On those who work around us, whose labor builds up the world,
Creating God, have mercy.

On the businesses and industries of this *city/town,*
Creating God, have mercy.

On the plants and animals of this urban ecosystem,
Creating God, have mercy.

On the parks and green spaces of this *city/town* and those who maintain them,
Creating God, have mercy.

On those who produce food and energy for this *city's/town's* people,
Creating God, have mercy.

On schools and places of learning, on all who care for and teach children and adults,
Creating God, have mercy.

On the poor and homeless residents of this *city/town,*
Creating God, have mercy.

On visitors and immigrants, and on all who offer welcome and shelter,
Creating God, have mercy.

On all places of reverence and prayer, on all who honor you and all who do not know you,
Creating God, have mercy.

On our ancestors and those who will come after us, and on all your people,
Creating God, have mercy.

On all creation returning praise to you,
Creating God, have mercy. *(The Episcopal Church)*

REFLECTION   JAMES HOWARD KUNSTLER

Though it's difficult to imagine in today's world of throwaway buildings in parking wastelands, Americans once did a spectacular job of honoring their own public life by endowing public space with beauty and grace. The recognition that we had suddenly become the world's leading industrial power prompted a "City Beautiful" movement [1890s and 1900s] to make America's urban centers worthy of our new status. In a remarkably short period, we got a burst of fantastic public architecture that captured the soaring confidence of that historical moment. Unlike the fractious political mood of our time, that period of extraordinary innovation and vitality was marked by a striking consensus across society about the need for this great endeavor of public building. Politicians, architects, business leaders, and artists overwhelmingly agreed on the agenda, and the transformation of our cities proceeded with stunning swiftness. American cities had been made healthful with vast sanitary networks and clean water, surpassing the achievements of ancient Rome. The great works of the City Beautiful movement were undertaken in a society that saw the human habitat as contiguous with nature, not necessarily inimical to it. The value of the human ecology was represented in artistry based on the fundamental mathematics of our world and all its parts. That holistic view of the human place in nature is waiting to be reclaimed by us. We can choose to surround ourselves with disposable clutter or reanimate American civic spirit with works of conscious artistry and adaptive permanence.

Social critic and author James Howard Kunstler (b. 1948) has written extensively about urban and suburban development, and most recently about how cities can creatively adapt to the challenges posed by the environment. Kunstler is best known for his books The Long Emergency *and* The Geography of Nowhere.

PRAYERS OF CONFESSION AND INTERCESSION

From cowardice that dares not face new truth; from laziness that is content with half truth; from arrogance that thinks it knows all truth, Good Lord, deliver us. **Amen.** *(Author unknown)*

Hear our prayer, compassionate God, for all whose lives are impoverished and beset by the problems of our inner cities. Guide those in local and central government, the planners, the administrators, the decision makers;

may they see the welfare of its citizens as the city's highest good. Raise up in such areas men and women of integrity and energy as leaders, ministers, and teachers; in industry and commerce, in health and social services, in the police and all the work of community and industrial relations. And this we ask for Jesus Christ's sake. **Amen.** *(Timothy Dudley-Smith)*

Gracious God, bless our cities and make them places of safety for all people, rich and poor. Give us grace to work for cities where neighborhoods remain vibrant and whole, where the lost and forgotten in society are supported, and where the arts flourish. Make the diverse fabric of the city a delight to all who live and visit there and a strong bond uniting people around common goals for the good of all; through Jesus Christ, our Savior and Lord. **Amen.** *(Evangelical Lutheran Church in America)*

HYMN   ERIK ROUTLEY

1. All who love and serve your city,
   all who bear its daily stress,
   all who cry for peace and justice,
   all who curse and all who bless,

2. in your day of loss and sorrow,
   in your day of helpless strife,
   honor, peace, and love retreating,
   seek the Lord, who is your life.

3. In your day of wrath and plenty,
   wasted work and wasted play,
   call to mind the word of Jesus,
   "I must work while it is day."

4. For all days are days of judgment,
   and the Lord is waiting still,
   drawing near a world that spurns him,
   offering peace from Calvary's hill.

5. Risen Lord! shall yet the city
   be the city of despair?
   Come today, our Judge, our Glory;
   be its name, "The Lord is there!"

Tune: CHARLESTOWN, 8.7.8.7.
Words © 1969 Stainer & Bell, Ltd. (admin. Hope Publishing)

Peace to the world, peace to the city, peace to the village, peace to the desert. Peace to Mother Earth. Peace to the cosmos, peace to you. Peace to my neighbor, peace to my enemy. Peace to all. Peace! Peace! Peace! *(Elizabeth Tapia)*

SOURCES

Psalm 127:1-2 from *The New Testament and Psalms: An Inclusive Version* (New York: Oxford University Press, 1995), an adaptation of the New Revised Standard Version Bible, copyright © 1989 National Council of the Churches of Christ in the United States of America. Used by permission. All rights reserved.

Jan S. Pickard, "God of our daily lives . . . ," in *Oceans of Prayer*, comp. Maureen Edwards and Jan S. Pickard (Nutfield, UK: National Christian Education Council, UK, 1991), 40, alt. © 1991 National Christian Education Council. Used by permission.

Alan Gaunt, "This is the place . . . " in *New Prayers for Worship* (Leeds, UK: John Paul the Preacher's Press, 1972), p. 1 of section 7, "Words and Prayers for Holy Communion," alt. Used by permission.

"A Litany for the Planet," in Standing Commission on Liturgy and Music, "Liturgical Materials Honoring God in Creation and Various Rites and Prayers for Animals," in *Report to the 77th General Convention* (Episcopal Church, July 5–12, 2012), 329, alt.

James Howard Kunstler, "City Beautiful: Reimagining Infrastructure," *Orion Magazine*, March/April 2015, https://orionmagazine.org/reimagining-infrastructure/. Used by permission.

Mordecai Kaplan [attrib.], "From the cowardice . . . ," in *Kol Haneshamah: Shabbat Vehagim*, 3rd ed. (Wyncote, PA: Reconstructionist Press, 1996), 173. Used by permission.

Timothy Dudley-Smith, "For Inner Cities," in *Chalice Worship*, ed. Colbert S. Cartwright and O. I. Cricket Harrison (St. Louis: Chalice, 1997), 366. Used by permission.

"Cities," in Evangelical Lutheran Church in America, *Evangelical Lutheran Worship*, Leaders Desk ed. (Minneapolis: Augsburg Fortress, 2006), 147. Used by permission.

Words by Erik Routley, "All Who Love and Serve Your City" © 1969 Stainer & Bell, Ltd. (admin. Hope Publishing Company, Carol Stream, IL 60188). All rights reserved. Used by permission.

Elizabeth Tapia, "Peace to the World," in *Timeless Prayers for Peace: Voices Together from around the World*, ed. Geoffrey Duncan (Cleveland: Pilgrim Press, 2003), 77, alt. Used by permission of Elizabeth Tapia.

26. NATIONS

Every person on earth is created equal in God's eyes, but nations—places of their naissance—are human constructs and they are often very unequal. People may be born in rich nations, or poor ones; in nations where the citizenry is respected and treated justly, or in nations where they live in fear and deprivation. The dream of God is that people of all nations will be gathered from every corner of the globe into one beloved community of love.

From one person God made all nations who live on earth, and he decided when and where every nation would be. *(Acts 17:26)*

Happy is the nation whose God is the Lord,
    the people whom he has chosen as his heritage. *(Psalm 33:12)*

PRAYERS OF PRAISE AND THANKSGIVING

We pray for the peace of all nations. Our prophets envisioned an age of blessing; still we yearn for it and work for it. As we have learned: Let justice dwell in the wilderness, righteousness in a fruitful field, for righteousness shall bring peace; it shall bring quietness and confidence for ever. Then all shall sit under their vines and under their fig trees, and none shall make them afraid. **Amen.** *(Central Conference of American Rabbis)*

God of all nations, we thank you for the life and history of every country, for the vast beauty of the world and the wealth of forest, plain, desert and sea. We praise you for its peoples, for the infinite variety of languages and cultures, and for the riches of its many spiritual and religious traditions. We pray for every country of the world, for our fellow members of the human family, and for our governments that, working together, we may face the future with confident hope and faith in your purpose for our world. In Jesus' name we pray. **Amen.** *(J. Allan McIntosh)*

PSALM 67

May God be gracious to us and bless us
    and make his face to shine upon us, . . .
that your way may be known upon earth,
    your saving power among all nations.
Let the peoples praise you, O God;
let all the peoples praise you.

Let the nations be glad and sing for joy,
    for you judge the peoples with equity
    and guide the nations upon earth. . . .
Let the peoples praise you, O God;
    let all the peoples praise you.

The earth has yielded its increase;
    God, our God, has blessed us.
May God continue to bless us;
    let all the ends of the earth revere him.

SCRIPTURE   MICAH 4:1-4

In days to come
    the mountain of the Lord's house
shall be established as the highest of the mountains,
    and shall be raised up above the hills.
Peoples shall stream to it,
    and many nations shall come and say:
"Come, let us go up to the mountain of the Lord,
    to the house of the God of Jacob;
that he may teach us his ways
    and that we may walk in his paths."
For out of Zion shall go forth instruction,
    and the word of the Lord from Jerusalem.
He shall judge between many peoples,
    and shall arbitrate between strong nations far away;
they shall beat their swords into plowshares,
    and their spears into pruning hooks;
nation shall not lift up sword against nation,
    neither shall they learn war any more;

> but they shall all sit under their own vines and under their own fig trees,
>> and no one shall make them afraid;
>> for the mouth of the LORD of hosts has spoken.

LITANY

Holy God, you abide in us.
May we know we abide in you.

We pray for countries where laws are being flouted. We pray for nations and peoples who are in danger of destroying themselves or others. We remember areas of civil strife, areas where people are misused or abused. We pray for all who seek to live in simplicity, gentleness and reverence, for all who suffer for doing good.
Holy God, you abide in us.
May we know we abide in you.

By your indwelling presence make our hearts and homes places of peace. We pray for our communities, for peace in our relationships, that your peace may spread throughout our world.
Holy God, you abide in us.
May we know we abide in you.

We pray for all who are captives to superstition or ignorance, for all who have no knowledge of God, for all whose lives are empty, or filled with the wrong things. We remember before you all whose lives are falling apart, all who are entering into darkness or sickness, that each in their weakness may know your strength.
Holy God, you abide in us.
May we know we abide in you.

Holy God, if we abide in you and you in us, we are already in the fullness of that life which is eternal. We rejoice in your presence, and pray for loved ones and friends who have gone before us.
Holy God, you abide in us.
May we know we abide in you. *(David Adam)*

REFLECTION   GRO HARLEM BRUNDTLAND

Scientists bring to our attention urgent but complex problems bearing on our very survival: a warming globe, threats to Earth's ozone layer, deserts consuming agricultural lands. Environmental degradation, first seen as mainly a problem of the rich nations and a side effect of industrial wealth, has become a survival issue for developing nations. It is part of the downward spiral of linked ecological and economic decline in which many of the poorest nations are trapped. If we do not succeed in putting our message of urgency through to today's parents and decision makers, we risk undermining our children's fundamental right to a healthy, life-enhancing environment. Unless we are able to translate our words into a language that can reach the minds and hearts of people young and old, we shall not be able to undertake the extensive social changes needed to correct the course of development.

Gro Harlem Brundtland (b. 1939), former prime minister of Norway, is a physician, diplomat, and international advocate for sustainable development. She chaired the United Nations Commission on Environment and Development, which conducted extensive world-wide public hearings on the state of the world and culminated in the 1987 report Our Common Future, *citing the links between poverty, inequality, and environmental degradation.*

PRAYERS OF CONFESSION AND INTERCESSION

God, the Creator and Provider, we confess the miserable failure of our human mechanisms for sharing the resources and opportunities of the earth. Give us, we pray, the insight to see the global divide between rich and poor for what it really is, the skill to persuade opinion-formers and decision-makers of that truth, and the integrity to accept for ourselves whatever limits our gospel of sharing. Grant to our own and other governments a vision of a just and caring world, the courage to move towards that vision with decisive action, and the ingenuity to work out new ways of bridging the gulf of poverty and debt. **Amen.** *(Alan Litherland)*

God our Father: In Jesus Christ you have ordered us to live as loving neighbors. Though we are scattered in different places, speak different words, or descend from different races, give us heartfelt concern, so that we may be one people, who share the governing of the world under your guiding purpose. May greed, war, lust for power be curbed, and all enter the community of love promised in Jesus Christ our Lord. **Amen.** *(Presbyterian Church, USA)*

HYMN   LLOYD STONE

1. This is my song, O God of all the nations,
   a song of peace for lands afar and mine.
   This is my home, the country where my heart is;
   here are my hopes, my dreams, my holy shrine;
   but other hearts in other lands are beating
   with hopes and dreams as true and high as mine.

2. My country's skies are bluer than the ocean,
   and sunlight beams on clover-leaf and pine;
   but other lands have sunlight too, and clover,
   and skies are everywhere as blue as mine.
   O hear my song, O God of all the nations,
   a song of peace for their land and for mine.

   Tune: FINLANDIA, 11.10.11.10.11.10.

As the earth keeps turning, hurtling through space; and night falls and day breaks from land to land, let us remember people—waking, sleeping, being born and dying—of one world and of one humanity. Let us go from here in peace. *(World Council of Churches)*

SOURCES

Acts 17:26 from *Contemporary English Version* (New York: American Bible Society, 1995). © 1995 American Bible Society.

"We pray for the peace . . . ," in *Gates of Prayer: The New Union Prayerbook* (New York: Central Conference of American Rabbis, 1975), 100, alt. © 1975, by Central Conference of American Rabbis, under the copyright protection of the Central Conference of American Rabbis and reprinted for use by permission of the CCAR. All rights reserved.

J. Allan McIntosh, "God of all . . . ," in United Church of Canada, *Celebrate God's Presence: A Book of Services for the United Church of Canada*, ed. Karen J. Verveda (Etobicoke, Ontario: United Church Publishing House, 2000), 532, alt.

David Adam, "Lord, you abide . . . ," in *Clouds and Glory: Prayers for the Church Year* (Harrisburg, PA: Morehouse, 2001), 71, alt. *Clouds and Glory: Prayers for the Church Year* © 2001 the Morehouse Publishing. Used by permission of Church Publishing Incorporated, New York, NY.

Gro Harlem Brundtland, "Chairman's Foreword," in World Commission on Environment and Development, *Our Common Future* (Oxford: Oxford University Press, 1987), xi, xiv. By permission of Oxford University Press. www.oup.com.

Alan Litherland, "Creator and Provider," in *Harvest for the World: A Worship Anthology on Sharing in the Work of Creation*, ed. Geoffrey Duncan (Cleveland: Pilgrim Press, 2003), 124, alt. © Alan Litherland.

"For World Community," in Presbyterian Church (USA), *The Worshipbook* (Philadelphia: Westminster Press, 1970), 179, alt. Used by permission.

Words by Lloyd Stone, "This Is My Song" © 1934 Lorenz Publishing Company (admin. by Music Services). All Rights Reserved. ASCAP.

"An Evening Litany," in *Let's Worship: A Risk Book*, ed. Fred Kaan, Doreen Potter, Konrad Raiser and Machteld van Vredenburch (Geneva: World Council of Churches, 1975), 23–25. Used by permission of World Council of Churches.

27. WORK

It is through our most human activities, in work and in love, that we become co-creators of the new Earth, the place we all call home. We may join Jesus in understanding that work is the way in which we are personally involved in God's ongoing creation and redemption of the world. (Dorothee Soelle)

Let the favor of the Lord our God be upon us,
    and prosper for us the work of our hands—
  O prosper the work of our hands! *(Psalm 90:17)*

PRAYERS OF PRAISE AND THANKSGIVING

O Lord God, our creator and keeper, giver of sunshine and rain; all that we are and all that we have is yours. In gratitude we offer to you, and for your work, the produce of our farms, businesses and employment. Accept and bless it for the furtherance of your work here and beyond. Bless your people in their daily work. Establish their work and multiply it to meet all their various needs. All for the glory and honor of your holy name. **Amen.** *(Anglican Church in Kenya)*

Almighty God, your Son Jesus Christ dignified our labor by sharing our toil. Guide us with your justice in the workplace, so that we may never value things above people, or surrender honor to love of gain or lust for power. Prosper all efforts to put an end to work that brings no joy, and teach us how to govern the ways of business to the harm of none and for the sake of the common good; through Jesus Christ our Lord. **Amen.** *(Evangelical Lutheran Church in America)*

PSALM 37:3-7, 10-11, 28A, 29

Trust in the Lord, and do good;
> so you will live in the land, and enjoy security.

Take delight in the Lord,
> **and he will give you the desires of your heart.**

Commit your way to the Lord;
> trust in him, and he will act.

He will make your vindication shine like the light,
> **and the justice of your cause like the noonday.**

Be still before the Lord, and wait patiently for him;
> **Do not fret over those who prosper in their way,**
> **over those who carry out evil devices.** . . .

Yet a little while, and the wicked will be no more;
> though you look diligently for their place, they will not be there.

But the meek shall inherit the land,
> **and delight in abundant prosperity.** . . .

For the Lord loves justice;
> he will not forsake his faithful ones.

The righteous shall be kept safe for ever, . . .

The righteous shall inherit the land,
> and live in it for ever.

SCRIPTURE   ECCLESIASTICUS (SIRACH) 38:25-32, 34

How will people become wise when they take hold of a plow or pride themselves in how well they handle an ox prod, when they drive cattle and are absorbed with their work, and their conversation is about bulls? Their hearts are given over to plowing furrows, and they lose sleep because they're concerned about supplying heifers with food. So it is also with every craftsperson and master artisan who carries over the day's work into the night, who carves figures on seals and works diligently to make diverse ornamentations. They will devote themselves to producing a lifelike painting, and they lose sleep in order to finish their work. So it is with smiths who sit near an anvil and who closely examine works of iron. The blast of the fire will melt their flesh, and they will struggle with the heat of the furnace. The sound of the hammer will strike their ears again and again, and their eyes are focused on the pattern of the object. They will devote themselves to finishing the work, and they lose sleep in order to complete its decoration. So it is with potters sitting at their work, turning the wheel at their feet. They lie down always feeling anxiety about their work, and every product of theirs is valued. They will mold the clay with their hands and work the wheel with their feet. They will devote themselves to finishing the glazing, and they lose sleep in order to clean the kiln. All of these have relied on their hands, and each one is skilled in their work. Without them a city can't be inhabited, and they neither go abroad to live as immigrants nor travel about. However, they aren't sought out when the people hold a council, . . . But they support the world from its foundations, and their prayer is concerned with their craft.

LITANY

God of the rough-worn hands, as we honor all workers,
Let us not forget all those whose work is without honor:

Homemakers who watch over children and homes, but are not recognized because they are not paid.
Those who are forced out of corporate jobs by corporate changes,

Those forced into retirement, those who are denied employment because of their age.
Those who live far from home, struggling to save a bit of money to send to their loved ones.

Those who must work illegally in order to survive and those who lose jobs because employers use undocumented labor.
Christ of the aching back, you worked the rough wood, you walked the long and dusty roads, you knew the bitter thirst of the poor.

Let our thirst become a passion for justice.
Help us to work towards transformation of economic policies that allow only a few nations to hoard the world's wealth, policies that pay women as only half a person or less,

Policies that do not recognize the worth of labor exacted without pay.
Spirit of creative power, move among us. Heal the wounds of those who labor to survive.
Renew our sense of vocation. Help us discern your Presence in even the lowliest tasks we face. **Amen.** *(O. I. Cricket Harrison)*

27. Work

REFLECTION   ANNE ROWTHORN

Whether we like it or not, we are identified by our work and, depending on what the job is and how we feel about it, we may be pleased or displeased to be so identified. If one were to ask the question, "Who are you?," the answer would almost certainly be given in terms of the job you do. Work can build up, enhance, beautify, glorify. It can also exploit, oppress, and violate. Because work is regarded as not only necessary but desirable and good, what about the unemployed? Because work is "good," unemployment must be "bad," and idleness worst of all. If work confers status, does that mean the unemployed have none? What about the fruits of labor, the products and conditions under which they are produced? Does it matter whether the worker makes bombs or bicycles, textbooks or toxic chemicals, mattresses or missiles? Are some jobs more morally or ethically acceptable than others in terms of what they produce? Are there some industries whose products are morally unquestionable but which engage in labor practices that oppress or exploit? Conflicts, questions and ambiguities surround work, yet we know that working is integral to being human, and that workers, in the words of the author of Ecclesiasticus, "maintain the fabric of the world, and their concern is for the exercise of their trade" (Eccl. 38:34; NRSV).

Anne Rowthorn wrote The Liberation of the Laity, *from which this reflection comes, out of the conviction that Christians best practice their faith through vibrant engagement in every aspect of society and that the best prayer is prayer in action performed faithfully and responsibly in the community, in political and family life, through daily endeavors and through works of justice and love.*

PRAYERS OF CONFESSION AND INTERCESSION

Our Maker God, we sinners confess to you what we are. We like the path of life to be easy, comfortable, untroubled. We like problems to melt away, hardships to be smoothed over, stones to turn into bread for us. We do not want the hard way that Jesus takes. We like every step to be free from fears. We like to see mighty power helping us at every turn. We like miracles to be happening for our benefit. We do not want the faithful way that Jesus takes. Merciful God, by all the grace of those forty desert days, arm us against those temptations, alert us to their corruption, forgive us our sins. Teach us to tread the way that Jesus takes; for his sake. **Amen.** *(Methodist Church)*

May the Lord give us peace in our work. God, send us into our work with new resolves. Help us to work out the problems that have perplexed us, and to serve the people we meet. May we see our work as part of your great plan and find significance in what we do. We do not know what any day will bring us, but we do know that the hour of serving you is always present. We dedicate our hearts, minds, and wills to your glory, through Jesus Christ our Lord. **Amen.** *(Unknown author)*

HYMN   JOHN A. DALLES

1. God, bless the work your people do
   throughout each working day,
   the contributions that they make,
   the talents they display.
   God, bless the work your people do,
   with minds and hands and hearts,
   to benefit the common good,
   the sciences and arts.

2. For all who have no respite, God,
   from labor without ease,
   for those for whom their work is filled
   with danger or disease,
   for all who labor without gain,
   or have no rest this day,
   for all who labor without hope,
   O God, we humbly pray.

3. We pray for those who cannot work,
   or seek for work in vain;
   great God, we pray your mercy shall
   encourage them, again!
   We pray for those whose work is hard,
   on body, spirit, soul,
   the under-paid, under-employed,
   who fill a vital role.

4. Grant unto each a day designed
   for worship, joy and rest;
   a Sabbath time of holiness,
   in which they may be blessed.
   As you achieved creation's work,
   then rested from your task,
   God bless the work your people do,
   and call it good, we ask!

Tune: RESIGNATION, C.M.D.

Whatever your task, put yourselves into it, as done for the Lord and not for your masters, since you know that from the Lord you will receive the inheritance as your reward; you serve the Lord Christ. *(Colossians 3:23-24)*

SOURCES

Dorothee Soelle with Shirley A. Cloyes, *To Work and to Love: A Theology of Creation* (Philadelphia: Fortress Press, 1984), 103 and 112. Used by permission.

"O Lord God our creator . . . ," in Anglican Church in Kenya, *Our Modern Services* (Nairobi, Kenya: Uzima Press, 2003), 216.

Ecclesiasticus 38:25-32 and 34 from the Common English Bible. © Copyright 2011 by the Common English Bible. All rights reserved. Used by permission. (www.CommonEnglishBible.com)

"Commerce and Labor," in Evangelical Lutheran Church in America, *Evangelical Lutheran Worship*, Leaders Desk ed. (Minneapolis: Augsburg Fortress, 2006), 148. Adapted from Charles Henry Brent, *Adventures in Prayer*, 38. Used by permission.

O. I. Cricket Harrison, "God of the rough-worn hands . . . ," in *Chalice Worship*, ed. Colbert S. Cartwright and O. I. Cricket Harrison (St. Louis: Chalice, 1997), 176, alt. Used by permission of Chalice Press.

Anne Rowthorn, *The Liberation of the Laity* (Wilton, CT: Morehouse, 1986), 82–83. © Anne Rowthorn.

"Lord, we sinners confess . . . ," in *Companion to the Lectionary 3: A New Collection of Prayers*, ed. Neil Dixon (London: Epworth Press, 1983), 68, alt.

"May the Lord give us . . . ," in *We Celebrate: Prayer Services for Special Occasions* (Notre Dame, IN: Ave Maria Press, 1990), 152. © 1990 by Ave Maria Press®, Inc., P.O. Box 428, Notre Dame, Indiana, 46556. Used with permission of the publisher. www.avemariapress.com.

Words by John A. Dalles, "God, Bless the Work Your People Do" © 2009 John A. Dalles. Used by permission.

28. SIMPLICITY

Lobsters grow by pushing to their limits. When the hard shell becomes too tight, the lobster sheds it in order that new growth may occur. Human beings also grow when they shed all that is superfluous in their lives, making room for new growth. Simplicity is a process of shedding all that is not necessary in order to embrace all that is.

"Do not store up for yourselves treasures on earth, where moth and rust consume and where thieves break in and steal; but store up for yourselves treasures in heaven, where neither moth nor rust consumes and where thieves do not break in and steal. For where your treasure is, there your heart will be also." *(Matthew 6:19-21)*

PRAYERS OF PRAISE AND THANKSGIVING

O God, we thank you for the many people throughout the ages who have followed your way of life joyfully; for the many saints and martyrs, men and women, who have offered up their lives, so that your life abundant may become manifest.

O God, we thank you for those who chose the way of Christ. In the midst of trial, they held out hope; in the midst of hatred, they kindled love; in the midst of persecutions, they witnessed to your power; in the midst of despair, they clung to your promise.

O God, we thank you for the truth they passed on to us; that it is by giving that we shall receive; it is by becoming weak that we shall be strong; it is by loving others that we shall be loved; it is by offering ourselves that the kingdom will unfold; it is by dying that we shall inherit life everlasting. O God, give us the courage to follow your way of life. For your love and faithfulness we praise you. **Amen**. *(National Council of Churches of the Philippines)*

CANTICLE   ISAIAH 35:1-7A, 8A, 10

The wilderness and the dry land shall be glad,
   the desert shall rejoice and blossom;
like the crocus it shall blossom abundantly,
   and rejoice with joy and singing. . . .
They shall see the glory of the Lord,
   the majesty of our God.

Strengthen the weak hands,
   and make firm the feeble knees.
Say to those who are of a fearful heart,
   "Be strong, do not fear!
Here is your God. . . .
   He will come and save you."

Then the eyes of the blind shall be opened,
   and the ears of the deaf unstopped;
then the lame shall leap like a deer,
   and the tongue of the speechless sing for joy.
For waters shall break forth in the wilderness,
   and streams in the desert;
the burning sand shall become a pool,
   and the thirsty ground springs of water; . . .

A highway shall be there,
   and it shall be called the Holy Way; . . .

And the ransomed of the Lord shall return,
   and come to Zion with singing;
everlasting joy shall be upon their heads;
   they shall obtain joy and gladness,
   and sorrow and sighing shall flee away.

SCRIPTURE   MARK 10:23-31

Jesus looked around and said to his disciples, "How hard it will be for those who have wealth to enter the kingdom of God!" And the disciples were perplexed at these words. But Jesus said to them again, "Children, how hard it is to enter the kingdom of God! It is easier for a camel to go through the eye of a needle than for someone who is rich to enter the kingdom of God." They were greatly astounded and said to one another, "Then who can be saved?" Jesus looked at them and said, "For mortals it is impossible, but not for God; for God all things are possible." Peter began to say to him, "Look, we have left everything and followed you." Jesus said, "Truly I tell you, there is no one who has left house or brothers or sisters or mother or father or children or fields, for my sake and for the sake of the good news, who will not receive a hundredfold now in this age—houses, brothers and sisters, mothers and children, and fields, with persecutions—and in the age to come eternal life. But many who are first will be last, and the last will be first."

LITANY

God of simplicity, God of justice: we have stored up treasures on earth that moths and rust are corroding. Open up our treasure houses and our hearts that we may freely share our possessions with all in need.
God of simplicity, God of justice: Open our hearts and hands.

God of simplicity, God of justice: Break down every gate, open every gated community, and crush every lock that keeps goods from those in need.
God of simplicity, God of justice: Open our hearts and hands.

God of simplicity, God of justice: Remove from our hearts the desire for more and more consumer goods.
God of simplicity, God of justice: Open our hearts and hands.

God of simplicity, God of justice: Strip us of what is excessive in our lives: clothing, jewelry, automobiles, electronics, the myriad purchases that do not satisfy.
God of simplicity, God of justice: Open our hearts and hands.

God of simplicity, God of justice: Turn us from being hoarders into sharers, for it is in giving that we become rich; it is in sharing that we become loving. Opening our hearts and our hands, may we stand with our sisters and brothers, freely giving and receiving. For where our treasure is, there our hearts are also.
God of simplicity and God of justice: Open our hearts and hands. *(Anne Rowthorn, inspired by Matthew 6:19-21)*

REFLECTIONS   DAVID KLINE AND VANDANA SHIVA

1. Maybe it is only carrying a rock off the field, or moving a piece of sod to some low spot to check possible erosion, or moving a killdeer's or horned lark's nest out of harm's way. These small acts of stewardship, multiplied a thousand times [on the farm], add up. Aldo Leopold once said that a good farm must be one where the wild flora and fauna have lost ground without losing their existence.

Even though much has been lost, we cherish what remains. And a farm is a good place to do this cherishing. Where else can one be so much a part of nature and the mysteries of God, the unfolding of the seasons, the coming and going of the birds, the pleasures of planting and the joys of harvest, the cycle of life and death? Where else can one still touch hands with an earlier people? Sure, there are periods of hard work. But it is labor with dignity, working together with family, neighbors, and friends. Here on our 120 acres I am a steward of the mysteries of God.

Writer, naturalist, and Amish farmer David Kline (1945) writes about his 120-acre family farm in Ohio. Environmentalism is a way of life for Kline. He does not drive a car, he uses only solar or wind power, and he farms organically. Every morning he milks forty cows. He grows hay and corn to feed them and he uses horses to plow and cultivate his fields.

2. Solutions are coming from those who know how to live lightly, who have never had an oil addiction, who do not define the good life as "shop till you drop," but rather define it as looking after Earth and their living community. Those who are being treated as disposable in the dominant system, which is pushing the planet's ecosystems to collapse and our species to extinction, carry the knowledge and values, the cultures and skills that give humanity a chance for survival.

Vandana Shiva (b. 1952) is a leading Indian philosopher, physicist, and author, whose father was a forester and whose mother was a farmer. She works to promote biodiversity in agriculture and the rights of local farmers. She gives voice to women farmers. She speaks against large-scale industrial agriculture, synthetic fertilizers and pesticides, genetically modified organisms and the corporate takeover of the world's seed supply.

PRAYERS OF CONFESSION AND INTERCESSION

Let us confess our sin against God and each other. Merciful God, we know that you love us and that you call us to fullness of life, but around us and within us we see the brokenness of the world and of our ways. Our successes leave us empty; our progress does not satisfy. Our prosperous land is not the promised land of our longing. Forgive our willful neglect of your word, our insensitivity to the needs of others, and our failure to feed the spirit that is within us; through Jesus Christ our Redeemer. **Amen.** *(United Church of Christ)*

Loving Father, as you made your love known in a single human life, lived for others and laid down, help us to meet Christ and greet him in every human face, to worship and serve him in every human need, until with him and every man and woman born into the world we share with you the kingdom, the power, and the glory forever. **Amen.** *(Alan Gaunt)*

HYMN   JOSEPH BRACKETT

1. 'Tis the gift to be simple,
   'tis the gift to be free,
   'tis the gift to come down
   where we ought to be,
   and when we find ourselves in the place just right,
   'twill be in the valley of love and delight.

2. When true simplicity is gained
   to bow and to bend we shan't be ashamed,
   to turn, turn, will be our delight
   till by turning, turning we come round right.

3. 'Tis the gift to be simple,
   'tis the gift to be free,
   'tis the gift to come down
   where we ought to be,
   and when we find ourselves in the place just right,
   'twill be in the valley of love and delight.

4. When true simplicity is gained
   to bow and to bend we shan't be ashamed,
   to turn, turn, will be our delight
   till by turning, turning we come round right.

Tune: SIMPLE GIFTS, Irregular with Refrain

May God who clothes the lilies and feeds the birds of the sky, who leads the lambs to pasture and the deer to water, who multiplied loaves and fishes and changed water into wine, lead us, feed us and change us to reflect the glory of our Creator through all eternity. Amen. *(Trevor Lloyd)*

SOURCES

"O God, we thank you . . ." in *Bread of Tomorrow*, ed. Janet Morley (Maryknoll, NY: Orbis Books, 2004), 111. Originally in National Council of Churches of the Philippines, *14th Biennial Convention Resource Book* (1989). Used by permission of National Council of Churches of the Philippines.

Anne Rowthorn, "God of Simplicity, God of Justice: Open Our Hearts and Hands" © 2016 Anne Rowthorn.

David Kline, "An Amish Perspective," in *Rooted in the Land: Essays on Community and Place*, ed. William Vitek and Wes Jackson (New Haven, CT: Yale University Press, 1996), 38–39, alt.

Vandana Shiva, *Soil Not Oil: Environmental Justice in an Age of Climate Crisis* (Berkeley: North Atlantic Books, 2015), 44. © 2008, 2015 by Vandana Shiva. Reprinted by permission of North Atlantic Books.

"Merciful God, we know . . . ," in United Church of Christ, *Book of Worship: United Church of Christ* (New York: United Church of Christ Office for Church Life and Leadership, 1986), 63, alt. Used by permission.

Alan Gaunt, "Loving Father . . . " in Alan Gaunt, *New Prayers for Worship* (Leeds, UK: John Paul the Preacher's Press, 1972), p. 30 of section 4, "Help." Used by permission.

Joseph Brackett, "Simple Gifts" (1848). Public domain.

Trevor Lloyd, "May God who clothes . . . ," in *Enriching the Christian Year*, ed. Michael Perham (Collegeville, MN: Liturgical Press), 161. © Trevor Lloyd. Used by permission.

29. COMPASSION

Compassion leads us to share the sufferings of others and to seek to alleviate their pain. Jesus had compassion whenever he saw people without food or without hope of healing, and he met their need.

In the tender compassion of our God, the morning sun from heaven will rise upon us, to shine on those who live in darkness, under the cloud of death, and to guide our feet into the way of peace. *(Luke 1:78-79)*

PRAYERS OF PRAISE AND THANKSGIVING

Creator, we give thanks that you long to sustain us, just as in the time of our ancestors you cared for them. Shield and care for us, as an eagle cares for its young. We give you thanks that you come to bring healing and nourishment to all. Help us to be open to all the ways you nourish us. May we be at peace with one another. **Amen.** *(United Church of Canada and Anglican Church of Canada)*

All-powerful God, you are present in the whole universe and in the smallest of your creatures. You embrace with your tenderness all that exists. Pour out upon us the power of your love, that we may protect life and beauty. Fill us with peace, that we may live as brothers and sisters, harming no one. O God of the poor, help us to rescue the abandoned and forgotten of this earth, so precious in your eyes. Bring healing to our lives, that we may protect the world and not prey on it, that we may sow beauty, not pollution and destruction. Touch the hearts of those who look only for gain at the expense of the poor and the Earth. Teach us to discover the worth of each thing, to be filled with awe and contemplation, to recognize that we are profoundly united with every creature as we journey towards your infinite light. We thank you for being with us each day. Encourage us, we pray, in our struggle for justice, love and peace. **Amen.** *(Pope Francis)*

PSALM 34:15-19

The eyes of the Lord are on the righteous,
   and his ears are open to their cry.
The face of the Lord is against evildoers,
   to cut off the remembrance of them from the earth.
When the righteous cry for help, the Lord hears,
   and rescues them from all their troubles.
The Lord is near to the brokenhearted,
   and saves the crushed in spirit.
Many are the afflictions of the righteous,
   but the Lord rescues them from them all.

PSALM 30:2, 8, 11-12

O Lord my God, I cried to you for help,
   and you have healed me. . . .
To you, O Lord, I cried,
   and to the Lord I made supplication: . . .
You have turned my mourning into dancing;
   you have taken off my sackcloth
   and clothed me with joy,
so that my soul may praise you and not be silent.
   O Lord my God, I will give thanks to you forever.

SCRIPTURE   LUKE 15:11-24

Jesus said, "There was a man who had two sons. The younger of them said to his father, 'Father, give me the share of the property that will belong to me.' So he divided his property between them. A few days later the younger son gathered all he had and traveled to a distant country, and there he squandered his property in dissolute living. When he had spent everything, a severe famine took place throughout that country, and he began to be in need. So he went and hired himself out to one of the citizens of that country, who sent him to his fields to feed the pigs. He would gladly have filled himself with the pods that the pigs were eating; and no one gave him anything. But when he came to himself he said, 'How many of my father's hired hands have bread enough and to spare, but here I am dying of hunger! I will get up and go to my father, and I will say to him, "Father, I have sinned against heaven and before you; I am no longer worthy to be called your son; treat me like one of your hired hands."' So he set off and went to his father. But while he was still far off, his father saw him and was filled with compassion; he ran and put his arms around him and kissed him. Then the son said to him, 'Father, I have sinned against heaven and before you; I am no longer worthy to be called your son.' But the father said to his slaves, 'Quickly, bring out a robe—the best one—and put it on him; put a ring on his finger and sandals on his feet. And get the fatted calf and kill it, and let us eat and celebrate; for this son of mine was dead and is alive again; he was lost and is found!' And they began to celebrate."

LITANY

Aware that great violence and injustice have been done to our environment and society, we are committed not to live in ways that are harmful to humans and nature. We will do our best to select livelihoods that help realize our ideal of understanding and compassion. Aware of global economic, political and social realities, we will take responsibility as consumers and citizens, not investing in companies that deprive others of their chance to live.
Holy One, make us mindful.

Aware that much suffering is caused by war and conflict, we will cultivate non-violence, understanding and compassion in our daily lives, promote peace education, mindful meditation, and reconciliation within families, communities and nations.
Holy One, make us mindful.

Aware of the suffering caused by exploitation, social injustice, stealing, and oppression, we will cultivate loving kindness, working for the well-being of people, animals, plants, and minerals. We will neither steal nor possess anything that should belong to others. We will try to prevent others from profiting from human suffering or the suffering of other beings.
Holy One, make us mindful.

Aware that true happiness is rooted in peace, solidarity, freedom, and compassion, we commit ourselves to living simply and sharing our time, energy, and material resources with those in need.
Holy One, make us mindful. *(Thich Nhat Hanh)*

REFLECTION   PAUL FARMER

I've chosen this very day to announce my discovery and naming of a new disease, which I've elected to call EDD. That stands for Empathy Deficit Disorder. I'm also announcing today a cure for EDD. Curing EDD will help untold millions whose unnecessary suffering may be averted or cured as long as our efforts are supported by a broad-based coalition of people able to link empathy to reason and action. That's my diagnosis and here's my prescription: We need to be part of that coalition. Ours is a nation still saddled with a big EDD problem.

You can be the cure for EDD in its chronic and acute forms. You can address local outbreaks of EDD and also the global pandemic, which has affected people in every single nation on this fragile and crowded planet. Indeed, ours is a world that requires nothing less than linking empathy and compassion to reasoned plans that harness it to meaningful action. . . . Even our short-term survival calls for deliberation and calculation and expertise. These will not be marshaled in adequate quantities nor for the public good unless we address the global pandemic of Empathy Deficit Disorder. And that is well within our grasp.

The physician Paul Farmer (b. 1959) first learned about the interlocking issues of inequality, extreme poverty, and environmental degradation when he visited Cange, a small remote village in Haiti, as a high school student. Inspired by what he observed, the goal of his life's work would become bringing health care to the most challenging places on earth. He cofounded Partners in Health in 1987 and its first location was Cange.

PRAYERS OF CONFESSION AND INTERCESSION

Save us, O Lord, from being idle bystanders—looking on and attempting to interpret the dilemmas of a broken world, yet rarely willing to act. Give us compassion for the lost and confused, the weary and the oppressed. Save us from slick and simplistic answers to human problems, which offer words but no real help. Unsettle us, and move us on from viewing the plight of sin-scarred people, to actions that promote spiritual and inward healing and liberating forgiveness. Cleanse our lives, that they may be instruments worthy of conveying your truth of abundant and everlasting life through Jesus Christ the Lord. We ask in his name. **Amen.** *(Michael Perry, Patrick Goodland, and Angela Griffiths)*

Lord Jesus Christ, you are alive in the world: among the poor and oppressed, the pavement dwellers and refugees of Africa, Asia, and Latin America. Amid the garbage and ruins, in depths of despair and suffering, there you are. The friendly face of a homeless child stares up at us; an old man smiles and blesses us; a beggar woman shares a handful of rice between her hungry children and the orphan who joins them. Of such is the kingdom. Lord Jesus Christ, we cannot see you as Thomas did, or touch you with our hands, but you come in unexpected ways and speak through people whose backgrounds and outlooks are different from our own. Help us to listen with respect to their experiences and reflect upon their insights. Free us from pride to find your dignity and presence wherever you are. **Amen.** *(Maureen Edwards)*

HYMN   MARY LOUISE BRINGLE

1. Touch that soothes and heals the hurting,
   hands that break a loaf of bread;
   steps that walk beside the weary,
   bearing burdens in their stead:

   Refrain:
   See my hands and feet, said Jesus,
   Love arisen from the grave.
   Be my hands and feet, said Jesus,
   live as ones I died to save.

2. Feed the hungry, clothe the naked,
   visit those in need of care,
   give the homeless warmth and shelter:
   Christ will find a welcome there.
   Refrain.

3. Love and serve without distinction
   all earth's people, first and least.
   Know that by each act of kindness
   hope and wholeness are increased.
   Refrain.

4. Hands that beckon little children,
   bind a wound, prepare a meal,
   feet that rush to share good tidings,
   Christ arisen still reveal. *Refrain.*

Tune: GENEVA, 8.7.8.7.D.

Stay close to the cracks, to the broken places, where people weep and cry out in pain.
Stay close to the cracks, where God's tears fall, and God's wounds bleed for love of us.
Stay close to the cracks where the light shines in, and grass pushes up through concrete.
Stay close to the cracks where wounds open doorways to healing and wholeness and life. *(Christine Sine)*

SOURCES

Luke 1:78-79 from the *New English Bible*, copyright © Cambridge University Press and Oxford University Press 1961, 1970. All rights reserved.

"Prayer of Thanks," from "Story Three: Respecting Different Traditions," *The Dancing Sun VI*, 17, quoted in *First Peoples Theology Journal* 4 (June 2006), 120. Used with permission of United Church Publishing House and Anglican Church of Canada.

Pope Francis, "A Prayer for Our Earth," in *Laudato Si'*, accessed December 1, 2017, Vatican.va. © Libreria Editrice Vaticana. Used by permission.

Adapted from "Ceremony to Recite the Fourteen Mindfulness Trainings," in *Plum Village Chanting and Recitation Book*, comp. Thich Nhat Hanh (Berkeley: Parallax Press, 2000), 79–80 and 76. Used with permission of Parallax Press, Berkeley, California, www.parallax.org.

Paul Farmer, "On Empathy and Reason" (commencement address, University of Delaware, Newark, DE, May 25, 2013). Used by permission.

Michael Perry, Patrick Goodland, and Angela Griffiths, "For Our Dedication to Christ's Mission," in *Prayers for the People*, ed. Michael Perry, Patrick Goodland, and Angela Griffiths, Leader's ed. (London: Marshall Pickering, 1992), 291–92. © The Jubilate Group (admin Hope Publishing Company, Carol Stream, IL 60188). All rights reserved. Used by permission.

Maureen Edwards, "Lord Jesus Christ . . . ," in *Oceans of Prayer*, comp. Maureen Edwards and Jan S. Pickard (Nutfield, UK: National Christian Education Council, UK, 1991), 86. © 1991 National Christian Education Council. Used by permission.

Words by Mary Louise Bringle, "See My Hands and Feet" © 2002, GIA Publications, Inc. Used by permission.

Christine Sine, "Stay Close to the Cracks," *Godspace*, last modified November 12, 2016, https://godspace-msa.com/2016/11/12/remembering-leonard-cohen-stay-close-to-the-cracks/. Used by permission.

30. SURVIVAL

Earth is such a tolerant mother, providing food, water, shelter, and protection. It is easy to forget that a return is expected—namely, that we will honor and protect her and follow the ancient Iroquois philosophy that all decisions are to be made on the basis of how the seventh generation will be affected. Forgetting this, the survival of humankind on this planet is called into question.

Give ear, O Lord, to my prayer;
> listen to my cry of supplication.

In the day of my trouble I call on you,
> for you will answer me. *(Psalm 86:6-7)*

PRAYERS OF PRAISE AND THANKSGIVING

Long live this wounded planet. Long live the good milk of the air. Long live the spawning rivers and the mothering oceans. Long live the juice of the grass and all the determined greenery of the globe. Long live the surviving animals. Long live the Earth, deeper than all our thinking. We have done enough killing. Long live the men. Long live the women who use both courage and compassion. Long live our children. **Amen.** *(Adrian Mitchell)*

Lord God, we praise you for those riches of your creation which we shall never see: for stars whose light will never reach the Earth; for species of living things that were born, that flourished and perished before mankind appeared in the world; for patterns and colors in the flowers, which only insect eyes are able to see; for strange, high music that humans can never hear. Lord God, you see everything that you have made and behold, it is very good. **Amen.** *(David Jenkins, Henry McKeating, and Michael Walter)*

PSALM 90:1-6, 17

Lord, you have been our dwelling place
    in all generations.
Before the mountains were brought forth,
    or ever you had formed the earth and the world,
    from everlasting to everlasting you are God.

You turn us back to dust,
    and say, "Turn back, you mortals."
For a thousand years in your sight
    are like yesterday when it is past,
    or like a watch in the night.

You sweep them away; they are like a dream,
    like grass that is renewed in the morning;
in the morning it flourishes and is renewed;
    in the evening it fades and withers. . . .
Let the favor of the Lord our God be upon us,
    and prosper for us the work of our hands—
    O prosper the work of our hands!

SCRIPTURE   DEUTERONOMY 11:8-17

Keep, then, this entire commandment that I am commanding you today, so that you may have strength to go in and occupy the land that you are crossing over to occupy, and so that you may live long in the land that the Lord swore to your ancestors to give to them and their descendants, a land flowing with milk and honey. For the land that you are about to enter to occupy is not like the land of Egypt, from which you have come, where you sow your seed and irrigate by foot like a vegetable garden. But the land that you are crossing over to occupy is a land of hills and valleys, watered by rain from the sky, a land that the Lord your God looks after. The eyes of the Lord your God are always on it, from the beginning of the year to the end of the year.

If you will only heed his every commandment that I am commanding you today—loving the Lord your God, and serving him with all your heart and with all your soul—then he will give the rain for your land in its season, the early rain and the later rain, and you will gather in your grain, your wine, and your oil; and he will give grass in your fields for your livestock, and you will eat your fill. Take care, or you will be seduced into turning away, serving other gods and worshiping them, for then the anger of the Lord will be kindled against you and he will shut up the heavens, so that there will be no rain and the land will yield no fruit; then you will perish quickly from the good land that the Lord is giving you.

LITANY

God, give us grace to build on sure foundations.
  We pray for the harvests of your world,
  that they may not be hoarded or squandered,
  that the land may be respected and cared for,
  that no one may hunger or be misused by others.
  We remember nations and individuals who are deeply in debt.
  We pray for all who have lost their freedom or their livelihood.
  God, give us grace to build on sure foundations.

We pray for our homes and our loved ones,
  that enmity and strife in our communities may be conquered,
  that forgiveness and mutual respect may be part of our lives.
  We pray for the renewal of broken relationships, and broken hearts.
  God, give us grace to build on sure foundations.

We remember all who have suffered from fraud, from robbery, from low wages,
  all who have suffered through injustice,
  all who have been slandered or maligned,
  all who have suffered mockery and scorn.
  We remember all whose lives are crumbling around them.
  God, give us grace to build on sure foundations.

That we may endure all, and come at last to your glorious kingdom,
  that we may share with our loved ones in glory,
  God, give us grace to build on sure foundations. *(David Adam)*

REFLECTION   ROGER ENGELMAN, WORLDWATCH INSTITUTE

The question of whether civilization can continue on its current path without undermining prospects for future well-being is at the core of the world's current environmental predicament. In the wake of failed international environmental and climate summits, when national governments take no actions commensurate with the risk of catastrophic environmental change, are there ways humanity might still alter current behaviors to make them sustainable? Is sustainability still possible? If humanity fails to achieve sustainability, when—and how—will unsustainable trends end? And how will we live through and beyond such endings? Whatever words we use, we need to ask these tough questions. If we fail to do so, we risk self-destruction. The stakes by their very nature are higher the younger someone is—and highest still for those who are not yet born. We are talking about the survival of human civilization as we know it, and possibly of the species itself.

Every year, Worldwatch Institute publishes State of the World, *an assessment of social and environmental trends affecting the world community. This is done in an effort to educate policymakers, concerned citizens, and the general public about trends in sustainable development. In 2013 they asked the question "Is sustainability still possible?"*

PRAYERS OF CONFESSION AND INTERCESSION

Creator God, maker and shaper of all that is, seen and unseen: You are in the expanse and depth of Creation, and in the processes that make life possible. Yet we are distracted by the gods we make for ourselves, and our lives become fractured and fragmented. In our brokenness we disturb the Earth's capacity to hold us. Instead we find climate uncertainty and global injustice. Call us back from the brink. Help us to choose love not fear, to change ourselves and not the planet; to act justly for the sake of the vulnerable; and to make a difference today for life tomorrow. In your name—Father, Son and Spirit. **Amen.** *(Martyn Goss)*

God, your Son Jesus Christ has taught us that power belongs to you. You have shared your power with us. Yet we confess we have not accepted the power you have given us. We have allowed others to use power to dominate people and nations, exploiting them, creating wars, and accumulating wealth. Today offer us your power, so that we can change the world, announce your kingdom, and acknowledge you, the source of all power and glory, forever and ever. **Amen.** *(Diego Frisch)*

HYMN   DAVID A. ROBB

1. Children from your vast creation,
   gather here for guidance, Lord;
   we of every tongue and nation
   yearn to see your earth restored.
   You have shown that your intention
   wills a world kept free from strife;
   open us to love's dimension
   filled with true abundant life.

2. We have grasped for more possessions,
   wanting things we do not need;
   help us, Lord, lest our obsessions
   soon consume us in our greed.
   Cure our tendency to plunder,
   scarring forests, wasting ore;
   come, and turn our schemes asunder;
   take away our lust for more.

3. We are learning how much damage
   spreads throughout the world from greed;
   though you made us in your image,
   we are less than you decreed:
   wanting ease and pleasure strongly,
   craving things your love deplores,
   asking not, or asking wrongly,
   we resort to waging wars.

4. Lord, we come as sisters, brothers,
   seeking your redemptive touch.
   Let unselfish love for others
   triumph, lest we want too much.
   Come to us amid life's scrimmage,
   help your people live as one:
   recreate us in your image;
   speed the day your will is done!

Tune: BLAENWERN, 8.7.8.7.D.

May you never become cynical. May you never become jaded. May you never lose heart. May you never let the bullies get you down. May you never lose faith. May you see light and good in everyone. May you remain open to wonder and mystery. May you stand firm in the assault of the powers, shielded with a sense of humor. May you stay rooted in hope. **Amen.** *(Neil Paynter)*

SOURCES

Adrian Mitchell, *Ride the Nightmare* (London: Jonathan Cape, 1971), 79, alt.

David Jenkins, Henry McKeating, and Michael Walter, "Lord God, we praise . . . ," in *Further Everyday Prayers*, ed. Hazel Snashall (Nutfield, UK: International Bible Reading Association 1987), 12. © 1987 National Christian Education Council. Used by permission.

David Adam, "Father, make us holy . . . ," in *Clouds and Glory: Prayers for the Church Year* (Harrisburg, PA: Morehouse, 2001), 39–40. *Clouds and Glory: Prayers for the Church Year* © 2001 the Morehouse Publishing. Used by permission of Church Publishing Incorporated, New York, NY.

Robert Engelman, "Beyond Sustainable," in *State of the World 2013: Is Sustainability Still Possible?*, ed. Worldwatch Institute (Washington, DC: Island Press, 2013), 4–5 and 15. © 2013 by Worldwatch Institute. Reproduced by permission of Island Press, Washington, DC.

Martyn Goss, "Call Us Back from the Brink," in *Season of Creation 2* (n.p.: Anglican Church of Southern Africa, 2013), 11, last modified August 2013, http://www.greenanglicans.org/wp-content/uploads/2013/08/Season-of-Creation-Two-low-res.pdf. Used by permission of the author.

Diego Frisch, "God, your Son . . . ," in *Oceans of Prayer*, comp. Maureen Edwards and Jan S. Pickard (Nutfield, UK: National Christian Education Council, UK, 1991), 62. © 1991 National Christian Education Council. Used by permission.

Words by David A. Robb, "Children from Your Vast Creation." Text: David A. Robb, 1992, rev. 1997 Text © 1997 Selah Publishing Co., Inc. www.selahpub.com All rights reserved. Used by permission. License no. 24641.

Neil Paynter, "May you never . . . ," in *Holy Ground: Liturgies and Worship Resources for an Engaged Spirituality*, ed. Neil Paynter and Helen Boothroyd (Glasgow: Wild Goose, 2005), 372. © Contributors, *Holy Ground* (2005), Wild Goose Publications, Glasgow. Used by permission. Note: The word "bullies" is substituted for the word "bastards" in the original.

31. THE LANGUAGE OF LOVE

Love is the language of the heart, the melody of the soul, freely flowing through the earth and gathering all the beloved into one magnificent song of creation.

The heavens are telling the glory of God;
    and the firmament proclaims his handiwork.
Day to day pours forth speech,
    and night to night declares knowledge.
There is no speech, nor are there words;
    their voice is not heard;
yet their voice goes out through all the earth,
    and their words to the end of the world. *(Psalm 19:1-4a)*

PRAYERS OF PRAISE AND THANKSGIVING

Love all of God's creation, the whole of it and every grain of sand, Love every leaf, every ray of God's light! Love the animals, love the plants, love everything. **Amen.** *(Fyodor Dostoyevsky)*

Creating God, your divine melodies fill the world. Every creature has a song. The wolf cries in the night, the songbird trills in the morning. You give voice to crickets and frogs, to coyotes, to large cats of the forest and cats of the hearth, to barking dogs and neighing horses, to the sweet song of the lark. You inspire human speech—voices of warning and wisdom, voices of justice, voices of comfort, hope and joy; voices that say, "I love you" when the night is dark and morning far off. Even the trees clap their hands in praise and the winds echo a rich refrain. We thank you for the language of love that unites us with all of creation in one unending song of praise to you. **Amen.** *(Anne Rowthorn)*

31. The Language of Love

CANTICLE   LUKE 6:27-30, 35B

"I say to you that listen, Love your enemies, do good to those who hate you,
bless those who curse you, pray for those who abuse you.

If anyone strikes you on the cheek, offer the other also;
and from anyone who takes away your coat do not withhold even your shirt.

Give to everyone who begs from you;
and if anyone takes away your goods, do not ask for them again. . . .

"But love your enemies, do good, and lend, expecting nothing in return.
Your reward will be great, and you will be children of the Most High."

CANTICLE   ROMANS 12:9-18

Let love be genuine; hate what is evil, hold fast to what is good;
love one another with mutual affection; outdo one another in showing honor.

Do not lag in zeal, be ardent in spirit, serve the Lord.
Rejoice in hope, be patient in suffering, persevere in prayer.

Contribute to the needs of the saints; extend hospitality to strangers.
Bless those who persecute you; bless and do not curse them.

Rejoice with those who rejoice, weep with those who weep.
Live in harmony with one another; do not be haughty, but associate with the lowly;

do not claim to be wiser than you are.
Do not repay anyone evil for evil, but take thought for what is noble in the sight of all.

If it is possible, so far as it depends on you, live peaceably with all.

SCRIPTURE   I CORINTHIANS 13:1-7, 13

If I speak in the tongues of mortals and of angels, but do not have love, I am a noisy gong or a clanging cymbal. And if I have prophetic powers, and understand all mysteries and all knowledge, and if I have all faith, so as to remove mountains, but do not have love, I am nothing. If I give away all my possessions, and if I hand over my body so that I may boast, but do not have love, I gain nothing. Love is patient; love is kind; love is not envious or boastful or arrogant or rude. It does not insist on its own way; it is not irritable or resentful; it does not rejoice in wrongdoing, but rejoices in the truth. It bears all things, believes all things, hopes all things, endures all things. . . . And now faith, hope, and love abide, these three; and the greatest of these is love.

LITANY

When long before time and the worlds were begun, when there was no earth and no sky and no sun, and all was deep silence and night reigned supreme, **and even our Maker had only a dream . . .**

. . . the silence was broken when God sang the Song, and love pierced the darkness and rhythm began, and with its first birth cries creation was born, **and creaturely voices sang praise to the morn.**

The sounds of the creatures were one with their Lord, their love-songs sweetly befitting the Word; the Singer was pleased as the earth sang the Song, **the choir of creatures re-echoed it long.**

Though, down through the ages, the Song disappeared—its harmonies broken and almost unheard—the Singer comes to us to sing it again . . . **Our God is singing of love without end.**

The language of love has returned as it came once before, the Song of the Lord is our own song once more . . .
. . . so let us sing with one heart and one voice the Song of the Singer in whom we rejoice. To you, God the Singer, our voices we raise, to you, Love Incarnate, we give you our praise. *(Peter W. A. Davison)*

REFLECTION   KATHLEEN DEAN MOORE

I held my granddaughter in my arms and sang to her an old lullaby. *Hush-a-bye, don't you cry. Go to sleep, you little baby. Birds and butterflies fly through the land.* She fell asleep in my arms, unafraid. But I was afraid! Poets warned us, writing of *the heartbreaking beauty that will remain when there is no heart to break for it.* What of the brokenhearted children who remain in a world without beauty? How will they find solace in a world without wild music?

How will they thrive without green hills edged with oaks? How will they forgive us for letting frog-song slip away? It isn't enough to love a child and wish her well. It isn't enough to open my heart to a bird-graced morning. Can I claim to love a morning if I don't protect what creates its beauty? Can I claim to love a child if I don't use all the power of my beating heart to preserve a world that nourishes children's joy? Loving is not a kind of *la-de-da*. Loving is a sacred trust. To love is to affirm the absolute worth of what you love and to pledge your life to its thriving—to protect it fiercely and faithfully, for all time.

Ring the angelus for the salmon and the swallows. Ring the bells for frogs floating in bent reeds. Ring the bells for all of us who did not save the songs. Holy Mary, mother of God, ring the bells for every sacred emptiness. Let them echo in the silence at the end of the day. I would pray only this: that our granddaughter would hear again the little lick of music, that grace note at the end of the meadowlark's song.

In an intimate letter to her infant granddaughter, the essayist and environmental philosopher Kathleen Dean Moore (b. 1947) imagines our world in the year 2025. It is a letter of prayer, warning, and hope.

PRAYERS OF CONFESSION AND INTERCESSION

We confess, Lord, that we have not loved you, or our neighbor, as we should. We have often neglected opportunities of good; sometimes we have done actual harm. Our consciences accuse us over trifles, but let us blithely ignore your weightier demands. We know that a mere apology will not do. We resolve to turn from the sins we know. We ask you to show us the sins we do not recognize. We resolve to forgive any who have wronged us, and to seek reconciliation with any from whom we are estranged. And now we beg your pardon and ask for your help. **Amen.** *(Anthony Coates, et al.)*

O God, be present among us, for the sake of all human beings on earth. Open our eyes that we may see the salvation that is in you, and reveal yourself to a blind humanity. Make your face shine upon those stricken with disease; give them your strength and your peace. All the poor ones, the weak, all those weighed down by want, may they have the knowledge of you, so as to lean on you and be filled to overflowing in you. To the mighty and the wealthy, grant the power they are lacking; give them a discerning spirit, that they may be freed by your freedom, and free to love others. To one and all of us, may you grant your life and your peace. **Amen.** *(Mamie Woungly-Massaga)*

HYMN — JEFFERY ROWTHORN

1. How precious is God's gift of speech,
   enriched by time and place;
   a thousand tongues that we may each
   rehearse and share what life will teach
   in syllables of grace,
   in syllables of grace.

2. So infants lisp and poets mold
   their ancient mother tongue.
   In it a people's dreams are clothed,
   the exploits of their past retold,
   their joys and sorrows sung,
   their joys and sorrows sung.

3. Yet all these bridges to your grace
   are barriers, Lord, to me.
   If unknown words allow no space
   to look beyond my neighbor's face,
   a stranger's all I see,
   a stranger's all I see.

4. Estranged, our world with fear is rife;
   its wars will never cease
   until we learn the words of life,
   with all our dialects of strife
   translated into peace,
   translated into peace.

5. Earth's thousand tongues, Lord, are your gift
   to bind, not keep apart,
   and so you came to heal the rift
   and taught us all, a world adrift,
   one language of the heart,
   one language of the heart.

6. Help us to practice daily, Lord,
   till, fluent in love's ways,
   our hearts interpret every word,
   and all our thousand tongues accord
   in grateful hymns of praise,
   in grateful hymns of praise.

Tune: REPTON, 8.6.8.8.6.6.
Words © 1996 Hope Publishing

May we hear today the song of God's grace unfolding, the music of the world becoming, the beating of Christ's own heart in, and with, and under all creation. *(Sam Hamilton-Poore)*

SOURCES

Fyodor Dostoyevsky, *The Brothers Karamazov*, trans. Constance Garnett (New York: Lowell Press, 1912), 354–55. Public domain.

Anne Rowthorn, "Divine Melodies of Love" © 2017 Anne Rowthorn.

Peter W. A. Davison, "The Singer and the Song," in *Dare to Dream: A Prayer and Worship Anthology from around the World*, ed. Geoffrey Duncan (London: HarperCollins, 1995), 185, alt. Used by permission.

Kathleen Dean Moore, "The Call to Forgiveness at the End of the Day," in *Moral Ground: Ethical Action for a Planet in Peril*, ed. Kathleen Dean Moore and Michael P. Nelson (San Antonio: Trinity University Press, 2010), 392–93, alt. Used by permission.

"We confess, Lord . . . ," in Anthony Coates et al., *Contemporary Prayers for Public Worship*, ed. Caryl Micklem (Grand Rapids, MI: William B. Eerdmans, 1967), 41, alt. Extract from *Contemporary Prayers for Public Worship* by Cathy Ross and Stephen B. Bevans is copyright © SCM Press 1967 and is reproduced by permission of Hymns Ancient & Modern Ltd.

Mamie Woungly-Massaga, "O God, be present . . . ," trans. René Robert, in *In Spirit and in Truth: A Worship Book* (Geneva: World Council of Churches, 1991), 22–23. Used by permission of World Council of Churches.

Words by Jeffery Rowthorn, "How Precious Is God's Gift of Speech" © 1996 Hope Publishing Company, Carol Stream, IL 60188. All rights reserved. Used by permission.

Sam Hamilton-Poore, "May we hear today . . . ," in *Earth Gospel: A Guide to Prayer for God's Creation* (Nashville: Upper Room Books, 2008), 171, alt. Reprinted from *Earth Gospel: A Guide to Prayer for God's Creation* by Sam Hamilton-Poore. Copyright © 2008. Used by permission of Upper Room Books. bookstore.upperroom.org.

The Whole Creation Groaning in Travail

32. EXPLOITATION OF THE EARTH

The land is ravaged; forests are clear-cut; wetlands are drained; deserts are increasing; polar ice is melting and oceans are rising and becoming more acidic; species are becoming extinct; we are choking on the air we breathe. Help! The whole creation is suffering. Come quickly, God of all creation, for our Mother Earth is dying.

Hear my cry, O God;
    listen to my prayer.
From the ends of the earth I call to you,
    when my heart is faint. . . .
Let me abide in your tent forever,
    find refuge under the shelter of your wings. *(Psalm 61:1-2a, 4)*

PRAYERS OF PRAISE AND THANKSGIVING

God of the universe, every atom, star, galaxy, and particle began and will end with your word. Your grace securely holds our lives in water and word. From our beginnings to our endings, living in you we need not fear anything. **Amen.** *(Jim Drury)*

Blessed are you, God of the universe. You have created us, and given us life. Blessed are you, God of the planet Earth. You have set our world like a radiant jewel in the heavens, and filled it with action, beauty, suffering, struggle and hope. Blessed are you, God of our nation, in all the peoples who live here, in all the lessons we have learned, in all that remains for us to do. Blessed are you because you need us; because you make us worthwhile; because you give us people to love and work to do for your universe, for your world and for ourselves. **Amen.** *(Anglican Church in New Zealand)*

CANTICLE   ISAIAH 24:19-23

The earth is utterly broken,
    the earth is torn asunder,
    the earth is violently shaken.
The earth staggers like a drunkard,
    it sways like a hut;
its transgression lies heavy upon it,
    and it falls, and will not rise again.

On that day the LORD will punish
    the host of heaven in heaven,
    and on earth the kings of the earth.
They will be gathered together
    like prisoners in a pit;
they will be shut up in a prison,
    and after many days they will be punished.
Then the moon will be abashed,
    and the sun ashamed;
for the LORD of hosts will reign
    on Mount Zion and in Jerusalem,
and before his elders he will manifest his glory. . . .

SCRIPTURE   LEVITICUS 26:3-6, 14, 20, 25

If you follow my statutes and keep my commandments and observe them faithfully, I will give you your rains in their season, and the land shall yield its produce, and the trees of the field shall yield their fruit. Your threshing shall overtake the vintage, and the vintage shall overtake the sowing; you shall eat your bread to the full, and live securely in your land. And I will grant peace in the land, and you shall lie down, and no one shall make you afraid; I will remove dangerous animals from the land, and no sword shall go through your land. . . . But if you will not obey me, and do not observe all these commandments, . . . Your strength shall be spent to no purpose: your land shall not yield its produce, and the trees of the land shall not yield their fruit. . . . I will bring the sword against you, executing vengeance for the covenant; and if you withdraw within your cities, I will send pestilence among you, and you shall be delivered into enemy hands.

LITANY

We have forgotten who we are. We have alienated ourselves from the unfolding cosmos. We have become estranged from the movements of the Earth. We have turned our backs on the cycles of life. We have sought our own security. We have exploited for our own ends. We have abused our power.
We have forgotten who we are.

Now the land is barren, and the waters are poisoned, and the air is polluted.
We have forgotten who we are.

Now the forests are dying, and the creatures are disappearing, and humans are despairing.
We have forgotten who we are.

We ask forgiveness. We ask for the gift of remembering. We ask for the strength to change.
We have forgotten who we are.

To bring new life to the land, to restore the waters, to refresh the air.
We have forgotten who we are.

To renew the forests, to care for the plants, to protect the creatures.
We have forgotten who we are.

To celebrate the seas, to rejoice in the sunlight, to sing the song of the stars.
We have forgotten who we are.

To recreate the human community, to promote justice and peace, to remember our children.
We have forgotten who we are.

We join together as many and diverse expressions of one loving mystery:
for the healing of the earth and the renewal of all life. *(United Nations Environment Programme)*

REFLECTION   ELIZABETH KOLBERT

In an extinction event of our own making, what happens to us? One possibility [follows the line of thinking that] humans remain dependent on the earth's biological and geochemical systems. By disrupting these systems—cutting down tropical rainforests, altering the composition of the atmosphere, acidifying the oceans—we're putting our own survival in danger. When a mass extinction occurs, it takes out the weak and also lays low the strong.

Another possibility is that human ingenuity will outrun any disaster human ingenuity sets in motion. There are serious scientists who argue that should global warming become too grave a threat, we can counteract it by reengineering the atmosphere. If things really go south, there are those who maintain people will still be OK; we'll simply decamp to other planets.

Right now, in the amazing moment that to us counts as the present, we are deciding, without quite meaning to, which evolutionary pathways will remain open and which will forever be closed. No other creature has ever managed this, and it will, unfortunately, be our most enduring legacy. The Sixth Extinction will continue to determine the course of life long after everything people have written and painted and built has been ground into dust and giant rats have—or have not—inherited the earth.

Since the origin of life on Earth some 3.8 billion years ago, the planet has endured five major mass extinctions. The last extinction, 66 million years ago, killed off the dinosaurs. Today, according to science writer Elizabeth Kolbert (b. 1961), the planet is experiencing a sixth mass extinction, this one of human making.

PRAYERS OF CONFESSION AND INTERCESSION

Lord, Jesus Christ, through whom and for whom the whole universe was created, we mourn with you the death of forests, fruitful lands that have become deserts, wild animals left without grass, plants, insects, birds, and animals threatened with extinction, lands ravaged by war, people left homeless. As the earth cries out for liberation, we confess our part in bringing it toward the brink of catastrophe. Through ignorance, but often willfully, we thought we could serve God and mammon, unable to resist the temptation to spend and acquire more and more possessions, with little thought of consequences for future generations. Savior of the world, you call us to repentance: to be transformed by your love, deny ourselves, take up the cross and follow in your way. **Amen.** *(Maureen Edwards)*

32. Exploitation of the Earth

O great creator of all life, you created vast galaxies and star systems, touching our minds with your majesty. You revealed yourself as a little child, touching our hearts with your love. Receive our thanksgiving. Consecrate our repentance. May the world be redeemed from exploitation and greed through our dedication to your will for wholeness throughout the created order. Help us bless the generations that follow us through our commitment to the health of everything you created. May children not inherit from us a broken, dying planet, sacrificed on the altar of human greed, but the cherished, beloved gift on which you looked that day when you found it very good. **Amen.** *(Frederick A. Styles)*

SONG   PETE SEEGER AND LORRE WYATT

1. When we look and we see things are not what they should be,
   God's counting on me, God's counting on you.
   When we look and we see things are not what they should not be,
   God's counting on me, God's counting on you.

   Chorus:
   Hoping we'll all pull through, hoping we'll all pull through,
   hoping we'll all pull through, me and you.

2. It's time to turn things around, trickle up, not trickle down!
   God's counting on me, God's counting on you.
   It's time to turn things around, trickle up, not trickle down!
   God's counting on me, God's counting on you.

   Hoping we'll all pull through, hoping we'll all pull though,
   hoping we'll all pull through, me and you.

3. And when "Drill, baby, drill!" turns to "Spill, baby, spill!"
   God's counting on me, God's counting on you.
   And when "Drill, baby, drill!" turns to "Spill, baby, spill!"
   God's counting on me, God's counting on you.

   Hoping we'll all pull through, hoping we'll all pull through,
   hoping we'll all pull through, me and you.

4. Yes, there's big problems to be solved, let's get ev'ryone involved.
   God's counting on me, God's counting on you.
   Yes, there's big problems to be solved, let's get ev'ryone involved.
   God's counting on me, God's counting on you.

   Hoping we'll all pull through, hoping we'll all pull through,
   hoping we'll all pull through, me and you.

5. Don't give up, don't give in, working together we all can win.
   God's counting on me, God's counting on you.
   Don't give up, don't give in, working together we all can win.
   God's counting on me, God's counting on you.

   Hoping we'll all pull through, hoping we'll all pull through,
   hoping we'll all pull through, me and you.
   Hoping we'll all pull through, hoping we'll all pull through,
   hoping we'll all pull through, me and you.

   Tune: GOD'S COUNTING ON ME, Irregular

Let us join with the Earth and each other—To bring new life to the land, to restore the waters, to refresh the air, to protect the animals, to treasure the trees, to gaze at the stars, to cherish the human community, to heal the Earth, to remember the children. Let us go forth to put our words into action. *(Diann L. Neu)*

SOURCES

Jim Drury, "Every Atom, Star, Galaxy," in *Bread for the Day: Daily Bible Readings and Prayers 2016* (Minneapolis: Augsburg Fortress, 2016), 361. Used by permission.

"A Thanksgiving for Our Country," in Church of the Province of New Zealand, *A New Zealand Prayer Book: He Karakia Mihinare o Aotearoa* (Auckland, New Zealand: William Collins, 1989), 142, alt. © 1989 The Provincial Secretary, The Church of the Province of New Zealand, Box 2148, Rotorua. Used by permission.

"We have forgotten . . . ," from "Only One Earth," a United Nations Environment Programme publication for "Environmental Sabbath/Earth Rest Day," June 1990.

Elizabeth Kolbert, *The Sixth Extinction: An Unnatural History* (New York: Henry Holt, 2014), 267–69. © 2014 Elizabeth Kolbert. Used by permission of the author.

Maureen Edwards, "Lord Jesus Christ . . . ," in *Oceans of Prayer*, comp. Maureen Edwards and Jan S. Pickard (Nutfield, UK: National Christian Education Council, UK, 1991), 63. © 1991 National Christian Education Council. Used by permission.

Frederick A. Styles, "O great creator . . . ," in United Church of Canada, *Celebrate God's Presence: A Book of Services for the United Church of Canada,* ed. Karen J. Verveda (Etobicoke, Ontario: United Church Publishing House, 2000), 632. Originally published in Frederick A. Styles, *Worship for an Easter People*, vol. 5. © 1995 Published by EnThusia Enterprises, Markham, Ontario. Used by permission of EnThusia Enterprises.

Words and music by Pete Seeger and Lorre Wyatt, "God's Counting on Me, God's Counting on You," abridged. © 2010 Pete Seeger and Lorre Wyatt, Roots and Branges Music.com, LorreWyattMusic@gmail.com. Used by permission.

Diann L. Neu, *Return Blessings: Ecofeminist Liturgies Renewing the Earth* (Cleveland: Pilgrim Press, 2003), 61. Used by permission.

33. THE CULTURE OF DEATH

The mystique of guns even after the slaughter of schoolchildren; the fear of people of different races, nationalities, and religions; national defense interpreted as military might; an economy based on consumerism; valuing private profit over the common good—this is the culture of death. Jesus breaks the chains of death and offers abundant life for all.

We light a light in the name of the Maker, who lit the world and breathed the breath of life for us. We light a light in the name of the Son, who saved the world and stretched out his hand to us. We light a light in the name of the Spirit, who encompasses the world and blesses our souls with yearning. *(Iona Community)*

PRAYERS OF PRAISE AND THANKSGIVING

We praise you, O Lord our God, Ruler of the universe, by whose word the shadows of evening fall. Your wisdom opens the gates of morning; your understanding orders the changes of time and seasons; your will controls the stars as they travel through the skies. You are the Creator of both night and day, making light recede before darkness, and darkness before light. You cause day to pass, and bring on the night, setting day and night apart. You are the Lord of hosts. Living and eternal God, rule over us always, to the end of time. Blessed are you, O Lord, whose word makes evening fall. **Amen.** *(Presbyterian Church, USA)*

Almighty God, through the rising of your Son from the grave, you broke the power of death and condemned death itself to die. As we celebrate this great triumph, may we also make it the model for our living. Help us to identify in our lives all that needs to die—harmful relationships, tired habits, fruitless longings. Resurrect in our lives faith, hope and love, as surely as you raised Jesus Christ from the grave. **Amen.** *(Church of Scotland)*

CANTICLE ISAIAH 13:6-11

Wail, for the day of the Lord is near;
 it will come like destruction from the Almighty!
Therefore all hands will be feeble,
 and every human heart will melt,
 and they will be dismayed.
Pangs and agony will seize them;
 they will be in anguish like a woman in labor.
They will look aghast at one another;
 their faces will be aflame.
See, the day of the Lord comes,
 cruel, with wrath and fierce anger,
to make the earth a desolation,
 and to destroy its sinners from it.
For the stars of the heavens and their constellations
 will not give their light;
the sun will be dark at its rising,
 and the moon will not shed its light.
I will punish the world for its evil,
 and the wicked for their iniquity;
I will put an end to the pride of the arrogant,
 and lay low the insolence of tyrants.

SCRIPTURE REVELATION 6:7-8 AND REVELATION 12:7-12

1. When he opened the fourth seal, I heard the voice of the fourth living creature call out, "Come!" I looked and there was a pale green horse! Its rider's name was Death, and Hades followed with him; they were given authority over a fourth of the earth, to kill with sword, famine, and pestilence, and by the wild animals of the earth.

2. And war broke out in heaven; Michael and his angels fought against the dragon. The dragon and his angels fought back, but they were defeated, and there was no longer any place for them in heaven. The great dragon was thrown down, that ancient serpent, who is called the Devil and Satan, the deceiver of the whole world—he was thrown down to the earth, and his angels were thrown down with him.

Then I heard a loud voice in heaven, proclaiming,
 "Now have come the salvation and the power
  and the kingdom of our God

> and the authority of his Messiah,
> for the accuser of our comrades has been thrown down,
> who accuses them day and night before our God.
> But they have conquered him by the blood of the Lamb
> and by the word of their testimony,
> for they did not cling to life even in the face of death.
> Rejoice then, you heavens
> and those who dwell in them!
> But woe to the earth and the sea,
> for the devil has come down to you
> with great wrath,
> because he knows that his time is short!"

LITANY

God of justice and compassion,
  we ask forgiveness for the widening gulf between rich and poor,
For the use of money as a measure of all things,

For the culture of self-gratification,
For the continuing disparities between those that have so much and those who have so little,

And for the suffering of those people who are excluded from the table of abundance.
Forgive us for our focus on material goods,

And our part in the worship of economic growth
**In a world where resources are limited
and where we are already using more than our fair share.**

Forgive us for going along with what is easy,
For failing to come to grips with the problems of change,

And to engage in the complexity of social issues.
Fill us with a living faith that we may become lively seeds of your kingdom,

Continually growing in your way of love,
Instruments of personal and social reconciliation,

Vehicles for a new dawn when those in poverty are welcomed to the table where compassion and justice meet.
Lord, in your mercy, hear our prayer. *(Education for Justice, based on a prayer by Alan Litherland)*

REFLECTION   DERRICK JENSEN

We as environmentalists work as hard as we can to protect the places we love, using the tools of the system the best we can. Yet we do not do the most important thing of all: we do not question the existence of this current death culture. We do not question the existence of an economic and social system that is working the world to death, that is starving it to death, that is imprisoning it, that is torturing it. We never question a culture that leads to these atrocities. We never question the logic that leads inevitably to clear cuts, murdered oceans, loss of topsoil, dammed rivers, poisoned aquifers, global warming. And we certainly don't act to bring it down.

We can fantasize all we want about some great turning, and if the people (including the nonhuman people) can't breathe, it doesn't matter. Nothing matters but that we stop this culture from killing the planet. The land is the source of everything. If you have no planet, you have no economic system, you have no spirituality. If you have no planet, nobody can ask any question at all.

It is long past time for brave women and men to do whatever it takes to protect this planet—our one and only home—from this culture's final solution. It is long past time we brought the industrial infrastructure down before it kills any more of this planet. It is long past time for us to be the miracle we've been waiting for.

Derrick Jensen (b. 1960) is a farmer, bee keeper, and environmental activist. In his many books and articles, he explores the hidden assumptions of dominant social and economic systems that are linked to the oppression of indigenous cultures and to ecological abuse.

PRAYERS OF CONFESSION AND INTERCESSION

You have given us life, intelligence and the beauty of Creation, O Lord. Your good gifts were given so we might be stewards of all that is alive. In our arrogance, we have unleashed fearful forces that destroy. We have brought down fierce fire from the sky.

Your children have been burned, your gentle green earth scorched. Fear rules us now, not Love; we have given in to evils, lesser and greater. In your mercy, help us turn from destruction, from the bombs and barricades. Lead us to Life again, to affirmation of all goodness and to international disarmament. With your grace, may we begin to dismantle the bombs, beat the swords into plowshares, and so transform the nuclear nightmare into the peace you have proposed. Hear our prayer, Lord, and guide us in your ways. **Amen.** *(Education for Justice)*

Our globe is nothing but a little star in the great universe. It is our duty to turn this globe into a planet whose creatures are not tormented by wars, nor tortured by hunger and fear, nor torn apart in senseless divisions according to race, color or creed. Give us the courage and foresight to begin this work even today, so that our children and grandchildren may one day take pride in being called human. **Amen.** *(Stephen Vincent Benét)*

HYMN   WILLIAM W. REID, JR.

1. O God of every nation,
   of every race and land,
   redeem your whole creation
   with your almighty hand.
   Where hate and fear divide us,
   and bitter threats are hurled,
   in love and mercy guide us
   and heal our strife-torn world.

2. From search for wealth and power
   and scorn of truth and right,.
   from trust in bombs that shower
   destruction through the night,
   from pride of race and station
   and blindness to your way,
   deliver every nation,
   eternal God, we pray.

3. Lord, strengthen those who labor
   that all may find release
   from fear of rattling saber,
   from dread of war's increase;
   when hope and courage falter,
   your still small voice be heard;
   with faith that none can alter,
   your servants undergird.

4. Keep bright in us the vision
   of days when war shall cease,
   when hatred and division
   give way to love and peace,
   till dawns the morning glorious
   when truth and justice reign,
   and Christ shall rule victorious
   o'er all the world's domain.

Tune: LLANGLOFFAN, 7.6.7.6. D.
Words © 1958, ren. 1986 The Hymn Society
(admin. Hope Publishing)

May God light in us a holy fire: Light a fire that is worthy of our ancestors. Light a fire that is worthy of our children. Light a fire that is worthy of our fathers. Light a fire that is worthy of our mothers. Light a fire that is worthy of God. Now let us go in peace, lighting holy fire wherever we go. *(Anne Rowthorn, inspired by an anonymous Masai prayer)*

SOURCES

Iona Community, "We light a light . . .," in *Iona Abbey Worship Book* (Glasgow: Wild Goose, 2001), 111. © Contributors, *Iona Abbey Worship* (2001), Wild Goose Publications, Glasgow. Used by permission.

"We praise you . . .," in Presbyterian Church (USA), *Book of Common Worship* (Louisville, KY: Westminster John Knox, 1993), 508. Reprinted by permission from *Book of Common Worship*, © 1993 Westminster John Knox Press.

"Almighty God . . .," in Church of Scotland, *Book of Common Order of the Church of Scotland* (Edinburgh: St. Andrew Press, 1994), 441. Extract is from *Book of Common Order of the Church of Scotland* © St Andrew Press, 1994 and is reproduced by permission of Hymns Ancient & Modern Ltd.

Education for Justice, "For Those in Poverty," inspired by prayer by Alan Litherland, *Center of Concern*, last modified September 12, 2012, https://www.coc.org/ef/twenty-fourth-sunday-ordinary-time, alt. © 2005–2017, Education for Justice, a project of Center for Concern. Used by permission.

Derrick Jensen, "You Choose," in *Moral Ground: Ethical Action for a Planet in Peril*, ed. Kathleen Dean Moore and Michael P. Nelson (San Antonio: Trinity University Press, 2010), 61, 64. Used by permission.

Education for Justice, "Prayer for Nuclear Disarmament," *Education for Justice*, accessed April 16, 2017, https://educationforjustice.org/node/1531, alt. © 2005–2017, Education for Justice, a project of Center for Concern. Used by permission.

Stephen Vincent Benét, "Our little globe . . .," in *Prayers Encircling the World: An International Anthology* (Louisville, KY: Westminster John Knox Press, 1998), 236.

Words by William Watkins Reid Jr., "O God of Every Nation" © 1958, ren. 1986 The Hymn Society (admin. Hope Publishing Company, Carol Stream, IL 60188). All rights reserved. Used by permission.

Anne Rowthorn, inspired by anonymous Masai prayer in F. Lynn Bachelder, *Canticles of the Earth: Celebrating the Presence of God in Nature* (Chicago, IL: Loyola, 2004), 156. © 2018 Anne Rowthorn.

34. THE LURE OF MONEY

Money talks! It is a blessing and a curse; a blessing when used to benefit the welfare of all; a curse when it is hoarded. Lurking at the root of hunger, poverty, injustice, war, the rupture of the social fabric, and so much more is the pervasive unequal distribution of wealth across the globe.

The lover of money will not be satisfied with money; nor the lover of wealth, with gain. *(Ecclesiastes 5:10)*

PRAYERS OF PRAISE AND THANKSGIVING

Thank you, Lord. You are the light that never goes out. You are the eye that never closes. You are the ear that is never shut. You are the mind that never gives up. You are the heart that never grows cold. You are the hand that never stops reaching. Thank you, Lord. And let us be receptive to you. **Amen**. *(Ronald J. Allen and Linda McKiernan-Allen)*

Let us pray for tenderness between people, in communities where economic activity is based in greed, where only the wealthy and ambitious are respected, where the poorest and weakest go unseen, and each feels alone. We give thanks for communities where the silent have found their voice, where the unseen work of many is affirmed with pride, where those who were treated as nothing have discovered that they matter. We give thanks for communities where the poor have pooled resources to support each other, where those with knowledge have used it to help others learn, where the interests of the strongest have been challenged with anger and courage and love. **Amen.** *(Christian Aid)*

34. The Lure of Money

CANTICLE   JOB 24:2-4, 13-17, 21, 24

The wicked remove landmarks;
>   they seize flocks and pasture them.
They drive away the donkey of the orphan;
>   **they take the widow's ox for a pledge.**
They thrust the needy off the road;
>   the poor of the earth all hide themselves. . . .
"There are those who rebel against the light,
>   **who are not acquainted with its ways,**
>   **and do not stay in its paths.**
The murderer rises at dusk
>   to kill the poor and needy,
>   and in the night is like a thief.
The eye of the adulterer also waits for the twilight,
>   **saying, 'No eye will see me';**
>   **and he disguises his face.**
In the dark they dig through houses;
>   by day they shut themselves up;
>   they do not know the light.
For deep darkness is morning to all of them;
>   **for they are friends with the terrors of deep darkness.** . . .
"They harm the childless woman,
>   and do no good to the widow. . . .
"They are exalted a little while, and then are gone;
>   **they wither and fade like the mallow;**
>   **they are cut off like the heads of grain."**

SCRIPTURE   JAMES 5:1-6

Come now, you rich people, weep and wail for the miseries that are coming to you. Your riches have rotted, and your clothes are moth-eaten. Your gold and silver have rusted, and their rust will be evidence against you, and it will eat your flesh like fire. You have laid up treasure for the last days. Listen! The wages of the laborers who mowed your fields, which you kept back by fraud, cry out, and the cries of the harvesters have reached the ears of the Lord of hosts. You have lived on the earth in luxury and in pleasure; you have fattened your hearts on a day of slaughter. You have condemned and murdered the righteous one, who does not resist you.

LITANY

Lord, must we starve our children to pay our debts?
Break the chains of debt!

How long must this go on?
Break the chains of debt!

It's one law for the rich and another for the poor.
Break the chains of debt!

Debt destroys our families and our way of life.
Break the chains of debt!

We defend our roots as our country's true base of growth.
Break the chains of debt!

Debt tears down our clinics and schools as in war.
Break the chains of debt!

Now external debt becomes eternal debt!
Break the chains of debt! *(Iona Abbey)*

REFLECTION   ECUMENICAL PATRIARCH BARTHOLOMEW I

We are obliged in the name of our faith and of truth to proclaim the need to change people's lifestyles and attitudes, to preach what is called in spiritual terms *metanoia* (or repentance), which implies justice and compassion. The lack of a sense of justice leads to greed and exploitation of the weaker by the more powerful, an abundance of wealth for the strong, and extreme poverty for the weak. Similarly, the lack of a spirit of compassion renders the soul indifferent to other people's pain and inaccessible to those things that kindle a sense of justice.

Therefore, we must broaden our notion of the environment to include the human and cultural environment. It would be a paradox to be concerned solely for the Earth while lacking interest in and concern for humanity and our cultural heritage. Just as the natural environment deserves our respect and protection, the human environment also deserves our attention and love. It is crucial that we recognize and respond to the interdependence between caring for the poor and caring for the Earth. Both in turn mirror the way we perceive the divine mystery in all people and things—the way we kneel in prayer before the living God.

Along with the Dalai Lama and Pope Francis, the Ecumenical Patriarch, Bartholomew I (b. 1940) has been the world's most ardent religious leader in his outspoken support for an expanded sense of caring for the whole creation, both human and physical.

PRAYERS OF CONFESSION AND INTERCESSION

God, who calls us to community: We pray as people committed to a new community in Christ. For the sake of the poor, your people of old did not reap to the edge of their field, or pick the loose ears, or the fallen grapes. But now forests are privatized and the poor can't pick up fallen branches, or hunt, or gather. The new idol, Profit, has made thieves of us all. We proclaim your love and justice, but we need your help lest we become deceivers, full of words, unable to do anything to strengthen the weak and share the burden of those for whom you have a special care. Have mercy on us. **Amen.** *(The Uniting Church in Australia)*

God of abundance, you have poured out a large measure of earthly blessings: our table is richly furnished, our cup overflows, and we live in safety and security. Teach us to set our hearts on you and not on these material blessings. Keep us from becoming captivated by prosperity, and grant us in wisdom to use your blessings to your glory and to the service of humankind; through Jesus Christ our Lord. **Amen.** *(Evangelical Lutheran Church in America)*

HYMN — MIRIAM THERESE WINTER

1. O for a world where everyone
   respects each other's ways,
   where love is lived and all is done
   with justice and with praise.

2. O for a world where goods are shared
   and misery relieved,
   where truth is spoken, children spared,
   equality achieved.

3. We welcome one world family
   and struggle with each choice
   that opens us to unity
   and gives our vision voice.

4. The poor are rich, the weak are strong,
   the foolish ones are wise.
   Tell all who mourn; outcasts belong,
   who perishes will rise.

5. O for a world preparing for
   God's glorious reign of peace,
   where time and tears will be no more,
   and all but love will cease.

Tune: AZMON, C. M., 8.6.8.6.

"Do not store up for yourselves treasures on earth, where moth and rust consume and where thieves break in and steal; but store up for yourselves treasures in heaven, where neither moth nor rust consumes and where thieves do not break in and steal. For where your treasure is, there your heart will be also." *(Matthew 6:19-21)*

SOURCES

Ronald J. Allen and Linda McKiernan-Allen, "Thank you, Lord . . . ," in *Chalice Worship*, ed. Colbert S. Cartwright and O. I. Cricket Harrison (St. Louis: Chalice, 1997), 302. Used by permission of Chalice Press.

"Tenderness between People," in *Harvest for the World: A Worship Anthology on Sharing in the Work of Creation*, ed. Geoffrey Duncan (Cleveland: Pilgrim Press, 2003), 41–43, alt. © Christian Aid.

Iona Abbey, "Break the chains . . . ," in *Holy Ground: Liturgies and Worship Resources for an Engaged Spirituality*, ed. Neil Paynter and Helen Boothroyd (Glasgow: Wild Goose, 2005), 282–83. © Contributors, *Holy Ground* (2005), Wild Goose Publications, Glasgow. Used by permission.

Patriarch Bartholomew I, "The Orthodox Church and the Environmental Crisis: Spiritual Insights and Personal Reflections," in *Holy Ground: A Gathering of Voices on Caring for Creation*, ed. Lyndsay Moseley et al. (San Francisco: Sierra Club Books, 2008), 40. © by the Sierra Club and individual authors as credited. Reprinted by permission of Counterpoint Press.

"Living with the New Economic Order," in *Harvest for the World: A Worship Anthology on Sharing in the Work of Creation*, ed. Geoffrey Duncan (Cleveland: Pilgrim Press, 2003), 131. © Uniting Church in Australia. Used by permission.

"The Proper Use of Wealth (2)," in Evangelical Lutheran Church in America, *Evangelical Lutheran Worship*, Leaders Desk ed. (Minneapolis: Augsburg Fortress, 2006), 151. Used by permission.

Miriam Therese Winter, "O for a World" © 1990 Medical Mission Sisters. Used by permission.

35. CLIMATE CHANGE

Droughts and desertification, heat waves, wildfires, rising sea levels and increasingly acidic oceans, snow upon snow, punishing summer storms, the extinction of species—well over half of the ecosystems of Earth have already been affected by climate change. There is overwhelming scientific evidence that climate change is largely induced by human beings, the most marvelous and the most dangerous creatures ever to inhabit the earth.

May the dawn light of the East enlighten your intellect. May the noon light of the South illuminate your passion. May the soul fire of the West strengthen your aspirations. May the night light of the North star bless your inspiration. *(Alla Renée Bozarth)*

PRAYERS OF PRAISE AND THANKSGIVING

Infinite God, Creator and Redeemer of all beings, you are most high, most near. We thank you that in all generations when we have cried out to you, you have heard our prayer. Now let your light and your truth appear to us and lead us. We shall not fear though the earth itself should shake, and though mountains fall into the heart of the sea; though its waters thunder and rage, though the winds lift its waves to the very vault of heaven. We shall not fear, for you are with us; in the shadow of your wings we shall sing with joy. **Amen.** *(Central Conference of American Rabbis)*

Author of creation: In wisdom you brought forth all that is, to participate in your divine being, and to change, adapt, and grow in freedom. You make holy the matter and energy of the universe that it may delight you and give you praise. We thank you for gathering all creation into your heart by the energy of your Spirit and bringing it through death to resurrection glory; through the One in whom all things have their being, Jesus Christ, your Wisdom and your Word. **Amen.** *(The Episcopal Church)*

35. Climate Change

PSALM 78:41-48, 50

They tested God again and again,
  and provoked the Holy One of Israel.
They did not keep in mind his power,
  or the day when he redeemed them from the foe;
when he displayed his signs in Egypt,
  and his miracles in the fields of Zoan.
He turned their rivers to blood,
  so that they could not drink of their streams.
He sent among them swarms of flies, which devoured them,
  and frogs, which destroyed them.
He gave their crops to the caterpillar,
  and the fruit of their labor to the locust.
He destroyed their vines with hail,
  and their sycamores with frost.
He gave over their cattle to the hail,
  and their flocks to thunderbolts. . . .
He made a path for his anger;
  he did not spare them from death,
  but gave their lives over to the plague.

SCRIPTURE   ISAIAH 24:1-6

The Lord is about to lay waste the earth and make it desolate,
  and he will twist its surface and scatter its inhabitants.
And it shall be, as with the people, so with the priest;
  as with the slave, so with his master;
  as with the maid, so with her mistress;
as with the buyer, so with the seller;
  as with the lender, so with the borrower;
  as with the creditor, so with the debtor.
The earth shall be utterly laid waste and utterly despoiled;
for the Lord has spoken this word.

The earth dries up and withers,
  the world languishes and withers;
  the heavens languish together with the earth.

The earth lies polluted
> under its inhabitants;
for they have transgressed laws,
> violated the statutes,
> broken the everlasting covenant.
Therefore a curse devours the earth,
> and its inhabitants suffer for their guilt;
therefore the inhabitants of the earth dwindled,
> and few people are left.

LITANY

In the face of the warming of Earth, rising sea levels, shrinking ice caps, and dispossessed peoples, we confess that by our action and inaction we have contributed to changes in our climate.

For our excessive use of motor vehicles
Forgive us, Lord

For our waste of energy and water
Forgive us, Lord

For our rampant consumerism
Forgive us, Lord

For our failure to embrace renewable energy resources
Forgive us, Lord

For our lack of respect for our oceans and forests
Forgive us, Lord

For our complacency and apathy
Forgive us, Lord

God, our Creator, as we view the mysteries of our climate, we have a sense of anxiety as well as wonder. Help us to see the deep powerful forces you have planted in creation as wondrous and natural. Teach us to recognize that the climate too is sustained by your wisdom and to rejoice with all the forces of nature. In the name of Christ who reconciles and renews all things in creation. **Amen.** *(Season of Creation)*

REFLECTION MARIE HAUSE

What will my daughter see, my great-granddaughter?

Will she go out to the forest and find only ragged stumps and hardened ground as brown as dried blood? Where once there was the flash of wing and flick of tail and calmness of cool green? Already fires have consumed trees, hurricanes toppled them, droughts drained them.

Will she go out to the ocean and find only the stagnancy of acidic waters as clouded as dead eyes? Where once there was the shimmer of silver scale and curl of clever tentacle and vibrancy of the reef? Already corals are becoming bare bone, shells struggle to form, rising waters drown out wetland life.

Will she fill her lungs and find only ash and smoggy skies as choking as the fumes of decay? Where once there was the buzz of bees and silent soaring and clarity of heaven? Already children cough in cities, animals flee overheated habitats, chaotic weather increases.

God, we have practiced our original human sin of reducing variety to lifeless uniformity not only on each other, but on the entire world.

Turn us toward wonder at the world that sings your praise. Shock us from our indifference before it becomes impossible that my daughter, my great-granddaughter, will ever sing in harmony with the world of your making.

Marie Hause (b. 1986) grew up in Bolivia and has a PhD in English literature from Florida State University. Her varied interests range from Shakespeare and Spenser to queer and feminist theology. Currently, Marie is a student at Yale Divinity School and research assistant for God's Good Earth.

PRAYERS OF CONFESSION AND INTERCESSION

Show us how to do things well today, so that others may not suffer, here or there, now or in the future. Show us how to make our contribution as we change the way we live, travel, make and consume, pack and unpack, use, misuse and re-use energy, heating and lighting. Show us how to do simple things well in our home, places of work and lifestyle choices. Show us how to protect the world you made, in all its diversity and goodness, from our carbon emissions, global warming and climate change, rising temperatures and sea levels, the displacement of peoples, environmental poverty, harm and destruction. Show us how and show us why, so that alone and with others our contribution will make a difference. **Amen.** *(Robin Morrison)*

O God, we pray for those places in the world where people suffer from extreme climatic conditions: places of intense cold, and heat and drought, places of great hardship and privation, where man, woman, and beast are constantly endangered by the elements and the environment. We give thanks for all that sustains and helps them, and pray that such may be multiplied in the hands of Jesus Christ and those who serve in his name. **Amen.** *(World Council of Churches)*

HYMN THOMAS H. TROEGER

1. Above the moon earth rises, a sunlit mossy stone,
   a garden that God prizes where life has richly grown,
   an emerald selected for us to guard with care,
   an isle in space protected by one thin reef of air.

2. The mossy stone is grieving, its tears are bitter rain,
   the garden is unleafing and all its harvests wane,
   the emerald is clouded, its luster dims and fades,
   the isle of life is shrouded in thick and stagnant haze.

3. O listen to the sighing of water, sky and land,
   and hear the Spirit crying the future is at hand:
   the moss and garden thinning portend a death or birth,
   the end or new beginning for all that lives on earth.

4. A death if hearts now harden, a birth if we repent
   and tend and keep the garden as God has always meant:
   to sow without abusing the soil where life is grown,
   to reap without our bruising this sunlit mossy stone.

   Tune: SALLEY GARDENS, 7.6.7.6. D.

May the God who shakes heaven and earth, whom death could not contain, who lives to disturb and heal us, bless us with power to go forth and proclaim the Gospel. **Amen.** *(Janet Morley)*

SOURCES

Alla Renée Bozarth, "An Everyday Birthfeast Blessing for Mind, Body, Soul and Spirit," in *Love's Alchemy* and *The Frequency of Light* © 2013 Alla Renée Bozarth. Used by permission.

"Infinite God . . . ," in *Gates of Prayer: The New Union Prayerbook* (New York: Central Conference of American Rabbis, 1975), 86, alt. © 1975, by Central Conference of American Rabbis, under the copyright protection of the Central Conference of American Rabbis and reprinted for use by permission of the CCAR. All rights reserved.

"God, the Source and Destiny of the Cosmos," in Standing Commission on Liturgy and Music, "Liturgical Materials Honoring God in Creation and Various Rites and Prayers for Animals," in *Report to the 77th General Convention* (Episcopal Church, July 5–12, 2012), 319.

"God, our Creator . . . ," in "Climate Sunday," *Season of Creation*, accessed May 12, 2016, https://seasonofcreation.com/wp-content/uploads/2010/08/Climate-Sunday.doc, alt. © Season of Creation, developed by Norm Habel and the Uniting Church in Australia, Synod of Victoria and Tasmania, 2004, seasonofcreation.com, used with permission.

Marie Hause © 2017 Marie Hause. Used by permission.

Robin Morrison, "A Morning Prayer," in *Season of Creation 2* (n.p.: Anglican Church of Southern Africa, 2013), 29, last modified August 2013, http://www.greenanglicans.org/wp-content/uploads/2013/08/Season-of-Creation-Two-low-res.pdf. Used by permission of the author.

"O God, we pray . . ." in *Celebrate God's Presence: A Book of Services for the United Church of Canada*, ed. Karen J. Verveda (Etobicoke, Ontario: United Church Publishing House, 2000), 627, altered from *With All God's People: The New Ecumenical Prayer Cycle*, comp. John Carden (Geneva: WCC Publications, 1989), 342. Used by permission of United Church Publishing House and World Council of Churches.

"Above the moon earth rises" by Thomas Troeger © Oxford University Press Inc. 2002. Assigned to Oxford University Press 2010. Reproduced by permission. All rights reserved.

Janet Morley, "May the God who shakes . . . ," in *All Desires Known*, 3rd ed. (Harrisburg, PA: Morehouse, 2006), 94. *All Desires Known*, 3rd edition © 2006 the Morehouse Publishing. Used by permission of Church Publishing Incorporated, New York, NY.

36. GLOBAL WARMING

Human actions have been the dominant cause of global warming since the mid-twentieth century. If life on Earth as we know it is to continue, carbon levels in the atmosphere need to be reduced to less than .350 parts per million (ppm). In March 2018 the level was .400 ppm and by mid-2018 it had risen to .411 ppm.

See how former predictions have come true. And now I declare new things! Before they spring forth, I tell them to you. *(Isaiah 42:9)*

PRAYERS OF PRAISE AND THANKSGIVING

Blessed are you, God of growth and discovery; yours is the inspiration that has altered and changed our lives; yours is the power that has brought us to new dangers and opportunities. Set us, your new creation, to walk through this new world, watching and learning, loving and trusting, until your kingdom comes. **Amen.** *(Anglican Church of New Zealand)*

God, you created the world with your dream of what it could be. You dreamed of people and plants, animals and air, all living in right relationship to you and to each other. Today we offer to you our dream for a world which is not threatened by a changing climate which harms our atmosphere, which wounds the poorest and most vulnerable, which leaves this wonderful planet in poor shape for future generations. Help us to listen to your voice, your Word, and your creation. **Amen.** *(Joan Weber)*

We thank you, Lord God, that all things are new in your grace and that the old passes away. We thank you for breaking our hold on familiar ways that you discard, and for giving us forward-looking courage to reach toward wiser ways. Lead us beyond ourselves to the new life promised in Jesus Christ, who is first and last, the beginning and the end. **Amen.** *(Presbyterian Church, USA)*

36. Global Warming

PSALM 105:29-35

> He turned their waters into blood,
>   and caused their fish to die.
> **Their land swarmed with frogs,**
>   **even in the chambers of their kings.**
> He spoke, and there came swarms of flies,
>   and gnats throughout their country.
> **He gave them hail for rain,**
>   **and lightning that flashed through their land.**
> He struck their vines and fig trees,
>   and shattered the trees of their country.
> **He spoke, and the locusts came,**
>   **and young locusts without number;**
> they devoured all the vegetation in their land,
>   and ate up the fruit of their ground.

SCRIPTURE   AMOS 4:1-2, 6-9

You mistreat and abuse the poor and needy. I, the Lord God, have sworn by my own name that your time is coming. Not one of you will be left—I, the Lord, took away the food from every town and village, but still you rejected me. Three months before harvest, I kept back the rain. Sometimes I would let it fall on one town or field but not on another, and pastures dried up. People from two or three towns would go to a town that still had water, but it wasn't enough. Even then you rejected me. I, the Lord, have spoken! I dried up your grain fields; your gardens and vineyards turned brown. Locusts ate your fig trees and olive orchards, but even then you rejected me. I, the Lord, have spoken!

LITANY

O God, your fertile soil is slowly being stripped of its riches,
Open our eyes to see.

O God, your living waters are slowly being choked with chemicals,
Open our eyes to see.

O God, your creatures are slowly dying and your people are suffering,
Open our eyes to see.

God, our maker, so move us by the wonder of your creation,
That we repent and care more deeply.

So move us to grieve the loss of life,
That we learn to walk with gentle footfalls upon your world. *(John Harrison)*

REFLECTION   BILL MCKIBBEN

The by-products—the pollutants—of one species have become the most powerful force for change on this planet. The change in quantity is so large that it becomes a change in quality. The story of our moment, of these few short decades when we happen to be alive, is the story of crossing a threshold. . . . This home of ours, the blessed link of rock and sky and biology that we were born onto, becomes each day a less complex and a more violent place; its rhythms of season shifted and shattered. We didn't create this world, but we are busy de-creating it. Still the sun rises; still the moon wanes and waxes; but they look down on a planet that means something different than it used to. Something less than it used to. This buzzing, blooming, mysterious, cruel, lovely globe of mountain, sea, city, forest; of fish and wolf and bug and man; of carbon and hydrogen and nitrogen—it has come unbalanced in our short moment on it.

When Bill McKibben (b. 1960) wrote The End of Nature *in 1989, it was the first book on climate change written for the general public. It has since been translated into twenty-four languages. In his more recent book,* Eaarth, *published in 2010, he said, "Twenty years ago, in 1989* The End of Nature *was mainly a philosophical argument. It was too early to see the practical effects of climate change but not too early to feel them. I described walking down a river near my home. Walking along this river today the evidence of destruction is all too obvious. Much more quickly than we would have guessed in the late 1980s, global warming has dramatically altered many things."*

PRAYERS OF CONFESSION AND INTERCESSION

We confess that we have polluted our own atmosphere, causing global warming and climate change that have increased poverty in many parts of our planet. We have contributed to global warming and been more concerned with getting gold than keeping our planet green. We have loved progress more than the planet. We are sorry. We are sorry. **Amen.** *(Season of Creation)*

36. Global Warming

Loving Father, we give thanks for the abundance of your creation. We pray for forgiveness when our greedy and unjust actions have harmed the environment and our neighbors. Please give us strength to change our behavior and courage to challenge others. Give us a passion for justice to support those affected by climate change and protect us when we face these challenges ourselves. Help us to see clearly the way to restore right and just relationships with the environment and each other, for the good of all. In Jesus' name we pray. **Amen.** *(Environmental Network of the Anglican Church of Southern Africa)*

HYMN   THOMAS H. TROEGER

1. How miniscule this planet
   amidst the stars at night,
   a mote that floats in vastness,
   mere dust that catches light,
   yet, God, you count of value,
   of boundless, precious worth,
   all creatures who inhabit
   this tiny, mite-sized earth.

2. Together faith and science
   extend what we can see.
   and amplify our wonder
   at all you bring to be:
   how energy and matter
   have coalesced in space
   as consciousness and meaning,
   and hearts that yearn for grace.

3. And from that wonder blossoms
   a wonder that exceeds
   the reach of human dreaming
   for meeting earth's deep needs:
   the Christ, in whom all matter,
   all energies cohere,
   is born upon this planet
   and dwelling with us here.

4. By Christ we are connected
   to every shining star,
   to every atom spinning,
   to all the things that are,
   and to your very being,
   around, below, above,
   suffusing each dimension
   with light and life and love.

Tune: LLANGLOFFAN, 7.6.7.6.D.

> Stand at the crossroads, and look,
> and ask for the ancient paths,
> where the good way lies; and walk in it,
> and find rest for your souls. *(Jeremiah 6:16)*

SOURCES

Isaiah 42:9 from *The Inclusive Bible* (Landham, MD: Rowman & Littlefield, 2007). A Sheed & Ward Book published by Rowman & Littlefield Publishers, Inc. All rights reserved. Used by permission.

"Blessed are you . . . ," in Church of the Province of New Zealand, *A New Zealand Prayer Book: He Karakia Mihinare o Aotearoa* (Auckland, New Zealand: William Collins, 1989), 465. © 1989 The Provincial Secretary, The Church of the Province of New Zealand, Box 2148, Rotorua. Used by permission.

"Your World," in *Climate Change Prayer Booklet,* comp. Caritas, Aotearoa New Zealand, http://www.caritas.org.nz/resource/2159. Adapted from Joan Weber, "God, you created . . . ," in *Friending Planet Earth* (Center for Ministry Development and Catholic Coalition for Climate Change), 8, http://www.usccb.org/issues-and-action/human-life-and-dignity/environment/upload/friending-planet-earth.pdf. Used by permission of Caritas, Aotearoa New Zealand, Center for Ministry Development, and Catholic Coalition for Climate Change.

"In a Time of Social Change," in United Presbyterian Church in the U.S.A., *The Worshipbook* (Philadelphia: Westminster Press, 1970), 180, alt. Used by permission.

Amos 4:1-2, 6-9 from *Contemporary English Version* (New York: American Bible Society, 1995). © 1995 American Bible Society.

John Harrison, "O God, your fertile earth . . . ," in "Footprints in the Cosmos," in *Holy Ground: Liturgies and Worship Resources for an Engaged Spirituality*, ed. Neil Paynter and Helen Boothroyd (Glasgow: Wild Goose, 2005), 251. Adapted from *Iona Abbey Worship Book*, 132–33. © Contributors, *Holy Ground* (2005), Wild Goose Publications, Glasgow. Used by permission.

Bill McKibben, *The End of Nature*, new introduction to the 10th anniversary ed. (New York: Doubleday Anchor Books, 1999), xxi and xxv. Used by permission of Penguin Random House.

Bill McKibben, *Eaarth* (New York: Henry Holt, 2010), xi–xii. © 2010 Bill McKibben. Used by permission of the author.

"As I hold this . . . ," in "Solar Sunday," Australian Version 1, *Season of Creation*, accessed May 12, 2016, https://seasonofcreation.com/wp-content/uploads/2010/04/solar-sunday-liturgy-australian-1.doc, alt. © Season of Creation, developed by Norm Habel and the Uniting Church in Australia, Synod of Victoria and Tasmania, 2004, seasonofcreation.com, used with permission.

Environmental Network of the Anglican Church of Southern Africa, "Facing the Challenges of Climate Change," in *Season of Creation 2* (n.p.: Anglican Church of Southern Africa, 2013), 9, last modified August 2013, http://www.greenanglicans.org/wp-content/uploads/2013/08/Season-of-Creation-Two-low-res.pdf. Used by permission.

"How Minuscule This Planet" by Thomas Troeger © Oxford University Press, 2015. Reproduced by permission. All rights reserved.

37. FORGOTTEN PEOPLE

In God's eyes no one is forgotten, no one lost. Jean Vanier and Mother Teresa hallow the lives of those who would be easy to ignore. The mentally ill Vincent Van Gogh brightens our days with his dazzling Provençal sunflowers and our nights with his Starry Night. Our spirits soar with deaf Beethoven's majestic melodies. Wheelchair-bound Stephen Hawking opens up the mysterious secrets of the universe. We live by the mutual sharing of our love, gifts, and talents.

"Give justice to the weak and the orphan;
    maintain the right of the lowly and the destitute.
Rescue the weak and the needy;
    deliver them from the hand of the wicked." *(Psalm 82:3-4)*

PRAYERS OF PRAISE AND THANKSGIVING

Jesus Christ, when multitudes of children and young people, marked for life by being abandoned, are strangers on this earth, some people ask: "Does my life still have meaning?" And you assure us of this: "Each time you alleviate the suffering of an innocent person, you do it for me, Christ." **Amen.** *(Brother Roger of Taizé)*

We bring before you, O Lord, the troubles and perils of people and nations, the sighing of prisoners and captives, the sorrows of the bereaved, the necessities of strangers, the helplessness of the weak, the despondency of the weary, the failing powers of the aged. O Lord, draw near to each, for the sake of Jesus Christ our Lord. **Amen.** *(St. Anselm)*

O God, you promise a world where those who now weep shall laugh; those who are hungry shall feast; those who are poor now, and the excluded, shall have your kingdom for their own. I want this world too. I renounce despair. I will act for change. I choose to be included in your great feast of life. **Amen.** *(Christian Aid)*

PSALM 147:1A, 2-11

Praise the LORD!
How good it is to sing praises to our God;
    for he is gracious. . . .
The LORD builds up Jerusalem;
    he gathers the outcasts of Israel. . . .
The LORD lifts up the downtrodden;
    he casts the wicked to the ground.

Sing to the LORD with thanksgiving;
    make melody to our God on the lyre.
He covers the heavens with clouds,
    prepares rain for the earth,
    makes grass grow on the hills.
He gives to the animals their food,
    and to the young ravens when they cry.
His delight is not in the strength of the horse,
    nor his pleasure in the speed of a runner;
but the LORD takes pleasure in those who fear him,
    in those who hope in his steadfast love.

SCRIPTURE   LUKE 10:29B-37

[A lawyer asked Jesus,] "Who is my neighbor?" Jesus replied, "A man was going down from Jerusalem to Jericho, and fell into the hands of robbers, who stripped him, beat him, and went away, leaving him half dead. Now by chance a priest was going down that road; and when he saw him, he passed by on the other side. So likewise a Levite, when he came to the place and saw him, passed by on the other side. But a Samaritan while traveling came near him; and when he saw him, he was moved with pity. He went to him and bandaged his wounds, having poured oil and wine on them. Then he put him on his own animal, brought him to an inn, and took care of him. The next day he took out two denarii, gave them to the innkeeper, and said, 'Take care of him; and when I come back, I will repay you whatever more you spend.' Which of these three, do you think, was a neighbor to the man who fell into the hands of the robbers?" He said, "The one who showed him mercy." Jesus said to him, "Go and do likewise."

LITANY

O Jesus, you sat at table with the betrayed and rejected of Palestine. We pray for those today who do not feel welcomed in their daily lives. Christ, in your mercy,
Hear our prayer.

O Jesus, you identified with the naked and with those who had no place to lay their heads. We pray for those thousands of homeless men and women, old and young, in our cities. Christ, in your mercy,
Hear our prayer.

O Jesus, you belonged to a refugee family. We pray for the millions of displaced people in our world, and for the opening of borders to the nationless. Christ, in your mercy,
Hear our prayer.

O Jesus, you cared for your companions and for the little ones who surrounded you. We pray for all people who are struggling everywhere, especially children who are journeying in great danger to promised lands. Christ, in your mercy,
Hear our prayer.

As the poor widow welcomed Elijah, let us be open to the richness and miracle in meeting others wherever they cross our paths. As Abraham and Sarah welcomed passing strangers, let us entertain the possibility of angels in disguise. Let our eyes be opened, that we may recognize in our neighbor the divine presence of Christ. **Amen.** *(Iona Community)*

REFLECTION   JEAN VANIER

The poor and the weak have revealed to me the great secret of Jesus. If you wish to follow him, you must not try to climb the ladder of success and power, becoming more and more important. Instead, you must walk *down* the ladder, to meet and walk with people who are broken and in pain. The light is there, shining in the darkness, the darkness of their poverty. The poor with whom you are called to share your life are the sick and the old, people out of work, young people caught up in the world of drugs, people angry because they were terribly hurt when they were young, people with disabilities or sick with AIDS, or just out of prison, people who are oppressed because of the color of their skin, people in pain.

In 1964, the Canadian humanitarian Jean Vanier (b. 1928) became aware of the thousands of people with developmental disabilities languishing in institutions. He felt God calling him to invite two such men, Raphael and Philippe, to share his household in the French village of Trosly-Bruil. From this modest beginning L'Arche (the Ark) was born. Today 147 L'Arche communities are located in thirty-five countries. Jean Vanier was awarded the Templeton Prize in 2015 for his innovative discovery of the central role of vulnerable people in the creation of a more just, inclusive, and humane society.

PRAYERS OF INTERCESSION AND THANKSGIVING

Gracious God, we acknowledge and confess in your presence the smallness of our love, the narrowness of our concern, the denial of our true humanity. Through our careless hands have slipped opportunities not taken, people not cared for, days not celebrated. We are ashamed and sorry for the ways of our unfaithfulness, and ask for reassurance and forgiveness. **Amen.** *(United Church of Canada)*

Almighty and most merciful God, we remember before you all poor and neglected persons whom it would be easy for us to forget: the homeless and the destitute, the old and the sick, and all who have none to care for them. Help us to heal those who are broken in body or spirit, and to turn their sorrow into joy. Grant this, Father, for the love of your Son, who for our sake became poor, Jesus Christ our Lord. **Amen.** *(The Episcopal Church)*

Make us worthy, Lord, to serve our fellow human beings throughout the world who live and die in poverty and hunger. Give them through our hands this day their daily bread, and by our understanding love, give peace and joy. **Amen.** *(Mother Teresa of Calcutta)*

37. Forgotten People

HYMN   DANIEL C. DAMON

1. Companion of the poor,
   God with us in our need:
   you know the pain of poverty,
   the cry that has no creed.

2. Companion of the poor:
   you do as love commands;
   you turn the tables of our greed
   with strong, determined hands.

3. Companion of the poor:
   by grace we change our ways,
   till justice rises from our lives,
   and mercy fills our days.

4. Companion of the poor:
   we learn to care and bless,
   and so, with you, we take to task
   the systems that oppress.

5. Companion of the poor:
   set every heart ablaze,
   until compassion fills the earth,
   and every song is praise.

Tune: ST. THOMAS (WILLIAMS), S.M., 6.6.8.6.

May you walk with the stars in your eyes, an epiphany of Divine Beauty flowing over you, giving you perspective and peace whatever your lot in life, wherever you are. *(Alla Renée Bozarth)*

SOURCES

Brother Roger of Taizé, "Does My Life Still Have Meaning?" in *Peace of Heart in All Things: Meditations for Each Day of the Year* (Chicago: GIA, 2004), 57. © Ateliers et Presses de Taizé, 71250 Taizé, France. Used by permission.

St. Anselm, "We bring before you . . . ," in *The Communion of Saints: Prayers of the Famous*, ed. Horton Davies (Grand Rapids, MI: Eerdmans, 1990), 124. Public domain.

"The Great Feast of Life," in *Harvest for the World: A Worship Anthology on Sharing in the Work of Creation*, ed. Geoffrey Duncan (Cleveland: Pilgrim Press, 2003), 130. © Christian Aid.

Iona Community, "O Christ, we bow . . . ," in *Iona Abbey Worship Book* (Glasgow: Wild Goose, 2001), 62–64, alt. © Contributors, *Iona Abbey Worship* (2001), Wild Goose Publications, Glasgow. Used by permission.

Jean Vanier, *The Broken Body: Journey to Wholeness* (London: Darton, Longman and Todd, 1993), 72–73. Published and copyright © 1993 by Darton Longman and Todd Ltd, London, and used by permission of the publishers.

"Prayers of Confession" in United Church of Canada, *Celebrate God's Presence: A Book of Services for the United Church of Canada*, ed. Karen J. Verveda (Etobicoke, Ontario: United Church Publishing House, 2000), 39. Adapted from *Service Book for the Use of Ministers* (Toronto: United Church of Canada, 1969), 111. Used with permission.

"For the Poor and Neglected," in Episcopal Church, *Book of Common Prayer* (New York: Church Publishing, 1986), 826.

Mother Teresa of Calcutta, quoted in Malcolm Muggeridge, *Something Beautiful for God: Mother Teresa of Calcutta* (London: William Collins Sons, 1971), 39.

Words by Daniel Charles Damon, "Companion of the Poor." © 2002 Abingdon Press (administered by Music Services). All Rights Reserved. BMI. Used by permission.

Alla Renée Bozarth, "May You Walk with the Stars" © 2015 Alla Renée Bozarth. Used by permission.

38. POVERTY

Poverty is more than hunger; it is a lack of nutrition. Poverty is high childhood mortality; it is lack of schooling, cooking fuel, sanitation, water, and electricity. Poverty is the unequal distribution of resources, both among nations and within them. Poverty is a scandal!

Jesus looked at his disciples and said, "God will bless you people who are poor. His kingdom belongs to you! God will bless you hungry people, you will have plenty to eat!" *(Luke 6:20-21)*

PRAYERS OF PRAISE AND THANKSGIVING

God, you have guided your people throughout their history. Guide us now as we turn to you, searching for your image and for a place of rest. Like a good friend, Lord, you are always with the poor. You make yourself a travel companion to wayfarers, to the undocumented, refugees and migrants, all pilgrims walking toward you. You call us to be witnesses of your love and examples of our faith in whatever land we make our home. Lord, may your spirit be renewed in us and may all peoples, races and languages be one in you. **Amen.** *(Mexican Episcopal Commission on Youth Ministry)*

We thank you, Jesus, our greatest treasure! You come in an explosion of true love. You shatter the proud fortresses of the arrogant and you unlock every gated community. You topple the powerful from their seats of power and you put your hand in the hand of the weak. You bring peace to the humble of heart and fill the hungry with good things. **Amen.** *(Anne Rowthorn)*

CANTICLE   ISAIAH 58:6-9

Is not this the fast that I choose:
>   to loose the bonds of injustice,
>   to undo the thongs of the yoke,
> **to let the oppressed go free,**
>   **and to break every yoke?**
> Is it not to share your bread with the hungry,
>   and bring the homeless poor into your house;
> **when you see the naked, to cover them,**
>   **and not to hide yourself from your own kin?**
> Then your light shall break forth like the dawn,
>   and your healing shall spring up quickly;
> **your vindicator shall go before you,**
>   **the glory of the Lord shall be your rear guard.**
> Then you shall call, and the Lord will answer;
> **you shall cry for help, and the Lord will say, Here I am.**

SCRIPTURE   LUKE 16:19-31

"There was a rich man who was dressed in purple and fine linen and who feasted sumptuously every day. And at his gate lay a poor man named Lazarus, covered with sores, who longed to satisfy his hunger with what fell from the rich man's table; even the dogs would come and lick his sores. The poor man died and was carried away by the angels to be with Abraham. The rich man also died and was buried. In Hades, where he was being tormented, he looked up and saw Abraham far away with Lazarus by his side. He called out, 'Father Abraham, have mercy on me, and send Lazarus to dip the tip of his finger in water and cool my tongue; for I am in agony in these flames.' But Abraham said, 'Child, remember that during your lifetime you received your good things, and Lazarus in like manner evil things; but now he is comforted here, and you are in agony. Besides all this, between you and us a great chasm has been fixed, so that those who might want to pass from here to you cannot do so, and no one can cross from there to us.' He said, 'Then, father, I beg you to send him to my father's house—for I have five brothers—that he may warn them, so that they will not also come into this place of torment.' Abraham replied, 'They have Moses and the prophets; they should listen to them.' He said, 'No, father Abraham; but if someone goes to them from the dead, they will repent.' He said to him, 'If they do not listen to Moses and the prophets, neither will they be convinced even if someone rises from the dead.'"

LITANY

O God, you have sown the seeds of love in my heart but I have not watered them with my tears—
Lord, forgive.

You have shown me hungry children and I have fed only my friends—
Lord, forgive.

You have shown me the homeless and I have cared only for my own home—
Lord, forgive.

You have shown me the naked but I have only clothed myself—
Lord, forgive.

You have shown me the wounded and I have only been concerned with my own pain—
Lord, forgive.

You have shown me the friendless and I have only nurtured my own friendships—
Lord, forgive.

You have shown me the bereaved and I have only sought out others to comfort me—
Lord, forgive.

You have shown me those who do not know your love and I have failed to share what you have given me—
Lord, forgive and help me to do your will. *(Ethel Jenkins)*

REFLECTION   BROTHER ROGER OF TAIZÉ

Today more than ever before, a call is rising to open paths of trust even in humanity's darkest hours. Can we hear that call?

More and more people throughout the world are becoming aware of how urgent it is to come to the aid of the victims of poverty, a poverty that is constantly on the rise. This is a basic necessity—to make peace on earth possible.

The disparity between the accumulation of wealth by some and the poverty of countless others is one of the most serious questions of our time. Will we do all in our power for the world economy to provide solutions? Neither misfortunes nor the injustice of poverty come from God; all God can do is to give his love. And so we are filled with astonishment when we discover that God looks at every human being with infinite tenderness and deep compassion.

When we realize that God loves us, that God loves even the most forsaken human beings, then our hearts open to others. We are made more aware of the dignity of the human person. However powerless we may be, are we not called to communicate a mystery of hope to those around us by the lives we live?

The founder of the Taizé Community in France, Brother Roger of Taizé (1915–2005) lived his whole life bringing about reconciliation—between religions, nations, classes, and people, especially the very poor and young people. He saw God in every human being he encountered and encouraged others to do the same. Thousands of young people visit Taizé every year where they live simply, study the Bible, pray, and participate in common worship. During one such service, packed with young people, Brother Roger was murdered by a deranged assailant. It would have been in his nature to forgive her.

PRAYERS OF CONFESSION AND INTERCESSION

Righteous God, we live in a world where human life is exploited and abused. Violence is taken lightly, and people are often viewed as objects. Images of hunger and war and murder flash before us until we become nearly hardened. If we have taken on these values of the world, forgive us. Give us tender hearts, help us to reflect upon your righteousness, and give us courage to challenge the wrongs we see; through the power of the Holy Spirit. **Amen.** *(Ruth C. Duck)*

Enlighten those who possess power and money that they may avoid the sin of indifference, that they may love the common good, advance the weak, and care for this world in which we live. The poor and the earth are crying out. O Lord, seize us with your power and light, help us to protect all life, to prepare for a better future, for the coming of your Kingdom of justice, peace, love and beauty. **Amen.** *(Pope Francis)*

38. Poverty

HYMN SHIRLEY ERENA MURRAY

1. I am standing waiting,
   waiting at your door,
   one of hunger's children
   from a billion poor;
   though you cannot see me,
   though I am so small,
   listen to my crying,
   crying for us all.

2. I stand at your table
   asking to be fed,
   holding up my rice bowl,
   begging for your bread;
   I stand at your schoolroom
   longing just to learn,
   hoping that you'll teach me
   ways to live and earn.

3. I stand at your clinic
   begging for vaccine,
   I stand at your wash-place
   where the water's clean,
   I stand at your office,
   beg the Heads of State;
   I am just a child,
   so I must hope and wait.

4. I stand in your churches,
   listen to your prayers,
   long to know a God
   who understands and cares.
   If there is a God,
   a God who loves the poor,
   I'm still standing waiting,
   waiting at your door.

Tune: KING'S WESTON or AU CLAIR DE LA LUNE, 6.5.6.5.D.
Words © 1992 Hope Publishing

Let your love be real; reject what is evil, hold fast to what is good. Love each other as sisters and brothers, and respect the dignity of one another.
(Romans 12:9-10)

SOURCES

Luke 6:20-21 from *Contemporary English Version* (New York: American Bible Society, 1995). © 1995 American Bible Society.

"Wayfarer's Prayer," in *Prayer without Borders: Celebrating Global Wisdom* (Baltimore: Catholic Relief Services, 2004), 51, alt. From *Companion of Hopes: Prayers for Migrant Youth* (Youth and Migration Program of the Mexican Episcopal Commission of Youth Ministry).

Anne Rowthorn, "We Thank You, Jesus, Our Greatest Treasure" © 2017 Anne Rowthorn.

Ethel Jenkins, "My Prayer," in *Dare to Dream: A Prayer and Worship Anthology from around the World*, ed. Geoffrey Duncan (London: HarperCollins, 1995), 57. © Ethel Jenkins.

Brother Roger of Taizé, "Creators of Solidarity," in *Brother Roger of Taizé: Essential Writings*, ed. Marcello Fidanzio (Maryknoll, NY: Orbis Books, 2006), 66–67. Used by permission.

Ruth C. Duck, "Righteous God . . . ," in *Bread for the Journey*, ed. Ruth C. Duck (New York: Pilgrim Press, 1981), 60. Used by permission.

Pope Francis, "A Christian Prayer in Union with Creation," in *Laudato Si'*, accessed December 1, 2017, Vatican.va. © Libreria Editrice Vaticana. Used by permission.

Words by Shirley Erena Murray, "I Am Standing Waiting" © 1992 Hope Publishing Company, Carol Stream, IL 60188. All rights reserved. Used by permission.

Romans 12:9-10 from *The New English Bible,* copyright © Cambridge University Press and Oxford University Press 1961, 1970. All rights reserved.

39. HUNGER

Husk an ear of corn and count: 800 kernels. Count the seeds in a pumpkin—500. Zucchini, cucumbers, and melons contain hundreds of seeds. Nature is abundant. Hunger is a scandal!

They shall feed along the ways,
>on all the bare heights shall be their pasture;
they shall not hunger or thirst,
>neither scorching wind nor sun shall strike them down,
for he who has pity on them will lead them,
>and by springs of water will guide them. *(Isaiah 49:9b-10)*

PRAYER OF PRAISE AND THANKSGIVING

Glory to you when you inspire us to serve our neighbors, and make humility shine in our souls; deep-piercing rays of light fall into the hearts of each one of us. Your rays glow, like iron in a furnace; we see your face, mysterious and elusive. Glory to you, transfiguring our lives with deeds of love. Glory to you, making wonderfully sweet each one of your commandments. Glory to you, present in fragrant compassion. Glory to you, sending us failures and afflictions to make us sensitive to other people's sufferings. Glory to you, promising high rewards for precious wholesome deeds. Glory to you, welcoming the impulse of our heart's love. Glory to you, for raising love above everything on earth. Glory to you, O Holy God, from age to age. **Amen.** *(Metropolitan Tryphon)*

PSALM 78:18-20, 23-29

They tested God in their heart
    by demanding the food they craved.
They spoke against God, saying,
    "Can God spread a table in the wilderness?
Even though he struck the rock so that water gushed out
    and torrents overflowed,
can he also give bread,
    or provide meat for his people?" . . .
Yet he commanded the skies above,
    and opened the doors of heaven;
he rained down on them manna to eat,
    and gave them the grain of heaven.
Mortals ate of the bread of angels;
    he sent them food in abundance.
He caused the east wind to blow in the heavens,
    and by his power he led out the south wind;
he rained flesh upon them like dust,
    winged birds like the sand of the seas;
he let them fall within their camp,
    all around their dwellings.
And they ate and were well filled,
    for he gave them what they craved.

SCRIPTURE   MARK 6:33-44

Many saw [the disciples] going and recognized them, and they hurried there on foot from all the towns and arrived ahead of them. As [Jesus] went ashore, he saw a great crowd; and he had compassion for them, because they were like sheep without a shepherd; and he began to teach them many things. When it grew late, his disciples came to him and said, "This is a deserted place, and the hour is now very late; send them away so that they may go into the surrounding country and villages and buy something for themselves to eat." But he answered them, "You give them something to eat." They said to him, "Are we to go and buy two hundred denarii worth of bread, and give it to them to eat?" And he said to them, "How many loaves have you? Go and see." When they had found out, they said, "Five, and two fish." Then he ordered them to get all the people to sit down in groups on the green grass.

So they sat down in groups of hundreds and of fifties. Taking the five loaves and the two fish, he looked up to heaven, and blessed and broke the loaves, and gave them to his disciples to set before the people; and he divided the two fish among them all. And all ate and were filled; and they took up twelve baskets full of broken pieces and of the fish. Those who had eaten the loaves numbered five thousand.

LITANY

For the hungry and the overfed
May we have enough.

For the mourners and the mockers
May we laugh together.

For the victims and the oppressors
May we share power wisely.

For the peacemakers and the warmongers
May clear truth and stern love lead us to harmony.

For the silenced and the propagandists
May we speak our own words in truth.

For the unemployed and the overworked
May our impress on the earth be kindly and creative.

For the troubled and the sleek
May we live together as wounded healers.

For the homeless and the cosseted
May our homes be simple, warm and welcoming.

For the vibrant and the dying
May we all die to live. *(Anglican Church of New Zealand)*

REFLECTION   GARY SNYDER

Eating is a sacrament. The grace we say clears our hearts and guides the children and welcomes the guest, all at the same time. We look at eggs, apples and stew. They are evidence of plenitude, excess, a great reproductive exuberance. Millions of grains of grass-seed that will become grass or flour, millions of codfish. Innumerable little seeds are sacrifices to the food chain. A parsnip in the ground is a marvel of living chemistry, making sugars and flavors from earth, air, water. And if we eat meat it is the life, the bounce, the swish, of a great alert being with keen ears and lovely eyes, with foursquare feet and a huge beating heart.

At our house we say a Buddhist grace. We are thankful for this meal, the work of many people, and the sharing of other forms of life. A grace is a plain, ordinary old-fashioned thing to do that connects us.

Pulitzer Prize winner Gary Snyder (b. 1930) is a poet, essayist, and environmental activist whose writings have been informed by Chinese, Indian, and Japanese religions and approaches to the natural world. Among his friends were Allen Ginsberg, Jack Kerouac, and Lawrence Ferlinghetti, collectively known as the "Beat Generation."

PRAYERS OF CONFESSION AND INTERCESSION

Lord, you made a world that is interrelated and interconnected. When we use toxic substances for our crops, we poison the food we harvest to put on our tables to eat. When we seek a higher yield through science, we poison the earth and generations to come. Polluted rivers and fields, polluted forests and countless ecosystems mean a polluted earth! Lord, teach us how to live in harmony with nature and one another for Christ's sake. **Amen.** *(Anglican Church in Kenya)*

All you who are thirsty, this is the place for water. All you who are hungry, this is the place to be fed. Why spend your earnings on what is not food? Why pay for that which fails to satisfy? Here without money, here without price, may all enjoy the bread of heaven. God speaks, and all who listen have life. **Amen.** *(Wild Goose Worship Group)*

39. Hunger

HYMN   BARBARA HAMM

1. God is still speaking when children beg for bread,
   roaming through city streets, their innocence long dead.
   How can we close our eyes, complacent in our greed?
   God, move our hearts of stone to serve a world in need.

2. God is still speaking when exiles cry in pain,
   forced from their homelands or enslaved for others' gain.
   How can we leave them to endure the wounds of hate?
   God, use our broken hearts, a new world to create.

3. God is still speaking when people pray for peace,
   seeing, through eyes of faith, the day when war will cease.
   How can we cling to hate as God's name we confess?
   God, let our hearts be changed by love, the world to bless.

Tune: BRANDON, 11.12.12.12.
Words © 2005 Hope Publishing

The Lord your God is bringing you to a rich land, a land of streams, of springs and underground waters gushing out in hill and valley, a land of wheat and barley, of vines, fig trees and pomegranates, a land of olives, oil and honey. It is a land where you will never live in poverty nor want for anything. *(Deuteronomy 8:7-9a)*

SOURCES

Metropolitan Tryphon [Prince Boris Petrovich Turkestanov], Ikos 9 of "An Akathist in Praise of God's Creation," in *SYNDESMOS Orthodoxy and Ecology Resource Book,* Annex 1, *Orthodox Services for the Creation*, ed. Alexander Belopopsky and Dmitri Oikonomou (Bialystok, Poland: Orthdruk Orthodox Printing House, 1996), 20–25, alt.

"For the hungry . . .," in Church of the Province of New Zealand, *A New Zealand Prayer Book: He Karakia Mihinare o Aotearoa* (Auckland, New Zealand: William Collins, 1989), 162. © 1989 The Provincial Secretary, The Church of the Province of New Zealand, Box 2148, Rotorua. Used by permission.

Gary Snyder, "Grace," in *The Practice of the Wild: Essays* (Washington, DC: Shoemaker & Hoard, 2003), 197. © 1990 by Gary Snyder. Reprinted by permission of Counterpoint Press.

"Ecological Concerns," in Anglican Church in Kenya, *Our Modern Services* (Nairobi, Kenya: Uzima Press, 2003), 298, alt.

Wild Goose Worship Group, "All you who are thirsty . . . ," in "Daytime Liturgy A," in *A Wee Worship Book*, fourth incarnation (Glasgow: Wild Goose, 1999), 43. © 1999 Wild Goose Resource Group. Used by permission.

Words by Barbara Hamm, "God Is Still Speaking" © 2005 Hope Publishing Company, Carol Stream, IL 60188. All rights reserved. Used by permission.

Deuteronomy 8:7-9a from *The New English Bible*, copyright © Cambridge University Press and Oxford University Press 1961, 1970. All rights reserved.

40. MIGRANTS

Migrants—people living in countries other than where they were born—are forced out by poverty, war, and political unrest. History's largest forced migration was the 350-year Atlantic slave trade when twelve million Africans were abducted from their homes. Among the newest migrants are those fleeing rising sea levels, droughts, deserts, and desertification. Pharaohs lurk along the way and many migrants do not reach the Promised Land of their dreams.

By the rivers of Babylon—
>there we sat down and there we wept
>when we remembered Zion. *(Psalm 137:1)*

PRAYERS OF PRAISE AND THANKSGIVING

O God, the guardian and guide of the Holy Family in their return and resettlement after exile in Egypt; we thank you for the dreams and visions and songs which sustain and guide so many exiles today; and we pray that they may be fully realized. To this end, O God, we ask your blessing and protection upon them and upon refugee resettlement workers and all others who, as companions and advocates and observers, travel with them to their journey's end. **Amen.** *(John Carden)*

Dear brothers and sisters, migrants and refugees! At the heart of the Gospel of mercy the encounter and acceptance by others are intertwined with the encounter and acceptance of God himself. Welcoming others means welcoming God in person! Do not let yourselves be robbed of the hope and joy of life born of your experience of God's mercy, as manifested in the people you meet on your journey! I entrust you to the Virgin Mary, Mother of migrants and refugees, and to Saint Joseph, who experienced the bitterness of emigration to Egypt. To their intercession I also commend those who invest so much energy, time and resources to the pastoral and social care of migrants. . . . **Amen.** *(Pope Francis)*

PSALM 145:14-20A

The Lord upholds all who are falling,
>and raises up all who are bowed down.

The eyes of all look to you,
>**and you give them their food in due season.**

You open your hand,
>satisfying the desire of every living thing.

The Lord is just in all his ways,
>**and kind in all his doings.**

The Lord is near to all who call on him,
>to all who call on him in truth.

He fulfills the desire of all who fear him;
>**he also hears their cry, and saves them.**

The Lord watches over all who love him.

SCRIPTURE   EXODUS 2:15-23

[Pharaoh] sought to kill Moses.

But Moses fled from Pharaoh. He settled in the land of Midian, and sat down by a well. The priest of Midian had seven daughters. They came to draw water, and filled the troughs to water their father's flock. But some shepherds came and drove them away. Moses got up and came to their defense and watered their flock. When they returned to their father Reuel, he said, "How is it that you have come back so soon today?" They said, "An Egyptian helped us against the shepherds; he even drew water for us and watered the flock." He said to his daughters, "Where is he? Why did you leave the man? Invite him to break bread." Moses agreed to stay with the man, and he gave Moses his daughter Zipporah in marriage. She bore a son, and he named him Gershom; for he said, "I have been an alien residing in a foreign land."

After a long time the king of Egypt died. The Israelites groaned under their slavery, and cried out. Out of their slavery their cry for help rose up to God.

LITANY

O God of all nations and peoples: You watched over your ancient people in exile,
You called them to the long journey home.

You watch over us when we are home or away,
You watch over us when home seems like a strange land.

You watch over a world in turmoil,
Your heart turns towards the homeless, the displaced, the refugee.

Walk with us, as we wait on your promise:
Come, O come, Emmanuel.

God of promise:
You called the Holy Family with signs and dreams;

You watched over them when they wandered as exiles.
You watch over us when we don't know where we are going.

You see those who wander as exiles in our world;
Take care, we pray, of all those who lack a place of safety.

You see those who seek a home:
Open our hearts to show mercy to those in need.

Walk with us, as we wait on your promise:
Come, O come, Emmanuel.

God of promise, you entered our world in human form,
You took flesh and became one of us.

You are with us when we hear the clarion call of your Word;
You watch over us when we cannot hear your voice.

We call out to you as we wait on your promise:
Come, O Come, Emmanuel. *(Maggi Dawn)*

REFLECTION   UNITED NATIONS GENERAL ASSEMBLY

Managing migration is one of the most urgent and profound tests of international cooperation in our time. Migration is an engine of economic growth, innovation and sustainable development. It allows millions of people to seek new opportunities each year, creating and strengthening bonds between countries and societies. Yet it is also a source of divisions within and between states and societies, often leaving migrants vulnerable to abuse and exploitation. In recent years, large movements of desperate people, including both migrants and refugees, have cast a shadow over the broader benefits of migration. It is time to reverse those trends, to recommit to protecting lives and rights of all migrants and to make migration work for all.

Child migrants deserve special attention. A great many migrant children, who experience violence, abuse and exploitation, are held in detention centers and deprived of education. Those who are separated from their families are often let down by weak guardianship systems and a lack of other options to protect them. Authorities can be slow to determine their status or assess their best interests, and sometimes they fail to do so altogether.

A forward-looking compact on migration, as well as a compact on refugees, must respond to the reality that climate change is likely to exacerbate economic, environmental and social pressures to migrate over the next few decades. It is also possible to foresee that other factors may increase the numbers of migrants in vulnerable situations in the years ahead. Individuals or whole populations may find themselves confronted with extreme deprivation, food scarcity, the onset of epidemics or the reality or threat of instability, forcing them to move, often without sufficient resources, knowledge or plans for the future.

This reflection was taken from the United Nations follow-up to the outcome of the Millennium Summit, 2015. The report focuses on making migration work for all, emphasizing its links to the 2030 Agenda for Sustainable Development.

PRAYERS OF CONFESSION AND INTERCESSION

Eternal God, Maker of the skies above, lowly Christ, born amidst the growing earth, Spirit of life, wind over the flowing waters, in earth, sea and sky, you are there. O hidden mystery, sun behind all suns, soul behind all souls, in everyone we meet, your presence is around us, and we give you thanks. But when we have not touched but trampled you in creation, when we have not met but missed you in one another, when we have not received but rejected you in the poor, forgive us, and hear now our plea for mercy. **Amen.** *(Iona Abbey)*

Loving God, we pray for millions of silent people today: the homeless, the refugees—forced to live in tents or shacks, often in camps, herded together. We pray for people whose harvest has failed for years, who listen to the sobs of children with daily hunger pains. Strengthen every missionary, every church organization, every national fund seeking to help the forgotten millions, and show us how we can best love these our neighbors in need. Hear our prayer and enliven our response, for Jesus' sake. **Amen.** *(Michael Perry)*

HYMN   ADAM M. L. TICE

1. Jesus entered Egypt
   fleeing Herod's hand,
   living as an alien
   in a foreign land.
   Far from home and country
   with his family,
   was there room and welcome
   for this refugee?

2. Jesus was a migrant
   living as a guest
   with the friends and strangers
   who could offer rest.
   Do we hold wealth lightly
   so that we can share
   shelter with the homeless,
   and abundant care?

3. Jesus crosses borders
   with the wandering poor,
   searching for a refuge,
   for an open door.
   Do our words and actions
   answer Jesus' plea:
   "Give the lowly welcome,
   and you welcome me"?

Tune: KING'S WESTON, 6.5.6.5.D.

God of the earth, protect us. God of the sky, protect us. God of the great shining waters, protect us. *(Rig-Veda)*

SOURCES

John Carden, "O God, the Guardian and Guide of the Holy Family," in *A Procession of Prayers: Meditations and Prayers from around the World*, ed. John Carden (Harrisburg, PA: Morehouse, 1998), 77, alt.

Pope Francis, "Message of His Holiness Pope Francis for the World Day of Migrants and Refugees," *The Holy See*, last modified September 12, 2015, https://w2.vatican.va/content/francesco/en/messages/migration/documents/papa-francesco_20150912_world-migrants-day-2016.html. © Libreria Editrice Vaticana. Used by permission.

Litany © Maggi Dawn, 2016. All rights reserved. Used by permission.

Report of the Secretary-General of the United Nations, "Making Migration Work for All," follow-up to the outcome of the Millennium Summit, December 12, 2017, Sections IA(1), II(17), IIIC(51), United Nations, accessed February 19, 2018, https://refugeesmigrants.un.org/sites/default/files/sg_report_en.pdf. © 2017 United Nations. Reprinted with the permission of the United Nations.

Iona Community, "Eternal God . . . ," in *Iona Abbey Worship Book* (Glasgow: Wild Goose, 2001), 51. © Contributors, *Iona Abbey Worship* (2001), Wild Goose Publications, Glasgow. Used by permission.

Michael Perry, "For the Marginalized," in *Chalice Worship*, ed. Colbert S. Cartwright and O. I. Cricket Harrison (St. Louis: Chalice Press, 1997), 374. © 1986 The Jubilate Group (admin. Hope Publishing Company, Carol Stream, IL 60188). All rights reserved. Used by permission.

Words by Adam M. L. Tice, "Jesus Entered Egypt" © 2009, GIA Publications, Inc. Used by permission.

The Golden Womb of the Sun: Rig-Vedic Songs in a New Translation, ed. P. Lal (Calcutta: Writers Workshop, 1970), alt. Used by permission of Writers Workshop (Calcutta, India).

41. VIOLENCE

Clear-cutting of forests, mountaintop removal, fracking, mining lands and ocean depths, polluting the waters, poisoning the atmosphere, economic injustice, rape, torture, genocide, murder, bullying, trafficking, domestic abuse, coercion, harassment—these are the many faces of violence; violence against God and against God's creation. Jesus weeps.

Out of the depths I cry to you, O God. God, hear my voice! Let your ears be attentive to the voice of my supplications! *(Psalm 130:1-2)*

PRAYERS OF PRAISE AND THANKSGIVING

We praise you, Lord, for the wonders of life on our planet, and we give you thanks for all that the earth provides for our food, shelter and well-being. We commit to you those areas of the world where the resources of nature have been plundered and people's livelihoods threatened; we pray for those who work to restore the land to people who most need its harvest. **Amen.** *(Christian Aid)*

O Christ, you are united to every human being without exception. Still more, risen from the dead, you come to heal the secret wounds of our souls. And for each of us there opens the gates of an infinite goodness of heart. Through such love, little by little our hearts are changed. **Amen.** *(Brother Roger of Taizé)*

PSALM 91:9-16

Because you have made the Lord your refuge,
    the Most High your dwelling place,
no evil shall befall you,
    no scourge come near your tent.

For he will command his angels concerning you
    to guard you in all your ways.
On their hands they will bear you up,
    so that you will not dash your foot against a stone.
You will tread on the lion and the adder,
    the young lion and the serpent you will trample under foot.

Those who love me, I will deliver;
    I will protect those who know my name.
When they call to me, I will answer them;
    I will be with them in trouble,
    I will rescue them and honor them.
With long life I will satisfy them,
    and show them my salvation.

SCRIPTURE   HABAKKUK 1:1-4; 2:1-4

O Lord, how long shall I cry for help,
    and you will not listen?
Or cry to you 'Violence!'
    and you will not save?
Why do you make me see wrongdoing
    and look at trouble?
Destruction and violence are before me;
    strife and contention arise.
So the law becomes slack
    and justice never prevails.
The wicked surround the righteous—
    therefore judgment comes forth perverted. . . .
I will stand at my watchpost,
    and station myself on the rampart;
I will keep watch to see what he will say to me,
    and what he will answer concerning my complaint.
Then the Lord answered me and said:

Write the vision;
> make it plain on tablets,
> so that a runner may read it.

For there is still a vision for the appointed time;
> it speaks of the end, and does not lie.

If it seems to tarry, wait for it;
> it will surely come, it will not delay.

Look at the proud!
> Their spirit is not right in them,
> but the righteous live by their faith.

LITANY

Almighty God, Judge of the nations and Protector of the helpless,
we come before you to ask for vision and courage and strength
as we witness in your Name against the evils of trafficking.

We pray first for the victims of trafficking, especially women and children, whose lot is slavery and whose future is despair.
Save us from weak resignation to the evils we deplore.
Grant us wisdom, grant us courage, for the facing of this hour.

We pray for those who traffic in human lives that they may know at first hand the wrath of God and, knowing it, may fear God and turn from their wickedness and live.
Save us from weak resignation to the evils we deplore.
Grant us wisdom, grant us courage, for the facing of this hour.

We pray for the exploiters whose relentless demand for forced labor and commercial sex spells doom for the innocent in many lands.
Save us from weak resignation to the evils we deplore.
Grant us wisdom, grant us courage, for the facing of this hour.

We pray for our governments who, having made a start, are left with much yet to do for the voiceless and wretched of the earth.
Save us from weak resignation to the evils we deplore.
Grant us wisdom, grant us courage, for the facing of this hour.

We pray for the religious leaders of all our communities that they may bear a bold and faithful witness to discomfort and challenge those who rest easy in the face of evil.
Save us from weak resignation to the evils we deplore.
Grant us wisdom, grant us courage, for the facing of this hour.

We pray finally for ourselves and for all people of compassion and goodwill that we may respect the dignity of every human being, loving our neighbors as ourselves.
Save us from weak resignation to the evils we deplore.
Grant us wisdom, grant us courage, for the facing of this hour. Amen.
(Jeffery Rowthorn)

REFLECTION   JEAN VANIER

Just as some of the purest and most cleansing substances come from things that are rotten—wine and alcohol from fermented fruit, penicillin from mold—and just as the earth is nourished by animal manure, so our hearts and inner brokenness are healed through communion with all that we have rejected and are afraid of: the poor and weak, enemies, strangers. Thus we come down to earth, to the dirt of reality. Because hidden in this earth is a light. Is it not now time to come back down to earth, to rediscover the beauty of our earth, of humanity, of each one of us? But this return to earth, to humanity, to a new form of solidarity where walls disappear, to communion with each person, demands a conversion. What can bring this about? How can we begin to change our world, one heart at a time? How can we set out on this journey home?

At the fiftieth anniversary of L'Arche in 2014, the founder, Jean Vanier (b. 1928), said, "There is a mystery behind people with disabilities. I find that in many ways they are the presence of Jesus. We see their fragility, their pain—and yet at the same time, we can say that they speak of God. As we enter into relationship with them, they change us."

PRAYERS OF CONFESSION AND INTERCESSION

God of life, forgive our denial of life, our destruction of its hopes, our denial of its needs, our distorting of its possibilities. Fill us with your Spirit of life, that we might be people of life, servants of life, encouragers of life, signs of Christ, the life of the world. In his name we pray. **Amen.** *(Baptist Union of Great Britain)*

God, father and mother of all the human race; God who lives within every human being, in every child, woman and man; God, broken by our divisiveness, hurt by our woundedness, dying on every battlefield. Vulnerable, holy God, we offer you ourselves as we come together here and we ask you to transform us from within; to heal our hurts and hates, and to lead us to ways of peace and growth. **Amen.** *(Hexham Abbey Youth Group and Bridget Hewitt)*

41. Violence

HYMN   NORMAN HABEL WITH INDIGENOUS FRIENDS

1. Hear the land crying, crying in darkness;
   hear the land crying, crying in pain:
   "Where are my people, torn from their homelands?
   People, my people, come back again!"

2. Hear the blood crying, crying for justice;
   hear the blood crying, out of the ground:
   "Massacres, murders, great names forgotten!
   Where is the healing? Where is it found?"

3. Hear mothers crying, crying for children;
   hear mothers crying, losing control!
   "Baby, my baby, why did they take you?
   Why did they steal my love from your soul?"

4. Hear fathers crying, sacrificed, dying;
   hear fathers crying after their death:
   "We gave our lives for good and for country.
   We shed our blood here, lest we forget."

5. Hear the land crying, crucified, crying;
   hear the land crying, gasping in pain:
   "I share your suffering! I offer healing!
   Will those who love me join my refrain?"

6. Hear the land calling those on a journey;
   hear the land calling, calling you home:
   "All who are sorry, sorry for stealing,
   I bring you healing, cover your shame."

   Tune: BUNESSAN, 5.5.5.4.D. or ROWTHORN, specially composed for this text by Don E. Saliers.

Be brave and steadfast, have no fear for Yahweh is the one who marches with you, and will never fail or forsake you. *(Deuteronomy 31:6)*

SOURCES

Psalm 130:1-2 from *The New Testament and Psalms: An Inclusive Version* (New York: Oxford University Press, 1995), an adaptation of the New Revised Standard Version Bible, copyright © 1989 National Council of the Churches of Christ in the United States of America. Used by permission. All rights reserved.

"We Praise You, Lord," in *Harvest for the World: A Worship Anthology on Sharing in the Work of Creation*, ed. Geoffrey Duncan (Cleveland: Pilgrim Press, 2003), 18. © Christian Aid.

Brother Roger of Taizé, "O Christ You Are United to Every Human Being," in *Peace of Heart in All Things: Meditations for Each Day of the Year* (Chicago: GIA, 2004), 15. © Ateliers et Presses de Taizé, 71250 Taizé, France. Used by permission.

Jeffery Rowthorn © 2008 Jeffery Rowthorn. The concluding line in each paragraph and the response to it are from Harry Emerson Fosdick's hymn, "God of Grace and God of Glory."

Jean Vanier, *Our Journey Home: Rediscovering a Common Humanity Beyond Our Differences*, trans. Maggie Parham (Canada: Novalis, 1997), 248, 250-51. © Plon, 1994. Used by permission.

Jean Vanier, interview by Alicia von Stamwitz, *United Church Observer*, October 2013, http://www.ucobserver.org/features/2013/10/jean_vanier/. Used by permission of Alicia von Stamwitz.

"God of life, forgive our denial . . . ," in Baptist Union of Great Britain, *Patterns and Prayers for Christian Worship* (Oxford: Oxford University Press, 1991), 53. Used by permission.

Hexham Abbey Youth Group and Bridget Hewitt, "God, father and mother . . . ," in "Help Us Make a Difference," in *Holy Ground: Liturgies and Worship Resources for an Engaged Spirituality*, ed. Neil Paynter and Helen Boothroyd (Glasgow: Wild Goose, 2005), 142. © Contributors, *Holy Ground* (2005), Wild Goose Publications, Glasgow. Used by permission.

Norman Habel and indigenous friends, "Hear the Land Crying" © 2000 Norman Habel. Used by permission.

Deuteronomy 31:6 from *The Inclusive Bible* (Landham, MD: Rowman & Littlefield, 2007). A Sheed & Ward Book published by Rowman & Littlefield Publishers, Inc. All rights reserved. Used by permission.

42. VICTIMS OF WAR

War has no winners, not even nations claiming victory. War's victims are the killed and the maimed and their families and friends; they are the innocents slaughtered by random gunfire and drones; they are the soldiers returning home, enduring the agonies of post-traumatic stress disorder and all too often resorting to suicide.

Jesus said to him, "Put your sword back into its place; for all who take the sword will perish by the sword. *(Matthew 26:52)*

PRAYERS OF PRAISE AND THANKSGIVING

Awesome God, you have turned the sea into dry land, tears into songs of joy, and death into life. In Christ you have freed us from sin, death, and the powers of the devil. We sing your praises! **Amen**. *(Robin McCullough-Bade)*

Eternal God, you are the power behind all things: behind the energy of the storm, behind the heat of a million suns. Eternal God, you are the power behind all minds: behind the ability to think and reason, behind all understanding of the truth. Eternal God, you are the power behind the cross of Christ: behind the weakness, the torture and the death, behind unconquerable love. Eternal God, we worship and adore you. **Amen.** *(Presbyterian Church, USA)*

Lord Jesus Christ, you know every sorrow of the heart. You suffer with the suffering; you grieve with those who are wounded and displaced by war; you are close to the broken-hearted. We thank you that through your great love you are with all the victims of war, wounded in body, mind and spirit. We thank you that you give them your solace and peace and the assurance that they are upheld in the compassionate community of the Beloved. **Amen.** *(Anne Rowthorn)*

PSALM 46:1-3, 6, 9-11

God is our refuge and strength,
    a very present help in trouble.
Therefore we will not fear, though the earth should change,
    though the mountains shake in the heart of the sea;
though its waters roar and foam,
    though the mountains tremble with its tumult. . . .

The nations are in an uproar, the kingdoms totter;
    he utters his voice, the earth melts. . . .

He makes wars cease to the end of the earth;
    he breaks the bow, and shatters the spear;
    he burns the shields with fire.
"Be still, and know that I am God!
    I am exalted among the nations,
    I am exalted in the earth."
The Lord of hosts is with us;
    the God of Jacob is our refuge.

SCRIPTURE   ISAIAH 9:2-7

The people who walked in darkness
have seen a great light;
those who lived in a land of deep darkness—
    on them light has shined.
You have multiplied the nation,
    you have increased its joy;
they rejoice before you
    as with joy at the harvest,
    as people exult when dividing plunder.
For the yoke of their burden,
    and the bar across their shoulders,
    the rod of their oppressor,
    you have broken as on the day of Midian.
For all the boots of the tramping warriors
    and all the garments rolled in blood
    shall be burned as fuel for the fire.

For a child has been born for us,
 a son given to us;
authority rests upon his shoulders;
 and he is named
Wonderful Counselor, Mighty God,
 Everlasting Father, Prince of Peace.
His authority shall grow continually,
 and there shall be endless peace
for the throne of David and his kingdom.
 He will establish and uphold it
with justice and with righteousness
 from this time onwards and for evermore.
The zeal of the LORD of hosts will do this.

LITANY

We pray for all who suffer because of the sale of arms: those caught up in war and conflict, those who go hungry, those who are persecuted, (remembering especially . . .).
O Lord, our God, have mercy upon us. Make us instruments of your peace.

We pray for the management, workers and shareholders of the armaments industry, that they may find other ways to use their skills—ways that celebrate life rather than threaten its destruction.
O Lord, our God, have mercy upon us. Make us instruments of your peace.

We pray for a conversion of hearts and minds from ways of war to ways of peace, especially remembering all decision-makers, and all those who carry out the decisions that are made.
O Lord, our God, have mercy upon us. Make us instruments of your peace.

We pray that the cry for peace will be heard above the clamor for war. And we pray for ourselves, that we will never tire of speaking up for peace. We pray for those who aren't free to speak out and protest.
O Lord, our God, have mercy upon us. Make us instruments of your peace. *(Author unknown)*

REFLECTION   WENDELL BERRY

How much poison are you willing
    to eat for the success of the free
    market and global trade? Please
    name your preferred poisons.

For the sake of goodness, how much
    evil are you willing to do?
    Fill in the following blanks
    with the names of your favorite
    evils and acts of hatred.

What sacrifices are you prepared
    to make for culture and civilization?
    Please list the monuments, shrines
    and works of art you would
    most willingly destroy.

In the name of patriotism and
    the flag, how much of our beloved
    land are you willing to desecrate?
    List in the following spaces
    the mountains, rivers, towns, farms
    you could most readily do without.

State briefly the ideas, ideals, or hopes,
    the energy sources, the kinds of security,
    for which you would kill a child.
    Name, please, the children whom
    you would be willing to kill.

The farmer, cultural critic, and prolific poet and essayist Wendell Berry (b. 1934) writes from the perspective of the land, his 125-acre farm near Port Royal, Kentucky.

PRAYERS OF CONFESSION AND INTERCESSION

God, you have entrusted us with the care of each other. Forgive us that we profit from the oppression and injury of our brothers and sisters. Forgive us that we develop so readily the means of destruction at the expense of the things that create community. Forgive us that when we are asked for bread we sell bombs, and that we have made the livelihood of so many dependent upon trading in death. Enable the victims of the arms race to forgive us. Enable us to give ourselves in commitment to the eradication of this evil. Enable us to help those with power to work for justice and peace. Lord, you have given us all we need; so now make us ready to forfeit all the hurtful things that are not needed. God, you are against the arms trade and for the people, give us your love. **Amen.** *(Campaign Against the Arms Trade)*

O God, judge eternal, you love justice and hate oppression, and you call us to share your zeal for truth. Give us courage to take our stand with all victims of bloodshed and greed, and, following your servants and prophets, to look to the pioneer and perfecter of our faith, your Son, Jesus Christ, our Savior and Lord. **Amen.** *(Evangelical Lutheran Church in America)*

HYMN   SYLVIA DUNSTAN

1. Blest are the innocents, Bethlehem's own,
   killed by a tyrant who clings to a throne.
   Not just by Herod, not just long ago,
   here and today voices cry from below.

2. Rachel is weeping, her child is no more,
   lost to the famine, the plague and the war;
   lost to the fist and the curse and the lie—
   in flesh or spirit the innocents die.

3. Where is the comfort for those who still mourn?
   Where is the assurance for those yet unborn?
   God, hear our blood crying out from the ground;
   shine on the shadows where secrets resound.

4. Where can we turn, Holy God, but to you?
   Lord, in your mercy, O make all things new!
   Cast down the arrogant, lift up the least.
   Gather your children and grant them your feast.

Tune: BETHLEHEM'S OWN, 10.10.10.10.

> They shall beat their swords into plowshares,
>   and their spears into pruning hooks;
> nation shall not lift up sword against nation,
>   neither shall they learn war any more. *(Isaiah 2:4b)*

SOURCES

Robin McCullough-Bade, "Tears into Songs," in *Bread for the Day: Daily Bible Readings and Prayers 2016* (Minneapolis: Augsburg Fortress, 2016), 208. Used by permission.

"Eternal God . . . ," in Presbyterian Church (USA), *Book of Common Worship* (Louisville, KY: Westminster John Knox, 1993), 21. Reprinted by permission from *Book of Common Worship*, © 1993 Westminster John Knox Press.

Anne Rowthorn, "Lord Jesus Christ, You Know Every Sorrow of the Heart" © 2017 Anne Rowthorn.

"We pray for all . . ." in "Prayer Vigil Outside BAE Systems Arms Factory, Warton, Lancashire," in *Holy Ground: Liturgies and Worship Resources for an Engaged Spirituality*, ed. Neil Paynter and Helen Boothroyd (Glasgow: Wild Goose, 2005), 178–79. © Contributors, *Holy Ground* (2005), Wild Goose Publications, Glasgow. Used by permission.

Wendell Berry, "Questionnaire," in *Leavings: Poems*, by Wendell Berry (Berkeley, CA: Counterpoint, 2010), 14. Copyright © 2010 by Wendell Berry. Reprinted by permission of Counterpoint Press.

Campaign against the Arms Trade, "Forgive us that we profit . . . ," in *Holy Ground: Liturgies and Worship Resources for an Engaged Spirituality*, ed. Neil Paynter and Helen Boothroyd (Glasgow: Wild Goose, 2005), 178. © Contributors, *Holy Ground* (2005), Wild Goose Publications, Glasgow. Used by permission.

"O God, judge eternal . . . ," in Evangelical Lutheran Church in America, *Evangelical Lutheran Worship*, Leaders Desk ed. (Minneapolis: Augsburg Fortress, 2006), 105. Altered from "Judge eternal . . . ," in *Revised Common Lectionary Prayers* (Minneapolis: Augsburg Fortress, 2002), 175. Used by permission.

Words by Sylvia Dunstan, "Blest Are the Innocents" © 1995, GIA Publications, Inc. Used by permission.

43. CONSEQUENCES

My mother warned, and perhaps yours did too, that "If you play with matches, you will start a fire," "If you don't turn down the heat, you will overheat the house," "If you don't turn off the water, you'll flood it." We have ignored the warnings. Now our earthly house is suffering—fires burn out of control and we have dangerously overheated our global home. Some lands are flooded, others too dry; sea levels are rising.

The beginning of human pride is to forsake the Lord;
>   the heart has withdrawn from its Maker.
For the beginning of pride is sin,
>   and the one who clings to it pours out abominations.
Therefore the Lord brings upon them unheard-of calamities,
>   and destroys them completely. *(Ecclesiasticus 10:12-13)*

PRAYERS OF PRAISE AND THANKSGIVING

Dear God, Creator of the earth, this sacred home we share: Give us new eyes to see the beauty all around and to protect the wonders of creation. Give us new arms to embrace the strangers among us and to know them as family. Give us new ears to hear and understand those who live off the land. Give us new hearts to recognize the brokenness in our communities and to heal the wounds we have inflicted. Give us new hands to serve the earth and its people and to shape the beloved community. For you are the One who seeks the lost, binds our wounds and sets us free, and it is in the name of Jesus the Christ we pray. **Amen.** *(Bishops of the Episcopal Church)*

PSALM 91:1-8

You who live in the shelter of the Most High,
    who abide in the shadow of the Almighty,
will say to the Lord, "My refuge and my fortress;
    my God, in whom I trust."
For he will deliver you from the snare of the fowler
    and from the deadly pestilence;
he will cover you with his pinions,
    and under his wings you will find refuge;
    his faithfulness is a shield and buckler.
You will not fear the terror of the night,
    or the arrow that flies by day,
or the pestilence that stalks in darkness,
    or the destruction that wastes at noonday.

A thousand may fall at your side,
    ten thousand at your right hand,
    but it will not come near you.
You will only look with your eyes
    and see the punishment of the wicked.

SCRIPTURE   DEUTERONOMY 28:1-2, 11-12, 15, 20-24, 28

If you will only obey the Lord your God, by diligently observing all his commandments that I am commanding you today, the Lord your God will set you high above all the nations of the earth; all these blessings shall come upon you and overtake you, if you obey the Lord your God. . . . The Lord will make you abound in prosperity, in the fruit of your womb, in the fruit of your livestock, and in the fruit of your ground in the land that the Lord swore to your ancestors to give you. The Lord will open for you his rich storehouse, the heavens, to give the rain of your land in its season and to bless all your undertakings. You will lend to many nations, but you will not borrow. . . . But if you will not obey the Lord your God by diligently observing all his commandments and decrees, which I am commanding you today, then all these curses shall come upon you and overtake you: . . . The Lord will send upon you disaster, panic, and frustration in everything you attempt to do, until you are destroyed and perish quickly, on account of the evil of your deeds, because you have forsaken me. The Lord will make the pestilence cling to you until it has consumed you from the land that you are entering to possess. The Lord will afflict you with consumption, fever, inflammation, with fiery heat and drought, and with blight and mildew; they shall pursue you until you perish. The sky over your head shall be bronze, and the earth under you iron. The LORD will change the rain of your land into powder, and only dust shall come down upon you from the sky until you are destroyed. . . . The LORD will afflict you with madness, blindness, and confusion of mind.

LITANY

Let us open ourselves to the grace of God, to the brokenness of our world, and to the call to be agents of healing and re-creation.
Where human greed has stripped the world of beauty and life, and robbed people of dignity and subsistence,
We pray, O God, for a new vision of abundance, and a new commitment to nurture the world that feeds us and share with those who do not have.

Where human hatred has severed relationships, and broken the connection that unites creation,
We pray, O God, for love to be renewed, and compassion to draw us back into union.

Where human loneliness, weakness, sickness and grief, and the suffering of our planet and its inhabitants hide the signs of your life,
We pray, O God, for healing, comfort and strength and for the courage to keep hoping for the renewed creation to come.

O God, restore our faith, revive our hope, rekindle our love, and hear our prayer, for we offer it in Christ's name. *(John van de Laar)*

REFLECTION   WILLIAM B. GAIL

Today, humans are for the first time knowingly altering nature on a global scale.

In many ways, society advances today because it can, not because advance has been deemed wise in any way. We do so without much thought. This cannot continue. Society's physical skills for advancing are now outstripping the ability of our minds to comprehend and manage those skills. The consequences for nature and society are potentially devastating.

One might argue that we live in a special time. If we don't pay attention to it and navigate a successful course past it, civilization, as we know it, will not survive. If we do we will prosper and endure.

Nature, in the form of climate change, is simply the canary in the cage. It is calling out for us to recognize the broader concern about humanity's global-scale reach and the issues that arise from it. We are hurtling toward a future where our old ways won't suffice to ensure civilization's ongoing prosperity and progress. New problems require new solutions. Our ancestors faced the same dilemma with the capture of fire and chose to move forward then. Humans need nature and must protect it, but they cannot allow it to limit them. Nature has a split personality. Many things it does disrupt our lives. At the same time, nature's great wisdom protects and promotes our prosperity. Civilization's challenge is to recognize which is which and with that knowledge advance society, ensuring nature's sustainability as well.

William B. Gail (b. 1958) is co-founder and chief technology officer of the Global Weather Corporation, a past president of the American Meteorological Society, and the author of Climate Conundrums: What the Climate Debate Reveals About Us *(2014).*

PRAYERS OF CONFESSION AND INTERCESSION

Enlarge within us, O God, the sense of fellowship with all the living things, our little brothers and sisters, to whom you have given this earth as their home in common with us. We remember with shame that in the past we have exercised our high dominion with ruthless cruelty, so that the voice of the Earth, which should have gone up to you in song, has been a groan of travail. May we realize that they live, not for us alone, but for themselves and for you, and that they love the sweetness of life even as we do, and serve you in their place better than we do in ours.

When our time in this world is over and we make room for others, may we not leave anything ravished by our greed or spoiled by our ignorance, but may we hand on our common heritage fairer and sweeter through our use of it, undiminished in fertility and joy, so that our bodies may return in peace to the great mother who nourished them and our spirits may round out the circle of a perfect life in you. **Amen.** *(Walter Rauschenbusch)*

Come, Lord God, and rule the world: all the nations are yours. Let laws be just, let justice be impartial; let the rights of the poor and of children be defended. Help us to rescue the innocent from the power of those who do evil; let the ignorant be taught, let corruption be purged, let righteousness prevail. Come, Lord God, and rule the world: all the nations are yours. **Amen.** *(Michael Perry)*

43. Consequences

HYMN   HERMAN STUEMPFLE, JR.

1. God, you see your loved creation
   tortured, torn by violent hands;
   watch unsleeping, while we ravage
   peaceful homes and fruitful lands.

2. God, you hear your peoples' groaning,
   crushed beneath oppression's weight;
   listen where their cries for mercy
   rise to you from flames of hate.

3. God, you know in deep compassion
   all earth's sorrow, all its pain;
   suffer with your wounded children
   long as want and fear remain.

4. God, come now with power to save us,
   as you came in Christ your Son.
   Call us, send us in your service
   till your kingdom's work is done.

5. Grant us eyes that see with pity,
   ears that hear your children's cry,
   hearts that ache for others' anguish,
   hands your gifts of love supply.

Tune: RESTORATION, 8.7.8.7.

May the Prince of Peace enter today into our minds and souls, helping us to transform conflict into peace in our own small corner of the globe. May we never doubt that good can triumph over evil throughout the whole of creation. *(Heather Johnston)*

SOURCES

"A Word to the Church from the Episcopal Church's House of Bishops," Episcopal Church, last modified September 27, 2017, https://www.episcopalchurch.org/posts/publicaffairs/word-church-episcopal-churchs-house-bishops, alt.

John van de Laar, "Prayers of the People," in *A Liturgy of Creation and Communion*, Sacredise, last modified September 2014, http://sacredise.com/wp-content/uploads/2014/09/A-Liturgy-of-Creation-and-Communion.pdf. Written by John van de Laar © 2007 Sacredise Publishing (sacredise.com). Used by permission.

William B. Gail, *Climate Conundrums: What the Climate Debate Reveals about Us* (Boston: American Meteorological Society, 2014), 5, 204, 205, and 216. © American Meteorological Society. Used with permission.

Walter Rauschenbusch, "For This World," in *For God and the People: Prayers of the Social Awakening* (Boston: Pilgrim Press, 1910), 47–48, alt. Public domain.

Michael Perry, "Come, Lord God, and rule . . . ," in *Bible Praying* (Grand Rapids, MI: Zondervan, 1992), 155, alt. © 1992 Hope Publishing Company, Carol Stream, IL 60188. All rights reserved. Used by permission.

Herman G. Stuempfle, Jr., "God, You See Your Loved Creation." Text: Herman G. Stuempfle, Jr. Text © 1998 Selah Publishing Co., Inc. www.selahpub.com All rights reserved. Used by permission. License no. 24641.

Heather Johnston, "A Blessing for Peace," in *Timeless Prayers for Peace: Voices Together from around the World*, ed. Geoffrey Duncan (Cleveland: Pilgrim Press, 2003), 294. © Heather Johnston.

44. JUDGMENT AND MERCY

Judgment is God's mercy at work, seeking to deliver us from all that robs us of harmony with God's creation and with each other.

Rise up, O God, judge the earth;
>for all the nations belong to you! *(Psalm 82:8)*

PRAYER OF PRAISE AND THANKSGIVING

Lord God of judgment and mercy, we adore you. You are the ground of all that is. You hold us in being, and without you we could not be. Before you were born, before time began, before the universe came into being, you were. When time is finished, when the universe is no more, you will still be. Nothing can take your power from you. And in your presence we can only be silent before the mystery of your being, for no words of ours can do justice to your grandeur.

Silence

Yet you have spoken to us. Out of universal silence your living word has sprung. You have spoken, and given form and beauty to the world. You have spoken, and given purpose to human life. You have spoken, and declared the forgiveness of sin. You have spoken, and freed us from the fear of death. Lord Jesus Christ, divine Word, speak to us now. Show us the beauty of life; unite us to your eternal purpose; conquer our fears; embolden us to make your justice known throughout the world. Speak and let us hear, for your name's sake. **Amen.** *(Anthony Coates et al.)*

PSALM 51:1-7

Have mercy on me, O God,
>   according to your steadfast love;
> according to your abundant mercy
>   blot out my transgressions.

Wash me thoroughly from my iniquity,
>   **and cleanse me from my sin.**

For I know my transgressions,
>   and my sin is ever before me.

Against you, you alone, have I sinned,
>   **and done what is evil in your sight,**
> **so that you are justified in your sentence**
>   **and blameless when you pass judgment.**

Indeed, I was born guilty,
>   a sinner when my mother conceived me.

You desire truth in the inward being;
>   **therefore teach me wisdom in my secret heart.**

Purge me with hyssop, and I shall be clean;
>   wash me, and I shall be whiter than snow.

SCRIPTURE   AMOS 5:10-15

They hate the one who reproves in the gate,
>   and they abhor the one who speaks the truth.
> Therefore, because you trample on the poor
>   and take from them levies of grain,
> you have built houses of hewn stone,
>   but you shall not live in them;
> you have planted pleasant vineyards,
>   but you shall not drink their wine.
> For I know how many are your transgressions,
>   and how great are your sins—
> you who afflict the righteous, who take a bribe,
>   and push aside the needy in the gate.
> Therefore the prudent will keep silent in such a time;
>   for it is an evil time.

Seek good and not evil,
> that you may live;
and so the LORD, the God of hosts, will be with you,
> just as you have said.
Hate evil and love good,
> and establish justice in the gate;
it may be that the LORD, the God of hosts,
> will be gracious to the remnant of Joseph.

LITANY

It is not true that this world and its inhabitants are doomed to die and be lost;
This is true: For God so loved the world that he gave his only Son so that everyone who believes in him shall not die but have everlasting life.

It is not true that we must accept inhumanity and discrimination, hunger and poverty, death and destruction;
This is true: I have come that they may have life, and have it abundantly.

It is not true that violence and hatred shall have the last word, and that war and destruction have come to stay for ever.
This is true: For to us a child is born, to us a son is given, in whom authority will rest, and whose name will be Prince of Peace.

It is not true that we are simply victims of the powers of evil that seek to rule the world;
This is true: To me is given all authority in heaven and on Earth and lo, I am with you always, to the end of the world.

It is not true that we have to wait for those who are specially gifted, who are the prophets of the church, before we can do anything;
This is true: I will pour out my spirit on all people, and your sons and daughters shall prophesy, your young people shall see visions, and your old folk shall dream dreams.

It is not true that our dreams of the liberation of humankind, our dreams of justice, of human dignity, of peace, are not meant for this earth and its history;
This is true: the hour comes, and it is now, that true worshippers will worship God in spirit and in truth. *(Alan Boesak)*

REFLECTION   WENDELL BERRY

Despite its protests to the contrary, modern Christianity has become willy-nilly the religion of the state and the economic status quo. Because it has been so exclusively dedicated to incanting anemic souls into Heaven, it has been made the tool of much earthly villainy. It has, for the most part, stood silently by while a predatory economy has ravaged the world, destroyed its natural beauty and health, divided and plundered its human communities and households. It has flown the flag and chanted the slogans of empire. It has assumed with the economists that "economic forces" automatically work for good and has assumed with the industrialists and militarists that technology determines history. It has assumed with almost everybody that "progress" is good, that it is good to be modern and up with the times. It has admired Caesar and comforted him in his depredations and defaults. But in its *de facto* alliance with Caesar, Christianity connives directly with the murder of Creation. For in these days, Caesar is no longer a mere destroyer of armies, cities, and nations. He is a contradictor of the fundamental miracle of life. A part of the normal practice of his power is his willingness to destroy the world. He prays, he says, and churches everywhere compliantly pray with him. But he is praying to a God whose works he is prepared at any moment to destroy. What could be more wicked than that, or mad?

Wendell Berry (b. 1934) is an ardent voice for the restoration of a holistic biblical understanding of creation and for the reformation of our economic system on the basis that creation matters.

PRAYERS OF CONFESSION AND INTERCESSION

Lord, forgive us, for we are fragmented persons. We go many directions at once. We seek opposite goals; we serve contradictory causes. We mouth liberation; we live oppression. We shout peace; we practice violence and anarchy. We shout justice; we walk injustice. We preach love; we practice hate. Through your compassion have mercy on us and make us whole. Enable us to discern your voice among dissonant voices. **Amen.** *(Unknown writer, Philippines)*

O living God, God of all the earth, send down the Spirit of your Son Jesus Christ; heal our wounded hearts; make peace in the place of conflict; grant love in the face of revenge; build hope where fear prevailed; establish trust across our divisions. Let the light of truth disperse the shadows, and the dawn of justice banish hatred, that our lives may be saved, our lands restored, and the love of God be known in joy for all. **Amen.** *(Peter Lee)*

44. Judgment and Mercy

HYMN   HERMAN STUEMPFLE, JR.

1. O God, your justice towers above our human plain,
   while nation vies with nation in restless search of gain.
   Where lust for wealth corrupts us, God, turn our hearts again.
   Let justice roll like waters, a mighty, cleansing stream!

2. O God, your eye, unsleeping, beholds inequity,
   while we, replete with riches, grow blind to poverty.
   Correct our darkened vision until the truth we see.
   Let justice roll like waters, a mighty, cleansing stream!

3. O God, your heart is breaking where wretched millions lie,
   where people wander homeless and famished children die.
   Renew in us compassion and teach our hearts to cry:
   "Let justice roll like waters, a mighty, cleansing stream!"

4. Where evil still is coursing, a foul, defiling stream,
   fulfill among earth's people your prophet's ancient dream!
   God, stir us with your passion; this wayward world redeem,
   till justice rolls like waters, a mighty, cleansing stream!

Tune: NYLAND, 7.6.7.6.D.

Let us humble ourselves, let us strive to know the Lord, whose justice dawns like morning light, and its dawning is as sure as the sunrise. It will come to us like a shower, like spring rains that water the earth. *(Hosea 6:3)*

SOURCES

"Lord God, we come . . . ," in Anthony Coates et al., *Contemporary Prayers for Public Worship*, ed. Caryl Micklem (Grand Rapids, MI: William B. Eerdmans, 1967), 17, alt. Extract from *Contemporary Prayers for Public Worship* by Cathy Ross and Stephen B. Bevans is copyright © SCM Press 1967 and is reproduced by permission of Hymns Ancient & Modern Ltd.

Alan Boesak, presentation on the assembly theme, in *Gathered for Life: Official Report*, VI Assembly World Council of Churches, Vancouver, Canada 24 July–10 August 1983, ed. David Gill (Geneva: WCC Publications, 1983), 228–29. Used by permission of World Council of Churches.

Wendell Berry, "Christianity and the Survival of Creation," in *The Art of the Commonplace: The Agrarian Essays of Wendell Berry* (Berkeley: Counterpoint Press, 2002), 319. © 2002 by Wendell Berry. Reprinted by permission of Counterpoint Press.

"A Call to Prayer and Meditation," in *What Does the Lord Require of Us? A Discussion Guide on the Current State of National Crisis in the Philippines*, ed. and comp. Ton Alcantara et al. (Quezon City, Philippines: ATS Center for Transformation Studies, Inc. and National Council of Churches in the Philippines, 1989), 42. Used by permission of National Council of Churches in the Philippines.

Peter Lee, "O living God . . . ," in *Prayers Encircling the World: An International Anthology* (Louisville, KY: Westminster John Knox Press, 1998), 237, alt.

Herman Stuempfle, Jr., "O God, Your Justice Towers." Text: Herman G. Stuempfle, Jr., 1996. Text © 1998 Selah Publishing Co., Inc. www.selahpub.com All rights reserved. Used by permission. License no. 24641.

Hosea 6:3 from *The New English Bible*, copyright © Cambridge University Press and Oxford University Press 1961, 1970. All rights reserved.

45. DEATH AND RESURRECTION

Salmon are born in the upper reaches of rivers. The yearlings swim to the ocean where they freely roam for two to seven years. In time, they will look for their home streams and begin the arduous journey back, sometimes swimming one thousand miles upstream. Those who make it will spawn their eggs in gravel pools and usually die shortly thereafter. The eternal cycle of death and resurrection continues.

They shall come and sing aloud on the height of Zion,
>and they shall be radiant over the goodness of the Lord,
over the grain, the wine, and the oil,
>and over the young of the flock and the herd;
their life shall become like a watered garden,
>and they shall never languish again. *(Jeremiah 31:12)*

PRAYERS OF PRAISE AND THANKSGIVING

God, our Creator, we celebrate with all life. Help us to see your presence, not only in human history but also in the stories of our kin in creation, the great community of life. Teach us to hear the good news of God's loving care ringing through human beings and the creatures of the wild. Rejoice with us as we behold the mysteries of your Wisdom implanted in all life. In the name of Christ who fills heaven and Earth. **Amen.** *(Season of Creation)*

O God, intimate and fearful, who carried us with tenderness within our mother's womb; who appointed us to speak when we were yet unborn: touch our mouths with your truth, and take away our fear, that we may find relief from our suffering and discern your love. Let the whole world see and know that things which were cast down have been raised up, and things which had grown old have been made new. **Amen.** *(Janet Morley)*

CANTICLE   ECCLESIASTES 3:1-8

For everything there is a season, and a time for every matter under heaven:
a time to be born, and a time to die;
a time to plant, and a time to pluck up what is planted;
a time to kill, and a time to heal;
a time to break down, and a time to build up;
a time to weep, and a time to laugh;
a time to mourn, and a time to dance;
a time to throw away stones, and a time to gather stones together;
a time to embrace, and a time to refrain from embracing;
a time to seek, and a time to lose;
a time to keep, and a time to throw away;
a time to tear, and a time to sew;
a time to keep silence, and a time to speak;
a time to love, and a time to hate;
a time for war, and a time for peace.

SCRIPTURE   EZEKIEL 37:7-14 AND JOHN 5:24-28

1. I prophesied as I had been commanded; and as I prophesied, suddenly there was a noise, a rattling, and the bones came together, bone to its bone. I looked, and there were sinews on them, and flesh had come upon them, and skin had covered them; but there was no breath in them. Then he said to me, "Prophesy to the breath, prophesy, mortal, and say to the breath: Thus says the Lord God: Come from the four winds, O breath, and breathe upon these slain, that they may live." I prophesied as he commanded me, and the breath came into them, and they lived, and stood on their feet, a vast multitude.

Then he said to me, "Mortal, these bones are the whole house of Israel. They say, 'Our bones are dried up, and our hope is lost; we are cut off completely.' Therefore prophesy, and say to them, Thus says the Lord God: I am going to open your graves, and bring you up from your graves, O my people; and I will bring you back to the land of Israel. And you shall know that I am the Lord, when I open your graves, and bring you up from your graves, O my people. I will put my spirit within you, and you shall live, and I will place you on your own soil; then you shall know that I, the Lord, have spoken and will act, says the Lord."

2. Very truly, I tell you, anyone who hears my word and believes him who sent me has eternal life, and does not come under judgment, but has passed from death to life.

"Very truly, I tell you, the hour is coming, and is now here, when the dead will hear the voice of the Son of God, and those who hear will live. For just as the Father has life in himself, so he has granted the Son also to have life in himself; and he has given him authority to execute judgment, because he is the Son of Man. Do not be astonished at this; for the hour is coming when all who are in their graves will hear his voice."

LITANY

I am Christ, the pioneer and perfecter of your faith;
The beginning and the end.

The atom and the universe;
The one and the many.

The birth and the death;
The rise and the fall.

The dawn and the dusk;
The spring and the winter;

The rain and the rainbow;
The seed and the harvest.

The quest and the return;
The dream and the remembrance.

The foundation and the spire;
The promise and the fulfillment.

The baptism and the requiem;
The silence and the word.

I am the Alpha and the Omega, who is and was and is to come:
Life forevermore! *(Phyllis Cole and Everett Tilson)*

REFLECTION   JOHN MUIR

One is constantly reminded of the infinite lavishness and fertility of Nature—inexhaustible abundance amid what seems enormous waste. And yet when we look into any of her operations that lie within reach of our minds, we learn that no particle of her material is wasted or worn out. It is eternally flowing from use to use, beauty to yet higher beauty; and we soon cease to lament waste and death, and rather rejoice and exult in the imperishable, unspendable wealth of the universe, and faithfully watch and wait for the reappearance of everything that melts and fades and dies about us, feeling sure that its next appearance will be better and more beautiful than the last.

No single American has done more to preserve our wilderness than John Muir (1838–1914), the Scottish-born naturalist and founder of the Sierra Club. Muir had already become the most ardent defender of the American wilderness by 1903 when he guided President Theodore Roosevelt on a three-day camping trip in Yosemite. As a result of this trip, Roosevelt went on to establish 148 million acres of national forest, five national parks, and twenty-three national monuments during his years in office.

PRAYERS OF CONFESSION AND INTERCESSION

Great God of the Universe, ruler of ages and atoms, of time and destiny, of cells and cyclones, of plankton and panther, who cares equally for the sequoia of a thousand years and the insect that lives less than a day—we confess our shortsighted vision, the narrowness of our love and care and our failure to understand the eternal cycles of life.

We have grieved over the deaths of beloved family members but ignored the extinction of species and the slowly dying oceans and all their creatures. We have sought to prolong some human life at the expense of the lives of other beings. We have bulldozed mountaintops and dug up your sacred earth, forgetting that the earth itself is living matter and home to innumerable species. We have polluted the sky around us and the birds that inhabit it.

Help us, we pray, to enlarge the range of our love, to quicken our passion for the wellbeing of all life. Help us to appreciate that death is essential to life, and that in dying all of creation and all of your beloved creatures are transformed to new life. **Amen.** *(Anne Rowthorn)*

Lord, help us to see in the groaning of creation not death throes but birth pangs; help us to see in suffering a promise for the future, because it is a cry against the inhumanity of the present. Help us to glimpse in protest the dawn of justice, in the Cross the pathway to resurrection, and in suffering the seeds of joy. **Amen.** *(Rubem Alves)*

HYMN   JOHN MACLEOD CAMPBELL CRUM

1. Now the green blade rises from the buried grain,
   wheat that in the dark earth many years has lain;
   love lives again, that with the dead has been:
   Love is come again, like wheat that springs up green.

2. In the grave they laid him, Love whom we had slain,
   thinking that he'd never wake to life again,
   laid in the earth like grain that sleeps unseen:
   Love is come again, like wheat that springs up green.

3. Up he sprang at Easter, like the risen grain,
   he that for three days in the grave had lain;
   up from the dead my risen Lord is seen:
   Love is come again, like wheat that springs up green.

4. When our hearts are saddened, grieving or in pain,
   by your touch you call us back to life again;
   fields of our hearts that dead and bare have been:
   Love is come again, like wheat that springs up green.

   Tune: NOEL NOUVELET, 11.10.10.11.

> When you pass through the waters, I will be with you;
>   and through the rivers, they shall not overwhelm you;
> when you walk through fire you shall not be burned,
>   and the flame shall not consume you. *(Isaiah 43:2)*

SOURCES

"God, our Creator . . . ," in "Fauna Sunday," Australian Version 1, *Season of Creation*, accessed May 12, 2016, https://seasonofcreation.com/wp-content/uploads/2010/04/liturgy-fauna-sunday-1.pdf, alt. © Season of Creation, developed by Norm Habel and the Uniting Church in Australia, Synod of Victoria and Tasmania, 2004, seasonofcreation.com, used with permission.

Janet Morley, "O God, intimate and fearful . . . ," in *All Desires Known*, 3rd ed. (Harrisburg, PA: Morehouse, 2006), 80–81. *All Desires Known*, 3rd edition © 2006 the Morehouse Publishing. Used by permission of Church Publishing Incorporated, New York, NY.

Phyllis Cole and Everett Tilson, "I Am Christ," in *Litanies and Other Prayers for the Revised Common Lectionary: Year B* (Nashville: Abingdon Press, 1993), 174–75, alt. © 2003 Abingdon Press. Used by permission. All rights reserved.

John Muir, *My First Summer in the Sierra* (Boston: Houghton Mifflin, 1911), 168. Public domain.

Anne Rowthorn, "We Confess Our Failure in Understanding Eternal Cycles of Life and Death," © 2016 Anne Rowthorn.

Rubem Alves, "Lord: Help us to see . . . ," in *Bread of Tomorrow*, ed. Janet Morley (Maryknoll, NY: Orbis Books, 2004), 101. Originally published in British Council of Churches, *All Year Round* (1987). Used by permission of Churches Together in Britain and Ireland.

John Macleod Campbell Crum, "Love Is Come Again," in *The Oxford Book of Carols*, ed. Percy Dearmer, R. Vaughan Williams, and Martin Shaw (London: Oxford University Press, 1964), 306–307, alt. "Now the green blade riseth" by J M C Crum (1872–1958) [altd]. Reproduced by permission of Oxford University Press. All rights reserved.

Hope and the Future

46. ECOLOGICAL CONVERSION

Whether Christian, Jain, Buddhist, Muslim, or a follower of an indigenous religious tradition, everyone needs two conversions: a conversion to God, and a conversion to God's magnificent natural world. Such a double conversion would touch the mind, the heart, and the soul to serve God in the human community, and would become a lens through which to see God revealed through the splendor of creation.

You shall go out in joy,
>and be led back in peace;
the mountains and hills before you
>shall burst into song,
>and all the trees of the field shall clap their hands. *(Isaiah 55:12)*

PRAYERS OF PRAISE AND THANKSGIVING

O Lord our God and Creator of all, we thank you for the beauty of creation; show us, we pray, how to respect the fragile balance of life. Guide by your wisdom those who have power to care for or to destroy the environment, that by the decisions they make life may be cherished and a good and fruitful earth be preserved for future generations; through Jesus Christ our Lord. **Amen.** *(Anglican Church in Kenya)*

Rejoice in the Creator who sustains the earth and each of us. Rejoice for the clouds that protect us from the sun, for the thunder at which the earth trembles, for lightning that splits the sky. Rejoice for the rain that falls by night and soaks the ground, causing dry roots to swell and the deep cracks in the earth to close. Rejoice for cool nights, budding flowers, the flourishing of trees and the tender, green grass. Rejoice for the great showers that fall at midday, for the small streams singing on their way from the hills into the valleys, making the rivers roar, filling the reservoirs and supplying cities and irrigation channels with water. Rejoice for the fruitfulness of the earth, for seeds planted in expectation and for the hope that comes with every new harvest. Rejoice and praise God who sustains the earth and each of us. **Amen.** *(Author unknown)*

PSALM 36:5-9

Your steadfast love, O Lord, extends to the heavens,
    your faithfulness to the clouds.
Your righteousness is like the mighty mountains,
    your judgments are like the great deep;
    you save humans and animals alike, O Lord.

How precious is your steadfast love, O God!
    All people may take refuge in the shadow of your wings.
They feast on the abundance of your house,
    and you give them drink from the river of your delights.
For with you is the fountain of life;
    in your light we see light.

PSALM 19:7-10, 14

The law of the Lord is perfect,
    reviving the soul;
the decrees of the Lord are sure,
    making wise the simple;
the precepts of the Lord are right,
    rejoicing the heart;
the commandment of the Lord is clear,
    enlightening the eyes;
the fear of the Lord is pure,
    enduring forever;
the ordinances of the Lord are true
    and righteous altogether.
More to be desired are they than gold,
    even much fine gold;
sweeter also than honey,
    and drippings of the honeycomb. . . .

Let the words of my mouth and the meditation of my heart
> be acceptable to you,
>> O Lord, my rock and my redeemer.

SCRIPTURE   ZEPHANIAH 3:9-13

I will change the speech of the peoples
> to a pure speech,
that all of them may call on the name of the Lord
> and serve him with one accord.
From beyond the rivers of Ethiopia
> my suppliants, my scattered ones,
>> shall bring my offering.

On that day you shall not be put to shame
> because of all the deeds by which you have rebelled against me;
for then I will remove from your midst
> your proudly exultant ones
and you shall no longer be haughty
> in my holy mountain.
For I will leave in the midst of you
> a people humble and lowly.
They shall seek refuge in the name of the Lord—
> the remnant of Israel;
they shall do no wrong
> and utter no lies,
nor shall a deceitful tongue
> be found in their mouths.
Then they will pasture and lie down,
> and no one shall make them afraid.

LITANY

We give you thanks and praise, O God of creation, for the grandeur of all that you have made, saying,
We thank you, God.

For the healing waters of creation, which bring pleasure and health, purity and life,
We thank you, God.

For the richness of the good Earth that brings forth fruits and flowers, a pleasure to taste and a joy to behold,
We thank you, God.

For the soaring birds of the air, the crawling creatures on the Earth, the gliding fish in the seas, for all creatures great and small with whom we share this precious web of life,
We thank you, God.

For the invigorating sunlight of day, the deepening mystery of night, the wonder of the stars, and the call of the unknown in the universe,
We thank you, God.

From heedless misuse and dishonoring of the wonders of your hand,
Good Lord, deliver us.

From squandering resources, abusing our companion species, and polluting the habitat we all share,
Good Lord, deliver us.

From the folly of imagining ourselves free from the fate of your whole creation,
Good Lord, deliver us.

For the courage and wisdom to confess how little we have cared for your gifts,
Strengthen us, O Spirit.

For the conviction that you have called us to love and restore the Earth,
Strengthen us, O Spirit.

For repentance and the determination to begin our stewardship anew,
Strengthen us, O Spirit. *(St. Thomas Episcopal Church, Medina, Washington)*

REFLECTION   POPE FRANCIS

The ecological crisis is a summons to profound interior conversion. All [are in need of] an "ecological conversion." Living our vocation to be protectors of God's handiwork is essential to a life of virtue; it is not an optional or a secondary aspect of our Christian experience. The ecological conversion needed to bring about lasting change is also a community conversion.

This conversion calls for a number of attitudes which together foster a spirit of generous care, full of tenderness. First, it entails gratitude, a recognition that the world is God's loving gift, and that we are called quietly to imitate his generosity in self-sacrifice and good works: "Do not let your left hand know what your right hand is doing and your Father who sees in secret will reward you" (Mt 6:3-4). It also entails a loving awareness that we are not disconnected from the rest of creatures, but joined in a splendid universal communion. As believers, we do not look at the world from without but from within, conscious of the bonds with which the Father has linked us to all beings. By developing our individual, God-given capacities, an ecological conversion can inspire us to greater creativity and enthusiasm in resolving the world's problems and in offering ourselves to God "as a living sacrifice, holy and acceptable" (Rom 12:1).

In Laudato Si', *Pope Francis makes clear his conviction that our only viable future is a shared future, that creation is a continuous revelation of the divine, and that we all need an "ecological conversion."*

PRAYERS OF CONFESSION AND INTERCESSION

Lord, your word gave us this marvelous creation. Forgive us for what we have done to it and for what we have not done to protect it. Empower our re-creative work to restore the joy, the exuberance, and the promise of your abundance. **Amen.** *(Jim Drury)*

We thank you, God of the sun and the moon; of the mountains, deserts and plains; God of the mighty oceans, of rivers, lakes and streams; God of all creatures that live in the seas and fly in the air; God of every living thing that grows and moves on this sacred Earth: Help us to love and respect all of creation, to repair what we have damaged, to care for what you have made good and holy. Give us the wisdom and the passion to change our minds and hearts and our ways. Let us be mustard seeds in our world, bringing about ecological conversion which grows and spreads to every corner of the earth for our sake now and for every generation which is to come. We ask this through Christ, our Lord. **Amen.** *(Catholic Earthcare Australia)*

HYMN   FRED PRATT GREEN

1. God out of love for us lent us this planet,
   gave it a purpose in time and in space;
   small as a spark from the fire of creation,
   cradle of life and the home of our race.

2. Thanks be to God for its bounty and beauty,
   life that sustains us in body and mind:
   plenty for all, if we learn how to share it,
   riches undreamed of to fathom and find.

3. Long have our human wars ruined its harvest;
   long has earth bowed to the terror of force.
   Now we pollute it, in cynical silence,
   poison the fountain of life at its source.

4. Casual despoilers, or high priests of Mammon
   selling the future for present rewards,
   careless of life and contemptuous of beauty;
   bid them remember the Earth is the Lord's.

5. Earth is the Lord's: it is ours to enjoy it,
   ours, as God's stewards, to farm and defend.
   From its pollution, misuse and destruction,
   good Lord, deliver us, world without end!

Tunes: ECOLOGY or WAS LEBET, 11.10.11.10.
Words © 1973 The Hymn Society (admin. Hope Publishing)

May all roads lead us home on the trail of peace. Happily may we all return. In beauty we walk. With beauty before us, we walk. With beauty behind us, we walk. With beauty above and about us we walk. It is finished in beauty. It is finished in beauty. *(Navajo Night Chant)*

SOURCES

"For the Environment," in Anglican Church in Kenya, *Our Modern Services* (Nairobi, Kenya: Uzima Press, 2003), 289.

Inspired by, "Rejoice in the Lord," a creation prayer from Africa, in *Sinfonia Oecumenica: Worship With the Churches in the World* (Basel, Switzerland: Gütersloher Verlagshaus, 1998), 844–45.

"We give you thanks . . ." in *Interfaith Worship Resources on Earth Stewardship* (n.p.: Sustainable Sanctuary Coalition, 2014), 12–13, last modified May 2014, https://www.ohipl.org/wp-content/uploads/2012/04/Worship-Resources-May-2014.pdf. Attributed to St. Thomas Episcopal Church, Medina, Washington.

Pope Francis, *Laudato Si'*, accessed December 1, 2017, Vatican.va, 217, 219, and 220. © Libreria Editrice Vaticana. Used by permission.

Jim Drury, "This Marvelous Creation," in *Bread for the Day: Daily Bible Readings and Prayers 2016* (Minneapolis: Augsburg Fortress, 2016), 349. Used by permission.

"Prayer for Ecological Conversion," Creation We Care, Brisbane Catholic Education, accessed October 13, 2017, http://www.bne.catholic.edu.au/creationwecare/Pages/CatholicTradition.aspx. Adapted from Catholic Earthcare Launch 2002.

Words by Fred Pratt Green, "God Out of Love for Us Lent Us this Planet" © 1973 The Hymn Society (admin. Hope Publishing Company, Carol Stream, IL 60188). All rights reserved. Used by permission.

"A Prayer of the Second Day of the Night Chant," in Washington Matthews, *Navajo Myths, Prayers, and Songs with Text and Translations*, ed. Pliny Earle Goddard (Berkeley: University of California Press, 1907), 48–49, alt. Public domain.

47. ACTION

Do something! Just like Martin Luther King, Jr., Dorothy Day, Wangari Maathai, Mother Teresa, Oscar Romero, Rigoberta Manchú, Chico Mendez, Malala Yousafzai, Berta Cácares, the Chipko women, Robert Kennedy. All these, and countless others, have acted for the sake of God's people and God's holy earth. Some of them lost their lives doing so.

My children, love must not be a matter of words or talk; it must be genuine, and show itself in action. *(1 John 3:18)*

PRAYERS OF PRAISE AND THANKSGIVING

Loving God, we thank you for the multitude of your faithful people throughout the ages who have mirrored your love in action at great cost to themselves. Now we come to you in our need. Create in us an awareness of the massive forces that threaten our world today. Give us a sense of urgency to activate the forces of goodness, of justice, of love and of peace. Where there is armed conflict, let us stretch our arms to our brothers and sisters. Where there is abundance, let there be simple lifestyles and sharing. Where there is poverty, let there be dignified living and constant striving for just structures. Where there are wounds of division, let there be unity and wholeness. Help us to be committed to building your kingdom—not seeking to be cared for but to care; not expecting to be served, but to place ourselves at the service of others; not aspiring to be materially secure, but to place our security in your love. Give us your spirit, for only in loving imitation of you can we discover the healing springs of life that will bring new birth to our world. **Amen.** *(Unknown author)*

We thank you, Lord, changing our words into action, our good intentions into commitment, our trackless wanderings into a pilgrimage. Lead us out to our brothers and sisters who need us the most, that we may catch their sense of urgency, share their courage against sin and corruption, their strength against oppression. **Amen.** *(United Reformed Church)*

PSALM 10:12-15, 17-18

Rise up, O Lord; O God, lift up your hand;
    do not forget the oppressed.
Why do the wicked renounce God,
    and say in their hearts, 'You will not call us to account'?

But you do see! Indeed you note trouble and grief,
    that you may take it into your hands;
the helpless commit themselves to you;
    you have been the helper of the orphan.

Break the arm of the wicked and evildoers;
    seek out their wickedness until you find none. . . .

O Lord, you will hear the desire of the meek;
    you will strengthen their heart, you will incline your ear
to do justice for the orphan and the oppressed,
    so that those from earth may strike terror no more.

SCRIPTURE   JAMES 2:5-8, 14-18

Listen, my beloved brothers and sisters. Has not God chosen the poor in the world to be rich in faith and to be heirs of the kingdom that he has promised to those who love him? But you have dishonored the poor. Is it not the rich who oppress you? Is it not they who drag you into court? Is it not they who blaspheme the excellent name that was invoked over you?

    You do well if you really fulfill the royal law according to the scripture, "You shall love your neighbor as yourself." . . . What good is it, my brothers and sisters, if you say you have faith but do not have works? Can faith save you? If a brother or sister is naked and lacks daily food, and one of you says to them, "Go in peace; keep warm and eat your fill," and yet you do not supply their bodily needs, what is the good of that? So faith by itself, if it has no works, is dead.

    But someone will say, "You have faith and I have works." Show me your faith apart from your works, and I by my works will show you my faith.

LITANY

For everything there is a season,
And a time for every matter under heaven.

Therefore, if this is a time to be born, let us emerge from the womb with a cry;
If this is a time to die, let us say farewell with a smile.

If this is a time to plant, let us scatter the seed with a prayer;
If this is a time to harvest, let us reap the grain with a song.

If this is a time to break down, let us topple the walls with a shout.
If this is a time to build up, let us raise the foundation with care.

If this is a time to mourn, let us catch the tears with a chalice;
If this is a time to dance, let us leap the moon with a laugh.

If this is a time to embrace, let us wrap the world with a ribbon;
If this is a time to stand alone, let us face the crowd with a mirror.

If this is a time to remain silent, let us proclaim the truth with a deed;
If this is a time to speak, let us counsel the words with the heart.

If this is a time to do battle, let us sustain the weak with a vision;
If this is a time to make peace, let us anoint the wounds with a balm.

For everything there is a season,
And a time for every matter under heaven; O Lord, teach us to know the times! *(Phyllis Cole and Everett Tilson)*

REFLECTION   ROBERT F. KENNEDY

Let no one be discouraged by the belief there is nothing one man or one woman can do against the enormous array of the world's ills—against misery and ignorance, injustice and violence. Few will have the greatness to bend history itself; but each of us can work to change a small portion of events, and in the total of all those acts will be written the history of this generation.

It is from the numberless diverse acts of courage and belief that human history is shaped. Each time a man stands up for an ideal, or acts to improve the lot of others, or strikes out against injustice, he sends a tiny ripple of hope, and crossing each other from a million different centers of energy and daring, those ripples build a current which can sweep down the mightiest walls of oppression and resistance.

Robert F. Kennedy (1925–1968), brother of President John F. Kennedy, worked tirelessly to address the issues of the poor and dispossessed in the United States. From urban ghettos to Indian reservations, from migrant workers' camps to the people of Appalachia and the Mississippi Delta, Robert Kennedy as attorney general of the United States sought to alleviate the problems of poverty in all its forms through legislation. Sadly, a bullet in a Los Angeles hotel on June 5, 1968, cut short his life and his brilliant career.

PRAYERS OF CONFESSION AND INTERCESSION

Holy God, in your gracious presence we confess our sin and the sin of this world. Although Christ is among us as liberation and peace, we are a people divided against ourselves, as we cling to the values of a broken world. The profit and pleasure we pursue lay waste the land and pollute the seas. The fears and jealousies that we harbor set neighbor against neighbor, and nation against nation. We abuse your gifts of imagination and freedom, of intellect and reason, and have turned them into bonds of oppression. Heal and forgive us. Set us free to serve you in the world as agents of your reconciling love. **Amen.** *(Presbyterian Church in Canada)*

Dear God, as we think of Jesus, we think not just of prayer and quiet retreat but of a life of action, of tables overturned, of lives touched and healed, endless walks through arid deserts to the next place of hurt and need. And as we consider our troubled, torn planet, even now on the brink of yet more death and destruction, stir us, we pray, to work for the transforming of this beautiful world. We pray for justice for those oppressed by tyrants, and for justice for those whose lives, even now, are blighted by endless forgotten wars. Give us wisdom, guide our actions. Make us fearless and passionate for the earth and all its suffering people. **Amen.** *(Iona Community)*

HYMN   CARL P. DAW, JR.

1. Till all the jails are empty and all the bellies filled,
   till no one hurts or steals or lies, and no more blood is spilled,
   till age and race and gender no longer separate,
   till pulpit, press and politics are free of greed and hate:

   Refrain: God has work for us to do.

2. In tenement and mansion, in factory, farm and mill,
   in board-room and in billiard hall, in wards where time stands still,
   in classroom, church and office, in shops or on the street;
   in every place where people thrive or starve or hide or meet:

   Refrain: God has work for us to do.

3. By sitting at a bedside to hold pale trembling hands,
   by speaking for the powerless against unjust demands,
   by praying through our doing and singing though we fear,
   by trusting that the seed we sow will bring God's harvest near:

   Refrain: God has work for us to do.

Tune: WORK TO DO, 7.6.7.6.D. and Refrain
Words © 1996 Hope Publishing

Go in peace: The wisdom of the Wonderful Counselor guide you, the strength of the Mighty God uphold you, the love of the Everlasting Father enfold you, the peace of the Prince of Peace be upon you. And the blessing of God, Father, Son and Holy Spirit, be upon you now and forevermore.
(Armenian Orthodox Church)

SOURCES

1 John 3:18 from *The New English Bible*, copyright © Cambridge University Press and Oxford University Press 1961, 1970. All rights reserved.

"Loving God, we thank you . . . ," in *Prayer without Borders: Celebrating Global Wisdom*, ed. Barbara Ballenger (Baltimore: Catholic Relief Services, 2004), 70, alt. Author unknown.

"Lord, change our Christianity . . . ," in *Encounters: Prayer Handbook 1988*, ed. Edmund Banyard (London: United Reformed Church, 1987), alt. © 1987, United Reformed Church Prayer Handbook 1988 Edition, United Reformed Church. Used by permission.

Phyllis Cole and Everett Tilson, "For Everything There Is a Season," in *Litanies and Other Prayers for the Revised Common Lectionary: Year B* (Nashville: Abingdon Press, 1993), 177–78. © 2003 Abingdon Press. Used by permission. All rights reserved.

Robert F. Kennedy, "June 6, 1966: Keynote Address: Day of Reaffirmation of Academic and Human Freedom (Cape Town, South Africa)," in *Classic Speeches 1830–1993: The Senate, 1789–1989*, ser. ed. Robert C. Byrd, vol. ed. Wendy Wolff, Bicentennial ed. (Washington, DC: U.S. Government Printing Office, 1994), 3:717, alt.

"Holy God, in your gracious presence . . . ," in Presbyterian Church in Canada, *Book of Common Worship* ([Don Mills, Ont.]: Presbyterian Church in Canada, 1991), 28, alt. © Presbyterian Church in Canada, used by permission.

Iona Community Resident Group, "A Call to Commitment and Action," in "Worship in a Time of War: Resources from Iona," in *Holy Ground: Liturgies and Worship Resources for an Engaged Spirituality*, ed. Neil Paynter and Helen Boothroyd (Glasgow: Wild Goose, 2005), 267, alt. © Contributors, *Holy Ground* (2005), Wild Goose Publications, Glasgow. Used by permission.

Words by Carl P. Daw, Jr. "Till All the Jails Are Empty" © 1996 Hope Publishing Company, Carol Stream, IL 60188. All rights reserved. Used by permission.

"Go in Peace," in *Timeless Prayers for Peace: Voices Together from around the World*, ed. Geoffrey Duncan (Cleveland: Pilgrim Press, 2003), 294. © Armenian Orthodox Church.

48. SCIENCE

How do we understand the earth and its place in the universe? How do we know its age and how it has changed over millennia? How do we know about climate cycles and the acid content of sea and sky? How can we measure what benefits and what harms the earth? Science minimizes bias, provides measurable data, and enables us to understand our world. What we do with this knowledge is up to us.

Blessed is God's name from age to age, for to God belongs wisdom and power! God changes the seasons and the times; God gives wisdom to the wise, and knowledge to those who have discernment. God reveals all mysteries! *(Daniel 2:20-22a)*

PRAYERS OF PRAISE AND THANKSGIVING

The outpouring of the Holy Spirit enlightens the thoughts of artists, poets and scientists. Their great minds receive from you prophetic insights into your laws, and reveal to us the depth of your creative wisdom. How great you are in all that you have created, how great you are in the people of earth! Glory to you, showing your unfathomable might in the laws of the universe! Glory to you, for all nature is permeated by your laws. Glory to you for what you have revealed to us in your goodness. Glory to you for all that remains hidden from us in your wisdom. Glory to you for the inventiveness of the human mind. Glory to you for the invigorating effort of work. Glory to you for the tongues of fire which bring inspiration. Glory to you, O Holy God, from age to age. **Amen.** *(Metropolitan Tryphon)*

O God, we thank you for this universe, our great home; for its vastness and its riches, and for the manifoldness of the life which teems upon it and of which we are a part. We praise you for the arching sky and the blessed winds, for the driving clouds and the constellations on high. We praise you for the salt sea and the running water, for the everlasting hills, for the trees, and for the grass under our feet. We thank you for our senses by which we can see the splendor of the morning, and hear the jubilant songs of love, and smell the breath of the springtime. Grant us, we pray, a heart wide open to all this joy and beauty, and save our souls from being so steeped in care or so darkened by passion that we pass heedless and unseeing when even the thorn-bush by the wayside is aflame with the glory of God. ***Amen.*** *(Walter Rauschenbusch)*

PSALM 19:1-4

The heavens are telling the glory of God;
> and the firmament proclaims his handiwork.

Day to day pours forth speech,
> **and night to night declares knowledge.**

There is no speech, nor are there words;
> their voice is not heard;

yet their voice goes out through all the earth,
> **and their words to the end of the world.**

PSALM 104:25-31

Yonder is the sea, great and wide,
> **creeping things innumerable are there,**
> **living things both small and great.**

There go the ships,
> and Leviathan that you formed to sport in it.

These all look to you
> **to give them their food in due season;**

when you give to them, they gather it up;
> **when you open your hand, they are filled with good things.**

When you hide your face, they are dismayed;
> when you take away their breath, they die
> and return to their dust.

When you send forth your spirit, they are created;
> **and you renew the face of the ground.**

May the glory of the LORD endure forever;
> **may the LORD rejoice in all his works.**

SCRIPTURE   JOEL 2:23-24, 26-28

O children of Zion, be glad
    and rejoice in the LORD your God;
for he has given the early rain for your vindication,
    he has poured down for you abundant rain,
    the early and the later rain, as before.
The threshing-floors shall be full of grain,
    the vats shall overflow with wine and oil. . . .
You shall eat in plenty and be satisfied,
    and praise the name of the Lord your God,
    who has dealt wondrously with you.
And my people shall never again be put to shame.
You shall know that I am in the midst of Israel,
    and that I, the Lord, am your God and there is no other.
And my people shall never again be put to shame.
    Then afterward
    I will pour out my spirit on all flesh;
your sons and your daughters shall prophesy,
    your old men shall dream dreams,
    and your young men shall see visions.

LITANY

Cosmic Christ, your presence fills the cosmos. Your presence pulses through all galactic space across light years of time.
Living Christ, make your presence felt among us.

We invite the cosmos to worship with us.
We invite glittering galaxies high in the sky to radiate the splendor of God's presence.

We call distant domains of space to celebrate with us.
We invite nebula, nova and black holes to thank God for their fascinating formation.

We summon that piece of stardust called Earth,
To pulse with the rhythm of God's presence and celebrate God's glory in this planet garden.

We invite millions of living species to dance with life,
The turtle, the toad and the elephant, the earthworm, the ant and the dragonfly.

We invite every creature in the web of creation to connect with others in this community called the cosmos.
Dance, creation, dance! Dance with cosmic energy! *(Season of Creation)*

REFLECTION   MARY EVELYN TUCKER AND BRIAN SWIMME

Over the past century, science has begun to weave together the story of a historical cosmos that emerged some 13.7 billion years ago. The magnitude of this universe story is beginning to dawn on humans as we awaken to a new realization of the vastness and complexity of this unfolding process. What is humankind in relation to this 13.7 billion years of universe history? What is our place in the framework of 4.6 billion years of Earth history? How can we foster the stability and integrity of the life process? These are critical questions underlying the new consciousness of the universe story. This is not simply a dynamic narrative of evolution; it is a transformative cosmological story which engages human energy for a future that is sustaining and sustainable. The goal of the universe story is to tell the story of cosmic and Earth evolution by drawing on the latest scientific knowledge in a way that makes it both relevant and moving. What emerges is an intensely poetic story that evokes emotions of awe and excitement, fear and joy, belonging and responsibility. A great transition is upon us that beckons the sense of a larger planetary whole—an emerging, multiform, planetary civilization. It requires a profound change of consciousness and values—both an expanded worldview of the universe story and a comprehensive global ethic that embraces the Earth community.

Brian Swimme (b. 1950), an evolutionary philosopher, and Mary Evelyn Tucker (b. 1949), a historian of religions and co-founder and co-director of the Forum on Religion and Ecology at Yale University, have collaborated on the book The Journey of the Universe *(Yale University Press, 2011). They draw together insights from science, cosmology, religion, and philosophy to expand our understanding of the evolutionary process. Their goal is to awaken a renewed sense of awe and gratitude for the uniqueness of the universe. It is a plea to act responsibly as global ecosystems rapidly unravel.*

PRAYERS OF CONFESSION AND INTERCESSION

God of all mercy, we confess that we have sinned against you, opposing your will in our lives. We have denied your goodness in each other, in ourselves, and in the world you have created. We repent of the evil that enslaves us, the evil we have done, and the evil done on our behalf. Forgive, restore, and strengthen us through our Savior Jesus Christ, that we may abide in your love and serve only your will. **Amen.** *(The Episcopal Church)*

Mysterious God, whose imagination and desire embrace all: We seek to discern you in the interplay of forces, in the order and the chaos of the universe, and in the complexities of every living system. Give us grace to honor your goodness in what we know and in what we do not know, in the world's harmonies and turbulence, and in its promise and change. For you are in, through, and beyond all that is: one God, made known to us in Jesus Christ, through the Holy Spirit, our inspiration and guide. **Amen.** *(The Episcopal Church)*

48. Science

HYMN — THOMAS H. TROEGER

1. Praise the Source of faith and learning
that has sparked and stoked the mind
with a passion for discerning
how the world has been designed.
Let the sense of wonder flowing
from the wonders we survey
keep our faith forever growing
and renew our need to pray.

2. God of wisdom, we acknowledge
that our science and our art
and the breadth of human knowledge
only partial truth impart.
Far beyond our calculation
lies a depth we cannot sound
where your purpose for creation
and the pulse of life are found.

3. May our faith redeem the blunder
of believing that our thought
has displaced the grounds for wonder
which the ancient prophets taught.
May our learning curb the error
which unthinking faith can breed
lest we justify some terror
with an antiquated creed.

4. As two currents in a river
fight each other's undertow,
till converging they deliver
one coherent steady flow,
blend, O God, our faith and learning
till they carve a single course,
till they join as one, returning
praise and thanks to you, their Source.

Tune: HYFRYDOL, 8.7.8.7.D.

The God who creates the cheetah and provides for its needs, the Spirit who breathes life into us and animates our living, the Word who is creating all life each moment, each day, guide you, feed you, protect and inspire you this day. *(Sam Hamilton-Poore)*

SOURCES

Daniel 2:20-22a from *The Inclusive Bible* (Landham, MD: Rowman & Littlefield, 2007). A Sheed & Ward Book published by Rowman & Littlefield Publishers, Inc. All rights reserved. Used by permission.

Metropolitan Tryphon [Prince Boris Petrovich Turkestanov], Ikos 7 of "An Akathist in Praise of God's Creation," in *SYNDESMOS Orthodoxy and Ecology Resource Book,* Annex 1, *Orthodox Services for the Creation*, ed. Alexander Belopopsky and Dmitri Oikonomou (Bialystok, Poland: Orthdruk Orthodox Printing House, 1996), 20–25, alt.

Walter Rauschenbusch, "For This World," in *For God and the People: Prayers of the Social Awakening* (Boston: Pilgrim Press, 1910), 47–48, alt. Public domain.

"Risen Christ . . . ," and "We invite the cosmos . . . ," in "Cosmos Sunday," Australian Version 1, *Season of Creation*, accessed May 12, 2016, https://seasonofcreation.com/wp-content/uploads/2010/04/liturgy-cosmos-sunday-1.pdf, alt. © Season of Creation, developed by Norm Habel and the Uniting Church in Australia, Synod of Victoria and Tasmania, 2004, seasonofcreation.com, used with permission.

Mary Evelyn Tucker and Brian Swimme, "The Universe Story and Planetary Civilization," in *Moral Ground: Ethical Action for a Planet in Peril*, ed. Kathleen Dean Moore and Michael P. Nelson (San Antonio: Trinity University Press, 2010), 412, 415, 416. Used by permission.

"God of all mercy . . . ," in Episcopal Church, *Enriching Our Worship 1* (New York: Church Publishing, 1998), 56. *Enriching Our Worship*, alt © 1998 the Church Publishing Incorporated. Used by permission of Church Publishing Incorporated, New York, NY.

"God of Order and Dynamic Change," in Standing Commission on Liturgy and Music, "Liturgical Materials Honoring God in Creation and Various Rites and Prayers for Animals," in *Report to the 77th General Convention* (Episcopal Church, July 5–12, 2012), 319.

"Praise the source of faith and learning" by Thomas Troeger © Oxford University Press Inc., 1986. Assigned to Oxford University Press, 2010. Reproduced by permission. All rights reserved.

Sam Hamilton-Poore, "The God who creates . . . ," in *Earth Gospel: A Guide to Prayer for God's Creation* (Nashville: Upper Room Books, 2008), 27. Reprinted from *Earth Gospel: A Guide to Prayer for God's Creation* by Sam Hamilton-Poore. Copyright © 2008. Used by permission of Upper Room Books. bookstore.upperroom.org.

49. HEALING OUR NATION

How beautiful are our spacious skies, amber waves of grain, majestic purple mountains, blooming deserts, verdant forests, rushing streams, rural towns, steel and alabaster cities. May all our strife and division be healed, and our nation be crowned with good that sees beyond the years.

It is good to give thanks to the Lord,
    to sing praises to your name, O Most High;
to declare your steadfast love in the morning,
    and your faithfulness at night. *(Psalm 92:1-2)*

PRAYERS OF PRAISE AND THANKSGIVING

O God, we thank you for the tremendous gift of living in this beautiful world. We thank you especially for the privilege of living in this nation we call home with all its richness of diversity and its opportunities to learn from and share with people from many different cultures. Likewise, we yearn for the healing of our beloved country. Bring its people out of fear, mistrust and resentment into wisdom, perception and action for good. Holy Spirit, remind us to think, speak and act with informed intelligence and with open hearts and minds. Keep us in humility and strength, in light and in patience, as our common desire for the healing of this nation overrides every temptation toward frustration or despair. We pray for our leaders and representatives in government and for all our citizens and residents. For the Love of Christ in all creation and in one another, we pray with confidence and thanks. **Amen.** *(Alla Renée Bozarth)*

Almighty God, we thank you for this nation and its citizens. You rule all the peoples of the earth. Inspire the minds of all women and men to whom you have committed the responsibility of government and leadership in the nations of the world. Give to them the vision of truth and justice, that by their counsel all nations and peoples may work together. Give to the people of our country zeal for justice and strength of forbearance, that we may use our liberty in accordance with your gracious will. Forgive our shortcomings as a nation; purify our hearts to see and love the truth. We pray all this through Jesus Christ. **Amen.** *(Andy Langford)*

PSALM 85:7-13

Show us your steadfast love, O Lord,
    and grant us your salvation.

Let me hear what God the Lord will speak,
    for he will speak peace to his people,
    to his faithful, to those who turn to him in their hearts.
Surely his salvation is at hand for those who fear him,
    that his glory may dwell in our land.

Steadfast love and faithfulness will meet;
    righteousness and peace will kiss each other.
Faithfulness will spring up from the ground,
    and righteousness will look down from the sky.
The Lord will give what is good,
    and our land will yield its increase.
Righteousness will go before him,
    and will make a path for his steps.

SCRIPTURE   ISAIAH 58:6-7, 10-12

Is not this the fast that I choose:
    to loose the bonds of injustice,
    to undo the thongs of the yoke,
to let the oppressed go free,
    and to break every yoke?
Is it not to share your bread with the hungry,
    and bring the homeless poor into your house;
when you see the naked, to cover them,
    and not to hide yourself from your own kin? . . .

If you offer your food to the hungry
  and satisfy the needs of the afflicted,
then your light shall rise in the darkness
  and your gloom be like the noonday.
The Lord will guide you continually,
  and satisfy your needs in parched places,
  and make your bones strong;
and you shall be like a watered garden,
  like a spring of water,
  whose waters never fail.
Your ancient ruins shall be rebuilt;
  you shall raise up the foundations of many generations;
you shall be called the repairer of the breach,
  the restorer of streets to live in.

LITANY

Almighty God, giver of all good things: We thank you for the natural majesty and beauty of this land. They restore us, though we often destroy them.
Heal us.

We thank you for the great resources of this nation. They make us rich, though we often exploit them.
Forgive us.

We thank you for the men and women who have made this country strong. They are models for us, though we often fall short of them.
Inspire us.

We thank you for the torch of liberty which has been lit in this land. It has drawn people from every nation, though we have often hidden from its light.
Enlighten us.

We thank you for the faith we have inherited in all its rich variety. It sustains our life, though we have been faithless again and again.
Renew us.

Help us, O Lord, to finish the good work here begun. Strengthen our efforts to blot out ignorance and prejudice, and to abolish poverty and crime. And hasten the day when all our people, with many voices in one united chorus, will glorify your holy Name.
Amen. *(The Episcopal Church)*

REFLECTION   POPE FRANCIS

The current global situation engenders a feeling of instability and uncertainty, which in turn becomes "a seedbed for collective selfishness." When people become self-centered and self-enclosed, their greed increases. The emptier a person's heart is, the more he or she needs things to buy, own and consume. It becomes almost impossible to accept the limits imposed by reality. In this horizon, a genuine sense of the common good also disappears. As these attitudes become more widespread, social norms are respected only to the extent that they do not clash with personal needs. So our concern cannot be limited merely to the threat of extreme weather events, but must also extend to the catastrophic consequences of social unrest. Obsession with a consumerist lifestyle, above all when few people are capable of maintaining it, can only lead to violence and mutual destruction.

Yet all is not lost. Human beings, while capable of the worst, are also capable of rising above themselves, choosing again what is good, and making a new start, despite their mental and social conditioning. We are able to take an honest look at ourselves, to acknowledge our deep dissatisfaction, and to embark on new paths to authentic freedom.

The interconnected relationships between God, neighbor, and earth are rooted in a biblical understanding of the universe; they are connected and cannot be separated.

In Laudato Si' *Pope Francis introduces the term "integral ecology," stating that "Since everything is closely interrelated, and today's problems call for a vision capable of taking into account every aspect of the global crisis, I suggest that we now consider some elements of an integral ecology, one which clearly respects its human and social dimensions."*

PRAYERS OF CONFESSION AND INTERCESSION

God of justice, you have shown us what is right: to act justly, to love mercy, and to walk humbly with you. Forgive all in the life of our nation that falls short of what you require. Forgive the poverty of body, mind, and spirit that still exists among us. Forgive all the broken lives and all the broken hearts that are not tended; forgive us for the lives of young children that are being perverted and degraded, and all the social casualties that are not lifted up. Forgive us as individuals and as a nation, for not being big enough, broad-minded enough, hopeful enough, or loving enough to create a just society. Forgive us and help us, so that our life as a nation, and the contribution we make to the life of the world, may honor you and do justice to your demands; through Jesus Christ our Lord. **Amen.** *(Alan Gaunt)*

Almighty God, you have given us this good land as our heritage. Make us always remember your generosity and constantly do your will. Bless our land with honesty in the workplace, truth in education, and honor in daily life. Save us from violence, discord, and confusion; from pride and arrogance; and from every evil course of action. When times are prosperous, let our hearts be thankful; and, in troubled times, do not let our trust in you fail. We pray in the name of Jesus Christ our Lord. **Amen.** *(Evangelical Lutheran Church in America)*

HYMN   MARTIN LECKEBUSCH

1. In an age of twisted values
   we have lost the truth we need.
   In sophisticated language
   we have justified our greed.
   By our struggle for possessions
   we have robbed the poor and weak.
   Hear our cry and heal our nation;
   your forgiveness, Lord, we seek.

2. We have built discrimination
   on our prejudice and fear.
   Hatred swiftly turns to cruelty
   if we hold resentments dear.
   For communities divided
   by the walls of class and race,
   hear our cry and heal our nation;
   show us, Lord, your love and grace.

3. When our families are broken,
   when our homes are full of strife,
   when our children are bewildered,
   when they lose their way in life,
   when we fail to give the aged
   all the care we know they need,
   hear our cry and heal our nation;
   help us show more love, we plead.

4. We who hear your word so often
   choose so rarely to obey.
   Turn us from our willful wandering;
   give us truth to light our way.
   In the power of your Spirit
   come to cleanse us, make us new;
   hear our cry and heal our nation
   till our nation honors you.

Tune: EBENEZER, 8.7.8.7.D.

May the God who dances in creation, who embraces us with human love, who shakes our lives like thunder, bless us and drive us out with power to fill the world with her justice. *(Janet Morley)*

SOURCES

Inspired by Katharine Lee Bates, "America the Beautiful," (1895). Public domain.

Alla Renée Bozarth, "A Prayer for the Healing of Our Nation" © 2017 Alla Renée Bozarth. Used by permission.

Andy Langford, "Almighty God, you rule all . . .," in United Methodist Church (US), *The United Methodist Book of Worship* (Nashville: The United Methodist Publishing House, 1992), no. 442, alt. © 1992 The United Methodist Publishing House. Used by permission. All rights reserved.

"Almighty God, Giver of All Good Things," in Episcopal Church, *Book of Common Prayer* (New York: Church Publishing, 1986), 838–39.

Pope Francis, *Laudato Si'*, accessed December 1, 2017, Vatican.va, 204–5. © Libreria Editrice Vaticana. Used by permission.

Pope Francis, *Laudato Si'*, accessed December 1, 2017, Vatican.va, 137. © Libreria Editrice Vaticana. Used by permission.

Alan Gaunt, "God of justice . . ." in *New Prayers for Worship* (Leeds, UK: John Paul the Preacher's Press, 1972), p. 3 of section 3, "Confession and Forgiveness." Used by permission.

"The Nation," in Evangelical Lutheran Church in America, *Evangelical Lutheran Worship*, Leaders Desk ed. (Minneapolis: Augsburg Fortress, 2006), 146. Used by permission.

Words by Martin Leckebusch, "In an Age of Twisted Values" © 1995 Kevin Mayhew Ltd. Used by permission. All rights reserved.

Janet Morley, "May the God who dances . . .," in *All Desires Known*, 3rd ed. (Harrisburg, PA: Morehouse, 2006), 94. *All Desires Known*, 3rd edition © 2006 the Morehouse Publishing. Used by permission of Church Publishing Incorporated, New York, NY.

50. PEACE

Peace is the absence of conflict, yes, and it is so much more. Peace is forgiveness and reconciliation, and the determination to promote the well-being of our neighbors nearby and far away. Peace is nations, communities, and individuals embodying God's eternal loving purposes today and always.

Mercy and truth have met together; justice and peace join hands. Truth springs up from the earth, and justice looks down from heaven. *(Psalm 85:10-11)*

PRAYERS OF PRAISE AND THANKSGIVING

O God, beautiful as the moon, warm as the sun, powerful as the earth, bestow your blessings upon us to uplift humankind. In this holy place, grant that peace may defeat discord, unselfishness may conquer greed, sincere words may overcome deceit, and respect surmount insults. Fill our hearts with joy, uplift our spirits, and fill our bodies with glory. Great God of the Universe, Great Light, Great Mover, bestow upon us who gather to worship you, upon those who strive to touch your heart, a new strength and glorious light. **Amen.** *(The Monks of Kurama Temple)*

Lord Jesus Christ, you are the way of peace. Come into the brokenness of our lives and our land with your healing love. Help us to be willing to bow before you in true repentance, and to bow to one another in real forgiveness. By the fire of your Holy Spirit, melt our hard hearts and consume the pride and prejudice which separate us. Fill us, O Lord, with your perfect love, which casts out our fear, and bind us together in that unity which you share with the Father and the Holy Spirit. **Amen.** *(Cecil Kerr)*

PSALM 122:1-4, 6-9

I was glad when they said to me,
   "Let us go to the house of the Lord!"
Our feet are standing
   within your gates, O Jerusalem.

Jerusalem—built as a city
   that is bound firmly together.
To it the tribes go up,
   the tribes of the Lord,
as was decreed for Israel,
   to give thanks to the name of the Lord. . . .

Pray for the peace of Jerusalem:
   "May they prosper who love you.
Peace be within your walls,
   and security within your towers."
For the sake of my relatives and friends
   I will say, "Peace be within you."
For the sake of the house of the Lord our God,
   I will seek your good.

SCRIPTURE   PHILIPPIANS 4:4-9

Rejoice in the Lord always; again I will say, Rejoice. Let your gentleness be known to everyone. The Lord is near. Do not worry about anything, but in everything by prayer and supplication with thanksgiving let your requests be made known to God. And the peace of God, which surpasses all understanding, will guard your hearts and your minds in Christ Jesus.

   Finally, beloved, whatever is true, whatever is honorable, whatever is just, whatever is pure, whatever is pleasing, whatever is commendable, if there is any excellence and if there is anything worthy of praise, think about these things. Keep on doing the things that you have learned and received and heard and seen in me, and the God of peace will be with you.

LITANY

Peace comes with every . . .
forgiving word
sincere welcome
refused war
clear understanding
universal truth
signed treaty
gentle treatment
honest thought
friendly smile
forgiven sin
forfeited revenge
granted reprieve
angry protest
accepting prayer
compassionate person
conscientious objection
family meal
attentive listening
just law
merciful judgment
wistful hope
social healing
shared good
reconciling gesture
kindly gift
non-violent experiment
peaceful endeavor
authentic disarmament
restrained deed
new day
open community
twinged conscience
patient concern
achieved ceasefire
failed aggression
harmonious achievement
loving action. *(David J. Harding)*

REFLECTION   JOHN YOUNG

When the last dove of peace has flown.
When the last olive branch of peace has been stretched out.
Will we realize what we have done?

When the last war is waged.
When the last terrorist act is carried out.
Will we hear the cry of the people?

When the last crime is committed.
When the last innocent person is imprisoned.
Will we be able to undo our wrongs?

When the last gun is fired.
When the last bomb has been set off.
Will we see the land we have left for children?

John Young was eighteen years old when he wrote this reflection, which was part of a liturgy created by the Iona Youth Festival in 2001. The group focused on issues of justice and peace as they experienced them in their own lives, rather than as abstract concepts.

PRAYERS OF CONFESSION AND INTERCESSION

Lord, let us not say "peace" where there is no peace, where children have gnawing hunger, where rural people are exploited, where city dwellers are crowded into slums, where those who speak for freedom are tortured. Deliver us from saying "peace" where there is injustice. Lead us into word and action that challenge oppression and call for true peace, your peace. **Amen.** *(John Johansen-Berg)*

Gracious God, grant peace among nations. Cleanse from our own hearts the seeds of strife: greed and envy, harsh misunderstandings and ill will, fear and desire for revenge. Make us quick to welcome ventures in cooperation among the peoples of the world, so that there may be woven the fabric of a common good too strong to be torn by the evil hands of war. In the time of opportunity, make us be diligent; and in the time of peril, let not our courage fail; through Jesus Christ our Lord. **Amen.** *(Evangelical Lutheran Church in America)*

50. Peace

O God, you are the unsearchable abyss of peace, the ineffable sea of love, the fountain of blessings, and the bestower of affection, who sends peace to those that receive it. Open to us this day the sea of your love and water us with plenteous streams from the riches of your grace and from the most sweet springs of your kindness. Make us children of quietness and heirs of peace; enkindle in us the fire of your love; strengthen our weakness by your power; bind us closely to you and to each other in our firm and indissoluble bond of unity. **Amen.** *(Syrian Clementine liturgy)*

HYMN   CARL P. DAW, JR.

1. O day of peace that dimly shines
   through all our hopes and prayers
      and dreams,
   guide us to justice, truth, and love,
   delivered from our selfish schemes.
   May swords of hate fall from our
      hands,
   our hearts from envy find release,
   till by God's grace our warring world
   shall see Christ's promised reign of
      peace.

2. Then shall the wolf dwell with the
      lamb,
   nor shall the fierce devour the small;
   as beasts and cattle calmly graze,
   a little child shall lead them all.
   Then enemies shall learn to love,
   all creatures find their true accord;
   the hope of peace shall be fulfilled,
   for all the earth shall know the Lord.

Tune: JERUSALEM, L.M.D., 8.8.8.8.8.8.8.8.
Words © 1982 Hope Publishing

Peace I leave with you; my peace I give to you. . . . Do not let your hearts be troubled, and do not let them be afraid. *(John 14:27)*

SOURCES

Psalm 85:10-11 from *The New English Bible*, copyright © Cambridge University Press and Oxford University Press 1961, 1970. All rights reserved.

"Prayer for Happiness to the Sonten of Kuramayama," trans. Tenko Matsushita, Kurama Temple, Kyoto, Japan, alt. Used by permission of Kurama Temple, Kyoto.

Cecil Kerr, "Lord Jesus Christ . . . ," in United Methodist Church (US), *The United Methodist Book of Worship* (Nashville: United Methodist Publishing House, 1992), no. 482. Prayer from Christian Renewal Centre, Northern Ireland.

David J. Harding, "Peace Comes with Every . . . ," in *Timeless Prayers for Peace: Voices Together from around the World*, ed. Geoffrey Duncan (Cleveland: Pilgrim Press, 2003), 43–44, alt. © David J. Harding.

John Young, "When the last dove . . . ," in "Help Us Make a Difference," in *Holy Ground: Liturgies and Worship Resources for an Engaged Spirituality*, ed. Neil Paynter and Helen Boothroyd (Glasgow: Wild Goose, 2005), 141. © Contributors, *Holy Ground* (2005), Wild Goose Publications, Glasgow. Used by permission.

John Johansen-Berg, "Do Not Say 'Peace,'" in *Timeless Prayers for Peace: Voices Together from around the World*, ed. Geoffrey Duncan (Cleveland: Pilgrim Press, 2003), 127. © John Johansen-Berg.

"Peace Among the Nations," in Evangelical Lutheran Church in America, *Evangelical Lutheran Worship: Occasional Services for the Assembly* (Minneapolis: Augsburg Fortress, 2009), 393. Used by permission.

"O God, you are . . . ," in *Chalice Worship*, ed. Colbert S. Cartwright and O. I. Cricket Harrison (St. Louis: Chalice, 1997), 271. From a Syrian Clementine liturgy. Used by permission of Chalice Press.

Words by Carl P. Daw Jr., "O Day of Peace" © 1982 Hope Publishing Company, Carol Stream, IL 60188. All rights reserved. Used by permission.

51. HOPE

Hope begets hope. Hope can heal illness, repair broken relationships, inspire a nation. Hope explodes in acts of love and service, often against overwhelming odds. A leader in ending apartheid in South Africa, Nelson Mandela was elected the country's first black president after being held captive for twenty-seven years, eighteen of them on Robben Island where he was forced into hard labor and was permitted just one visitor a year for thirty minutes. Hope!

If we hope for what we do not see, we wait for it with patience. . . . We know that all things work together for good for those who love God, who are called according to his purpose. . . . If God is for us, who is against us? . . . Rejoice in hope, be patient in suffering, persevere in prayer. *(Romans 8:25, 28, 31b; 12:12)*

PRAYERS OF PRAISE AND THANKSGIVING

Lord Jesus Christ, you are the true sun of the universe, ever rising, never setting. You are the source of all life and health. With your glance you generate, preserve, nourish, sustain and inspire all things both in heaven and on earth. Dawn in our souls, that the night of our misdeeds and the clouds of our errors may be dispelled. With your light within us and before us, may we go through all of life without offence, walking soberly as in the day, made pure from all the works of darkness. **Amen.** *(Erasmus)*

Creator of mists and mystery: you roll away the stones to open us to your life, to let your story shine out in all the world. Give us hope, living God—hope in our hands to open doors; hope in our eyes to see possibilities; hope in our hearts to live by faith. We pray this in the name of Jesus Christ, the hope of the world. **Amen.** *(Janet Lees)*

PSALM 130:1-2, 5-7

Out of the depths I cry to you, O Lord.
    Lord, hear my voice!
Let your ears be attentive
    to the voice of my supplications! . . .

I wait for the Lord, my soul waits,
    and in his word I hope;
My soul waits for the Lord
    more than those who watch for the morning,
    more than those who watch for the morning.

O Israel, hope in the Lord!
    For with the Lord there is steadfast love,
    and with him is great power to redeem.

CANTICLE   ISAIAH 40:28-29, 31

Have you not known? Have you not heard?

The Lord is the everlasting God,
    the Creator of the ends of the earth.
He does not faint or grow weary;
    his understanding is unsearchable.
He gives power to the faint,
    and strengthens the powerless. . . .

but those who wait for the Lord shall renew their strength,
    they shall mount up with wings like eagles,
they shall run and not be weary,
they shall walk and not faint.

SCRIPTURE   AMOS 9:13-15 AND 2 CORINTHIANS 4:16; 5:17-19

1. The time is surely coming, says the Lord,
    when the one who plows shall overtake the one who reaps,
    and the treader of grapes the one who sows the seed;
the mountains shall drip sweet wine,
    and all the hills shall flow with it.
I will restore the fortunes of my people Israel,
    and they shall rebuild the ruined cities and inhabit them;

they shall plant vineyards and drink their wine,
> and they shall make gardens and eat their fruit.
I will plant them upon their land,
> and they shall never again be plucked up
out of the land that I have given them,
> says the LORD your God.

2. We do not lose heart. Even though our outer nature is wasting away, our inner nature is being renewed day by day. . . . So if anyone is in Christ, there is a new creation: everything old has passed away; see, everything has become new! All this is from God, who reconciled us to himself through Christ, and has given us the ministry of reconciliation; that is, in Christ God was reconciling the world to himself, not counting their trespasses against them, and entrusting the message of reconciliation to us.

LITANY

To have hope
> **is to believe that history continues open to the dream of God and to human creativity.**

To have hope
> **is to continue affirming that it is possible to dream a different world, without hunger, without injustice, without discrimination.**

To have hope
> **is to be a messenger of God, tearing down walls, destroying borders, building bridges,**

To have hope
> **is to believe in the revolutionary potential of faith.**

To have hope
> **is to leave the door open so that the Spirit can enter and make all things new.**

To have hope
> **is to believe that life wins over death.**

To have hope
> **is to begin again as many times as necessary.**

To have hope
> **is to believe that hope is not the last thing that dies.**

To have hope
> **is to believe that hope cannot die, that hope no longer dies.**

To have hope
> **is to live.** *(Missionary Sisters of St. Charles Borromeo, Honduras)*

REFLECTION   PAUL HAWKEN

What I see everywhere in the world are ordinary people willing to confront despair, power, and incalculable odds in order to restore some semblance of grace, justice, and beauty to this world. The poet Adrienne Rich wrote, "My heart is moved by all I cannot save: so much has been destroyed. I cast my lot with those who, age after age, perversely, with no extraordinary power, reconstitute the world." Humanity is coalescing. It is reconstituting the world, and the action is taking place in classrooms, farms, jungles, villages, campuses, companies, refugee camps, deserts, fisheries, and slums.

You join a multitude of caring people. No one knows how many are working on the most salient issues of our day: climate change, poverty, deforestation, peace, water, hunger, conservation, human rights, and more. This is the largest movement the world has ever seen.

The generations before you failed. They got distracted and lost sight of the fact that life is a miracle every moment of existence. Nature beckons you to be on her side. The most unrealistic person in the world is the cynic, not the dreamer. Hope makes sense only when it doesn't make sense to be hopeful. Take it and run with it as if your life depends on it.

The environmental activist and author Paul Hawken (b. 1946) is executive director of Project Drawdown, a nonprofit organization dedicated to researching how global warming can be reversed. This selection is taken from Hawken's 2009 speech to graduating seniors at the University of Portland. It was named by PBS as the best commencement address of the year.

PRAYERS OF CONFESSION AND INTERCESSION

Gracious God, our sins are too heavy to carry, too real to hide, and too deep to undo. Forgive what our lips tremble to name, what our hearts can no longer bear, and what has become for us a consuming fire of judgment. Set us free from a past that we cannot change; open to us a future in which we can be changed; and grant us grace to grow more and more in your likeness and image; through Jesus Christ, the light of the world. **Amen.** *(United Church of Christ)*

51. Hope

Spirit of Life and Love, be with us in this time, as people suffer, as parents grieve, as violence rages. Be with us who feel the pain of loss, who feel anger at injustice.

Stand with the oppressed and change the heart of the oppressor, for we know that both are joined in their humanity, no matter how often we forget it. Help us to remember the hope we had, the hope we have, and the hope we will have; help us to remember joy in the midst of sadness, success in the midst of challenge, and the good in the midst of the bad. **Amen.** *(Christian Schmidt)*

HYMN   GEORGIA HARKNESS

1. Hope of the world, O Christ of great compassion,
   speak to our fearful hearts by conflict rent.
   Save us, your people, from consuming passion,
   who by our own false hopes and aims are spent.

2. Hope of the world, God's gift from highest heaven,
   bringing to hungry souls the bread of life:
   still let your Spirit unto us be given
   to heal earth's wounds and end our bitter strife.

3. Hope of the world, afoot on dusty highways,
   showing to wandering souls the path of light:
   walk now beside us lest the tempting byways
   lure us away from you to endless night.

4. Hope of the world, who by your cross has saved us
   from death and deep despair, from sin and guilt:
   we render back the love your mercy gave us;
   take now our lives, with them your kingdom build.

5. Hope of the world, O Christ, o'er death victorious,
   who by this sign has conquered grief and pain:
   we would be faithful to your gospel glorious.
   You are our Lord! You shall forever reign!

Tune: DONNE SECOURS, 11.10.11.10.
Words © 1954, ren. 1982 The Hymn Society (admin. Hope Publishing)

May the God of hope fill you with all joy and peace in believing, so that you may abound in hope by the power of the Holy Spirit. *(Romans 15:13)*

SOURCES

Adapted from Erasmus, *Prayers of Erasmus*, trans. and ed. C.S. Coldwell (London: John Hodges, 1872), 11–12. Public domain.

Janet Lees, "Creator of Mists and Mystery," in *Dare to Dream: A Prayer and Worship Anthology from around the World*, ed. Geoffrey Duncan (London: HarperCollins, 1995), 232, alt. Used by permission of Janet Lees.

Missionary Sisters of St. Charles Borromeo, Honduras, "To Have Hope," in *Prayer without Borders: Celebrating Global Wisdom* (Baltimore: Catholic Relief Services, 2004), 7. Used by permission.

Paul Hawken, "The Most Amazing Challenge," in *Moral Ground: Ethical Action for a Planet in Peril*, ed. Kathleen Dean Moore and Michael P. Nelson (San Antonio: Trinity University Press, 2010), 465, 468. Used by permission.

"Gracious God . . ." in United Church of Christ, *Book of Worship: United Church of Christ* (New York: United Church of Christ Office for Church Life and Leadership, 1986), 211. Used by permission.

Christian Schmidt, "A Prayer for Hard Times," *Unitarian Universalist Association*, accessed January 28, 2016, http://www.uua.org/worship/words/prayer/prayer-hard-times, alt. Used by permission of Christian Schmidt.

Words by Georgia Harkness, "Hope of the World" © 1954, ren. 1982 The Hymn Society (admin. Hope Publishing Company, Carol Stream, IL 60188). All rights reserved. Used by permission.

52. REPLENISHING GOD'S GOOD EARTH

Our ancestors hunted and gathered their food, recycling remnants and continually replenishing the earth. For five hundred years humankind has ravaged it. Now, like Johnny Appleseed and Wangari Maathai, we are challenged to replant on ancient ruins and replenish our planet home.

The pastures of the wilderness overflow,
    the hills gird themselves with joy,
the meadows clothe themselves with flocks,
    the valleys deck themselves with grain,
        they shout together for joy. *(Psalm 65:12-13)*

PRAYERS OF PRAISE AND THANKSGIVING

God of power, God of people, you are the life of all that lives, the energy that fills the earth, the vitality that brings to birth, the impetus in making whole whatever is broken. In you we grow to know the truth that sets all creation free. You are the song the whole earth sings, the promise liberation brings, now and forever. **Amen.** *(Miriam Therese Winter)*

Almighty and everlasting God, you made the universe with its marvelous order and chaos, its atoms, worlds, and galaxies, and the infinite complexity of living creatures. We give you thanks for all who increase knowledge of and wonder at your works. Grant that as we explore the mysteries of your creation, we may come to know you more truly and serve you more humbly; in the name of Jesus Christ our Risen Savior. **Amen.** *(The Episcopal Church)*

CANTICLE   ISAIAH 45:8, 12, 18A

Shower, O heavens, from above,
    and let the skies rain down righteousness;
let the earth open, that salvation may spring up,
    and let it cause righteousness to sprout up.
    I the Lord have created it. . . .

I made the earth,
    and created humankind upon it;
It was my hands that stretched out the heavens,
    and I commanded all their host. . . .

For thus says the Lord,
who created the heavens
    (he is God!),
who formed the earth and made it . . .

PSALM 104:14-18, 24, 27-30

You cause the grass to grow for the cattle,
    and plants for people to use,
to bring forth food from the earth,
    and wine to gladden the human heart,
oil to make the face shine,
    and bread to strengthen the human heart.
The trees of the Lord are watered abundantly,
    the cedars of Lebanon that he planted.
In them the birds build their nests;
    the stork has its home in the fir trees.
The high mountains are for the wild goats;
    the rocks are a refuge for the coneys. . . .

O Lord, how manifold are your works!
    In wisdom you have made them all;
    the earth is full of your creatures. . . .

These all look to you
    to give them their food in due season;
when you give to them, they gather it up;
    when you open your hand, they are filled with good things.

When you hide your face, they are dismayed;
   when you take away their breath, they die
   and return to their dust.
When you send forth your spirit, they are created;
   and you renew the face of the earth.

SCRIPTURE   JOB 5:8-13, 15-16, 22-27

If I were you, I'd appeal to God;
I'd state my case before the Most High.
The works of God are great beyond reckoning—
miracles without number.
It is God who gives rain to the earth,
and sends water out into the fields.
God rescues the lowly
and lifts up the downcast to joyful heights;
and God thwarts the plans of the cunning
so that their hands achieve no success.
God traps these "wise people" in their own devices,
and makes fools of their shrewd counselors. . . .
God sees that they have swords in their mouths,
and protects the needy from their treacherous hands.
So the poor have hope,
and injustice shuts its mouth. . . .
You will laugh at destruction and famine,
and have no dread of the beasts of the wild.
You will have a covenant with the stones of the field,
and the animals of the wilderness will be at peace with you.
You will know that your dwelling place is secure,
and when you inspect your flocks, you won't find any missing.
You will witness the growth of your extended family,
and your offspring will be as the grass in the meadows.
You will approach the grave at a ripe old age,
like a harvest gathered at just the right time.

Look closely—
we have examined all this, and it is true.
Listen carefully—and know it for yourself.

LITANY

In the name of all that is we come together.
In the name of the stars and galaxies;
in the name of the planets, moons and the sun;
in the name of all that is we come.

In the name of all that is we come together.
In the name of the oceans and the sea;
in the name of the mountain, desert and plain;
in the name of all that is we come.

In the name of all that is we come together.
In the name of the buffalo and bear;
in the name of the turtle, eagle and whale;
in the name of all that is we come.

In the name of all that is we come together.
In the name of the cactus and the fern;
In the name of the flower, tree and herb;
in the name of all that is we come.

In the name of all that is we come together.
In the name of the elements of life;
in the name of the soil, water and air;
in the name of all that is we come.

In the name of all that is we come together.
In the name of the children of earth;
in the name of the spirit breathing in all things;
in the name of all that is we come. *(Jan Novotka)*

REFLECTIONS   WANGARI MAATHAI AND POPE FRANCIS

1. We need to rediscover our common experience with other creatures on Earth, and recognize that we have gone through an evolutionary process with them. They may not look like us, with their wings and scales and fur. We may not like some; others like mosquitoes we may detest. But they are part of the process of life beginning and being sustained on this planet. An apt analogy is Noah in Genesis, who found a pair of each species and two by two placed them into his ark, mosquitoes and reptiles among them. Noah was not commanded to pick only those that were useful to him; he sheltered

them all. God recognized that they are part of us; they needed the chance to survive as well. And in giving them this chance, God gave us a chance too. Now we must give that chance back to ourselves, and replenish the earth.

The Kenyan environmentalist Wangari Maathai (1940–2011) began the Greenbelt Movement in 1977 with the single idea that paying women to plant trees would lift them out of poverty and reforest the land. The movement has planted more than thirty million trees; it has expanded around the world and helped nearly 900,000 women. In 2004, Maathai was the first African woman to win the Nobel Peace Prize.

2. What kind of world do we want to leave to those who come after us, to children who are now growing up? What is the purpose of our life in this world? Why are we here? What is the goal of our work and all our efforts? What need does the earth have of us? It is no longer enough, then, simply to state that we should be concerned for future generations. We need to see that what is at stake is our own dignity. Leaving an inhabitable planet to future generations is, first and foremost, up to us. The issue is one which dramatically affects us, for it has to do with the ultimate meaning of our earthly sojourn.

In his Encyclical Laudato Si', *Pope Francis offers a bold challenge to all the citizens of the world.*

PRAYERS OF CONFESSION AND INTERCESSION

God, forgive us for being so locked into our own experiences in life that we have not tried to understand the depth of the horrors others around the world have known in theirs. Open our eyes to see something of what they have seen, our ears to hear something of what they have heard, our hearts to feel something of what they have felt. By the miracle of your grace help us to understand the ways of your redemptive love in such a world as this, and show us how we can be agents of that love. In Jesus' name we pray. **Amen.** *(Mark H. Landfried)*

God of abundant harvest, help us to recognize and maintain the balance of nature for the common good. Let us not exhaust the earth by constant sowing and reaping without rest for the fields; let us not expect more from the earth than we are prepared to give it. As the land blesses us with its produce, so may we enrich it with water and minerals. God of goodness, inspire us to give and to receive in our relationship with Mother Earth. **Amen.** *(John Johansen-Berg)*

God of all creation, of all that live in soil, in seas and air, you weave with great variation the web of life, so fragile, still so fair. Give us knowledge, that we may mend it. Give us wisdom, that we may tend it. Give us love and true compassion, that we may care for all your life in all its forms. *(Per Harling)*

HYMN   THOMAS H. TROEGER

1. Every planet, star and stone,
   every atom charged and spinning,
   every cell of blood and bone
   trace to you, God, their beginning.
   To exist in time and space
   is itself a gift of grace.

2. But as if our breath and birth
   and the joy of simple living
   were not gifts enough for earth,
   you outdo yourself in giving:
   from your Word that made all things
   love unbounded flows and springs.

3. Sweeping currents stir and guide
   and renew our rich tradition
   through the nurture they provide
   for our church's work and mission.
   Drinking from Christ's constant streams,
   we gain strength to live our dreams.

4. For each planet, star and stone,
   for the gift of our existence,
   for your love that we have known
   as a flowing stream's persistence,
   we will live and end our days,
   every heartbeat giving praise!

Tune: GROSSER GOTT, 7.8.7.8.7.7.

Deep peace, pure white of the moon to you. Deep peace, pure green of the grass to you. Deep peace, pure brown of the earth to you. Deep peace, pure gray of the dew to you. Deep peace, pure blue of the sky to you. Deep peace of the Son of Peace to you. *(Fiona MacLeod)*

SOURCES

Miriam Therese Winter, "God of power . . . ," in *WomanPrayer, WomanSong: Resources for Ritual* (Oak Park, IL: Meyer Stone Books, 1987), 171–72, alt. © 1987 Medical Mission Sisters. Used by permission.

"A Rogation Day Procession and Liturgy: For Scientists, Explorers, Teachers, and Learners," in Standing Commission on Liturgy and Music, "Liturgical Materials Honoring God in Creation and Various Rites and Prayers for Animals," in *Report to the 77th General Convention* (Episcopal Church, July 5–12, 2012), 332, alt.

The Inclusive Bible (Landham, MD: Rowman & Littlefield, 2007). A Sheed & Ward Book published by Rowman & Littlefield Publishers, Inc. All rights reserved. Used by permission.

Jan Novotka, "In the Name of All That Is" © Jan Novotka. Used by permission.

Wangari Maathai, *Replenishing the Earth: Spiritual Values for Healing Ourselves and the World* (New York: Doubleday, 2010), 194–95.

Pope Francis, *Laudato Si'*, accessed December 1, 2017, Vatican.va, 160. © Libreria Editrice Vaticana. Used by permission.

Mark H. Landfried, "God, forgive us . . . ," in *Let Us Pray: Reformed Prayers for Christian Worship*, ed. Martha S. Gilliss (Louisville, KY: Geneva Press, 2002), 65. Used by permission.

John Johansen-Berg, "Creator God," in *Harvest for the World: A Worship Anthology on Sharing in the Work of Creation*, ed. Geoffrey Duncan (Cleveland: Pilgrim Press, 2003), 39–40. © John Johansen-Berg.

Per Harling, "God of All Creation," in *Timeless Prayers for Peace: Voices Together from around the World*, ed. Geoffrey Duncan (Cleveland: Pilgrim Press, 2003), 20, alt. © Per Harling, Uppsala, Sweden. Used by permission.

"Every Planet, Star and Stone" by Thomas Troeger © Oxford University Press 2015. Reproduced by permission. All rights reserved.

Fiona MacLeod [William Sharp], *The Dominion of Dreams: Under the Dark Star* (New York: Duffield, 1910), 423–24. Public domain.

INDEX OF PSALMS AND OTHER BIBLICAL READINGS

All passages are taken from the New Revised Standard Version of the Bible (NRSV) *unless otherwise stated in the sources.*

Old Testament

Selected Passage	Liturgy
Genesis 1:1-5; 26-27; 31a	2
Genesis 1:9-10, 20-23	8
Genesis 1:11-12, 21-22, 24-25, 27, 29-31a	16
Exodus 2:15-23	40
Exodus 3:2-5, 7-8a	17
Exodus 19:16-19	11
Leviticus 25:8-12	23
Leviticus 26:3-6, 14, 20, 25	32
Deuteronomy 8:7-8a	12
Deuteronomy 8:7-10, 17-19	22
Deuteronomy 11:8-17	30
Deuteronomy 24:19-21	23
Deuteronomy 28:1-2, 11-12, 15, 20-24, 28	43
Job 5:8-13, 15-16, 22-27	52
Job 9:4-10	14
Job 12:7-10	23
Job 24:2-4, 13-17, 21, 24	34
Job 28:24-28a	19
Job 37:5, 14-24	5
Job 38:4-7, 25-27, 37a	13
Job 38:41; 39:1-6, 9-12, 19-20a, 26-29	20
Psalm 10:12-15, 17-18	47
Psalm 19:1-4	48
Psalm 19:7-10, 14	46

Psalm 30:2, 8, 11-12	29
Psalm 34:15-19	29
Psalm 36:5-9	46
Psalm 37:3-7, 10-11, 28a, 29	27
Psalm 46:1-3, 6, 9-11	42
Psalm 51:1-7	44
Psalm 65:5b-7, 9-13	2
Psalm 66:1-9	3
Psalm 67	26
Psalm 78:18-20, 23-29	39
Psalm 78:41-48, 50	35
Psalm 84:1, 3-8, 10-12	5
Psalm 85:7-13	49
Psalm 90:1-6, 17	30
Psalm 91:1-8	43
Psalm 91:9-16	41
Psalm 96:1-3, 9-12	10
Psalm 97:1-2, 4-6, 10-12	9
Psalm 98	16
Psalm 100	7
Psalm 104:1, 2b-5, 10-13	19
Psalm 104:14-18, 24, 27-30	52
Psalm 104:25-31	48
Psalm 105:29-35	36
Psalm 107:35-38	4
Psalm 121	11
Psalm 122:1-4, 6-9	50
Psalm 126	15
Psalm 130:1-2, 5-7	51
Psalm 145:14-20a	40
Psalm 147:1a, 2-11	37
Psalm 147:7-9, 12-18	14
Psalm 147:12-18	1
Psalm 148:1-13a	12
Proverbs 8:22-31	3
Ecclesiastes 3:1-8	45
Isaiah 2:2-3a	11
Isaiah 11:6-9	18
Isaiah 9:2-7	42
Isaiah 13:6-11	33
Isaiah 24:1-6	35
Isaiah 24:19-23	32
Isaiah 32:16-18, 20	23

Isaiah 35:1-10	13
Isaiah 35:1-7a, 8a, 10	28
Isaiah 40:28-29, 31	51
Isaiah 41:18-20	10
Isaiah 42:5-8a, 10-12	1
Isaiah 45:8, 12-18a	52
Isaiah 55:1-3a, 4b-5	4
Isaiah 55:6-13	6
Isaiah 58:6-7, 10-12	49
Isaiah 58:6-9	38
Isaiah 60:1-5, 11a, 18, 20-21, 22a	17
Isaiah 61:1-4	25
Isaiah 65:17, 21-25	21
Jeremiah 29:1, 4-14	25
Ezekiel 37:7-14	45
Ezekiel 47:7-9, 12	24
Joel 2:23-24, 26-28	48
Amos 4:1-2, 6-9	36
Amos 5:10-15	44
Amos 9:13-15	51
Micah 4:1-4	26
Habakkuk 1:1-4; 2:1-4	41
Zephaniah 3:9-13	46

Apocrypha

Judith 16:13-16	1
Ecclesiasticus (Sirach) 38:25-32, 34	27
Ecclesiasticus (Sirach) 43:1-12	9
Song of the Three Young Men: 35-51	6
Song of the Three Young Men: 52-60	8

New Testament

Matthew 4:1-4	10
Mark 6:33-44	39
Mark 9:33-37; 10:13-16	18
Mark 10:23-31	28
Luke 6:27-30, 35b	31
Luke 10:29b-37	37
Luke 15:11-24	29
Luke 16:19-31	38
John 4:7-15	4
John 5:24-28	45
Acts 17:21-28a	15

Romans 12:9-18	31
1 Corinthians 13:1-7, 13	31
2 Corinthians 9:6b-11a	22
2 Corinthians 4:16; 5:17-19	51
Galatians 5:16-18, 22-23; 6:2, 9-10a	21
Philippians 4:4-9	50
Colossians 1:15-17, 19-20a	14
James 2:5-8, 14-18	47
James 5:1-6	34
Revelation 6:7-8	33
Revelation 7:9-17	7
Revelation 7:16-17; 21:1a, 3-5	24
Revelation 12:7-12	33

Extra-Biblical Readings

Atharva Veda—Hymn to the Earth	19
Dead Sea Scrolls	12

INDEX OF CONTEMPORARY REFLECTIONS

	Liturgy
Edward Abbey	10, 13
Patriarch Bartholomew I	16, 24, 34
Thomas Berry	2, 9
Wendell Berry	22, 42, 44
Gro Harlem Bruntland	26
Rachel Carson	5
Francis S. Collins	1
The Dalai Lama	17
Vine Deloria, Jr.	19
Paul Farmer	29
Pope Francis	15, 46, 49, 52
William B. Gail	43
António Guterres	18
Marie Hause	35
Paul Hawken	51
Thor Heyerdahl	8
Alexander von Humboldt	12
Wes Jackson	3, 23
Derrick Jenson	33
Robert Kennedy	47
David Kline	28
Erazim Kohák	6
Elizabeth Kolbert	32
James Howard Kunstler	25
Lao-Tsu	15
Wangari Maathai	52
Bill McKibben	23, 36
Thomas Merton	7
Kathleen Dean Moore	31

John Muir	20, 45
Robert O'Rourke	11
Brother Roger of Taizé	38
Anne Rowthorn	4, 14, 27
Jeffrey Sachs	21
Vandana Shiva	28
Gary Snyder	39
Brian Swimme	48
Stephen Trimble	10
Mary Evelyn Tucker	48
United Nations General Assembly	40
Jean Vanier	37, 41
Worldwatch Institute	30
John Young	50

INDEX OF HYMNS

First Line	Author	Liturgy
Above the moon earth rises	Thomas H. Troeger	35
All creatures of our God most high	St. Francis; Tr. William Draper	2
All things bright and beautiful	Cecil Frances Alexander	16
All who love and serve your city	Erik Routley	25
As conflicts rage and lives are lost	Jeffery Rowthorn	17
Blest are the innocents	Sylvia Dunstan	42
Children from your vast creation	David A. Robb	30
Companion of the poor	Daniel C. Damon	37
Creative God, you spread the earth	Ruth Duck	3
Earth is full of wit and wisdom	Adam M. L. Tice	5
Every planet, star and stone	Thomas H. Troeger	52
For beauty of meadows	Walter Farquharson	12
Go, be justice to God's people	Martin Willett	21
God, bless the work your people do	John A. Dalles	27
God is still speaking when children beg for bread	Barbara Hamm	39
God out of love for us	Fred Pratt Green	46
God's counting on me	Pete Seeger/Lorre Wyatt	32
God the sculptor of the mountains	John Thornburg	11
God, you see your loved creation	Herman Stuempfle, Jr.	43
Hear the land crying	Norman Habel with Indigenous Friends	41
Hope of the world	Georgia Harkness	51
How miniscule this planet	Thomas H. Troeger	36
How precious is God's gift of speech	Jeffery Rowthorn	31

I am standing waiting	Shirley Erena Murray	38
In an age of twisted values	Martin Leckebusch	49
In the beginning God played with the planets	Andrew Pratt	8
Jesus entered Egypt	Adam M. L. Tice	40
Learn from all the songs of earth	Thomas H. Troeger	6
Night and day this planet sings	Thomas H. Troeger	1
Now the green blade rises	John Macleod Campbell Crum	45
O day of peace that dimly shines	Carl P. Daw, Jr.	50
O for a world where everyone	Miriam Therese Winter	34
O God of every nation	William W. Reid, Jr.	33
O God, your creatures fill the earth	Carolyn Winfrey Gillette	20
O God, your justice towers	Herman Stuempfle, Jr.	44
Praise God for the harvest	Brian Wren	23
Praise the Source of faith and learning	Thomas H. Troeger	48
Pray for the wilderness	Daniel C. Damon	10
Restless Weaver, ever spinning	O. I. Cricket Harrison	15
Shall we gather at the river	Robert Lowry	4
Sing praise to God	John L. Bell and Graham Maule	7
Sing praise to God, you heavens!	Herman Stuempfle, Jr.	9
Stars and planets flung in orbit	Herman Stuempfle, Jr.	14
The thirsty cry for water, Lord	Herman Stuempfle, Jr.	24
The whole creation is a song	Jeffery Rowthorn	19
There is no child so small	Shirley Erena Murray	18
This is my song	Lloyd Stone	26
Till all the jails are empty	Carl P. Daw, Jr.	47
'Tis the gift to be simple	Joseph Brackett	28
Touch that soothes and heals	Mary Louise Bringle	29
We plow the fields and scatter	Matthias Claudius; tr. Jane Montgomery Campbell	22
When, in awe of God's creation	Jane Parker Huber	13

SUPPLEMENTARY HYMNS

All praise to you, O God of all creation
    Omer Westendorf   11.10.11.10.11.10.   FINLANDIA

As waters rise around us
    Mary Louise Bringle   8.7.8.7. 12.7.7.   BRYN CALFARIA

Children of God, reach out to one another!
    John Greenleaf Whittier   11.10.11.10.   DONNE SECOURS

Christ has changed the world's direction!
    Shirley Erena Murray   8.7.8.7.6.7.   MICHAEL

Christ, you call us all to service
    Joy F. Patterson   8.7.8.7.D.   IN BABILONE

Come to us, creative Spirit
    David Mowbray   8.5. 8.5.8.7.   CASTLEWOOD

Community of Christ
    Shirley Erena Murray   6.6.8.4.D.   LEONI

Creating God, your fingers trace
    Jeffery Rowthorn   LM   DEUS TUORUM MILITUM

Creation sings a hymn of joy
    Herman Stuempfle, Jr.   Common Meter Double   FOREST GREEN

Dream on, dream on
    Hae Jong Kim   Irregular Meter   DREAM ON

Everything that has voice, sing for peace
    Shirley Erena Murray   6.3.3.6.3.3.7.7.6.3.   SING FOR PEACE

For everyone born a place at the table
    Shirley Erena Murray   11.10.11.10. and Refrain   TABLESONG

For the fruit of all creation
    Fred Pratt Green   8.4.8.4.8.8.8.4.   AR HYD Y NOS

For the healing of the nations
    Fred Kaan   8.7.8.7.8.7.   REGENT SQUARE

For the music of creation			
	Shirley Erena Murray	8.7.8.7.D.	HYME TO JOY
From all that dwell below the skies			
	Isaac Watts	LM with Alleluias	LASST UNS ERFREUEN
Gentle Jesus, loving Shepherd			
	Lurline DuPre	8.7.8.7.D.	NETTLETON
God of freedom, God of justice			
	Shirley Erena Murray	8.7.8.7.87.	REGENT SQUARE
God of futures yet unfolding			
	Mary Louise Bringle	8.7.8.7.D.	HYFRYDOL
God of grace and God of glory			
	Harry Emerson Fosdick	8.7.8.7.8.7.7.	CWM RHONDDA
God of wisdom, truth, and beauty			
	Jane Parker Huber	8.7.8.7.D.	AUSTRIAN HYMN
God who stretched the spangled heavens			
	Catherine Cameron	8.7.8.7.D.	HOLY MANNA
God, who touches earth with beauty			
	Mary S. Edgar	8.5.8.5.	GENEVA *C.H. Lowden, composer*
God, whose farm is all creation			
	John Arlott	8.7.8.7.	STUTTGART
God, you spin the whirling planets			
	Jane Parker Huber	8.7.8.7.D.	PLEADING SAVIOR
God, your music filled the cosmos			
	Herman Stuempfle, Jr.	8.7.8.7.8.7.7.	CWM RHONDDA
God, your power still creating			
	Herman Stuempfle, Jr.	8.7.8.7.8.7.	REGENT SQUARE
Heaven and earth, and sea and air			
	Joachim Neander	7.7.7.7.	GOTT SEI DANK
Here am I			
	Brian Wren	3.7.6.5.D.	HERE AM I
How can we sing our songs of faith			
	Fred Pratt Green	Common Meter Double	RESIGNATION
How great thou art			
	Stuart K. Hine	11.10.11.10. with Refrain	HOW GREAT THOU ART
How long, O Lord, how long			
	Herman Stuempfle, Jr.	6.6.8.6.	SOUTHWELL
I sing the mighty power of God			
	Isaac Watts	Common Meter Double	FOREST GREEN

Supplementary Hymns

I, the Lord of sea and sky			
	Daniel Schutte	7.7.7.4.D. and Refrain	HERE I AM
In Bethlehem a newborn boy			
	Rosamond Herklots	8.8.8.8.	IN BETHLEHEM
In labor all creation groans			
	Delores Dufner	8.6.8.6.	MORNING SONG
In the midst of new dimensions			
	Julian B. Rush	8.7.8.7. and Refrain	NEW DIMENSIONS
It is God who holds the nations			
	Fred Pratt Green	15.15.15.7.	VISION
Jesu, Jesu, fill us with your love			
	Tom Colvin	7.7.9. and Refrain	CHEREPONI
Join the song of praise and protest			
	Michael Forster	8.7.8.7.D.	BLAENWERN
Let all things now living			
	Katherine K. Davis	6.6.11.6.6.11.D.	ASH GROVE
Let there be peace on earth			
	Sy Miller and Jill Jackson	Irregular Meter	WORLD PEACE
Let wonder be reborn			
	Thomas H. Troeger	Short Meter Double	DIADEMATA
Light dawns on a weary world			
	Mary Louise Bringle	7.6.6.7.8. and Refrain	TEMPLE OF PEACE
Lord God, in whom all worlds			
	Fred Pratt Green	6.6.6.6.8.8.	MARLEE
Lord, whose love through humble service			
	Alfred F. Bayly	8.7.8.7.D.	HYFRYDOL
Maker God who breathed creation			
	Jacque B. Jones	8.7.8.7. and Refrain	TRUST ALONE
Many and great, O God, are thy works			
	Joseph R. Renville	Irregular Meter	LACQUIPARLE
Mighty God who called creation			
	Carl P. Daw, Jr.	8.7.8.7.D.	NETTLETON
Morning has broken			
	Eleanor Farjeon	5.5.5.4.D.	BUNESSAN
Mountain brook with rushing waters			
	William W. Reid, Jr.	8.7.8.7.D.	BLAENWERN
O God of all creation			
	Michael Forster	13.13.13.13.13.13.	THAXTED
O God of creation, we see all around us			
	Carolyn Winfrey Gillette	12.11.12.11.D.	THE ASH GROVE

Title / Author	Meter	Tune
O God of earth and altar G. K. Chesterton	7.6.7.6.D.	LLANGLOFFAN
O God of love, O God of peace Henry W. Baker	LM	ERHALT UNS, HERR
O Lord, our God, how excellent Fred R. Anderson	CM	WINCHESTER OLD
O who will speak for justice Betsy Phillips Fisher	7.6.7.6.D.	LLANGLOFFAN
Praise the Lord! God's glories show Henry Francis Lyte	7.7.7.7. with Alleluias	LLANFAIR
Praise with joy the world's Creator John L. Bell	8.7.8.7.8.7.	LAUDA ANIMA
Reckless extravagance, laughter and daring Andrew Pratt	11.10.11.10.	WAS LEBET
Sing a new world into being Mary Louise Bringle	8.7.8.7. D.	HYMN TO JOY
Sing of a God in majestic divinity Herbert O'Driscoll	12.10.12.10.	WAS LEBET
Teach us, O loving heart of Christ Shirley Erena Murray	CM	DAVIDSON
Thank you, God Brian Wren	9.10.10.9.	AMSTEIN
The earth belongs to God alone Adam M. L. Tice	CM	SIMMONS
The earth is the Lord's Maggi Dawn	Irregular	THE EARTH IS THE LORD'S
The earth is the Lord's Carolyn Winfrey Gillette	8.7.8.7.D.	ST. DENIO
The garden needs our tending now Mary Louise Bringle	8.6.8.6.8.8. and Refrain	UNE JEUNE PUCELLE
The God who set the stars in space Timothy Dudley-Smith	Common Meter Double	KINGSFOLD
The kingdom of God is justice and joy Bryn A. Rees	10.10.11.11.	LAUDATE DOMINUM
The works of the Lord are created in wisdom Christopher Idle	12.11.12.11.	KREMSER
Through all the world, a hungry Christ Shirley Erena Murray	LM	DE TAR

Supplementary Hymns

To bless the earth
    New Metrical Version   7.6.7.6.   CHRISTUS, DER IST
    of the Psalms   MEIN LEBEN

Touch the earth lightly
    Shirley Erena Murray   5.5.10.D.   TENDERNESS

Walls mark our boundaries and keep us apart
    Ruth Duck   10.10.10.10.   PENROSE
                                   and Refrain

We cannot own the sunlit sky
    Ruth Duck   8.7.8.7.D.   HOW CAN I KEEP
                                              FROM SINGING

We shall overcome
    African American Spiritual   Irregular Meter   WE SHALL OVERCOME

We thank you, God, for water, soil, and air
    Brian Wren   10.10.10. 9.   YOGANANDA

When all is ended, time and troubles past
    Brian Wren   10.10.10.4.   ENGELBERG

When children wake to tears
    Mary Louise Bringle   11.11.11.5.   ISTE CONFESSOR

When the present holds no promise
    Thomas Troeger   8.7.8.7.D.   BEACH SPRING

When the sword and spear are broken
    Adam M.L. Tice   8.7.8.7.8.7.7.   CWM RHONDDA

When will people cease their fighting?
    Constance Cherry   8.7.8.7.D.   RUSTINGTON

Where armies scourge the countryside
    Herman Stuempfle, Jr.   8.6.8.6.8.6.   MORNING GLORY

Where cross the crowded ways of life
    Frank Mason North/
    Ruth Duck   LM   GERMANY

Who put the colors in the rainbow?
    Paul Booth   Irregular meter   AUDREY-GREEN

Will the circle be unbroken
    Tony E. Alonso   8.7.8.7.D.   TONY E. ALONSO
                                               Composer

Wind of the Spirit
    Herman Stuempfle, Jr.   11.10.11.10.11.10.   FINLANDIA

With humble justice clad and crowned
    Brian Wren   Long Meter Double   SWEET HOUR

Womb of life and source of being
    Ruth Duck   8.7.8.7.D.   RAQUEL

ACKNOWLEDGMENTS

We have many people to thank for helping us in numerous ways in compiling *God's Good Earth*. Primarily we thank authors of litanies, hymns, prayers, and reflections whose works constitute much of the content of this book. Friends and colleagues contributed their original works without charge and we thank them all, in particular Scott Allen, Talitha Arnold, Edmund Banyard, Alla Renée Bozarth, Brothers of Weston Priory, Anthony G. Burnham, Janet Cawley, Francis S. Collins, Kate Compston, Cecil Corbett, John A. Dalles, Peter W. A. Davison, Timothy Dudley-Smith, Paul Farmer, William B. Gail, Alan Gaunt, Carolyn Winfrey Gillette, Martyn Goss, Norman Habel, Per Harling, Marie Hause, Linda Jones, Elizabeth Kolbert, Pat Kozak, Trevor Lloyd, Bill McKibben, Robin Morrison, Jan Novotka, Robert O'Rourke, Gail Ramshaw, Gabriel (Jay) Rochelle, Laura Rasplica Rodd, Janet Schaffran, Christian Schmidt, Carolyn Sharp, Christine Sine, Elizabeth Tapia, John Thornburg, Stephen Trimble, John van de Laar, Alicia von Stamwitz, Miriam Therese Winter, and also Marcia Holroyd for use of her late husband Peter's litany. William McKeown and Constance Coles shared their collection of biblical invocations and benedictions with us. Don E. Saliers composed a new tune, ROWTHORN, for the hymn in Liturgy 41, "Violence."

The following organizations, churches, and groups also contributed works *gratis*: Anglican Church of Canada, Anglican Consultative Council, Ateliers et Presses de Taizé, Augsburg Fortress, Baptist Union of Great Britain, Bloomsbury Continuum, Brandt & Hochman, Caritas (Aotearoa New Zealand), Catholic Agency for Overseas Development (CAFOD), Catholic Coalition for Climate Change, Catholic Relief Services, Center for Ministry Development, Church of the Province of New Zealand, Church of Scotland, Churches Together in Britain and Ireland, Columbia University Press, Counterpoint Press, Creation Justice Ministries, Darton, Longman and Todd, EnThusia Enterprises, Environmental Network of the Anglican Church in Southern Africa, Evangelical Lutheran Church in Canada, Inner Traditions International and Bear and Co., International Justice Mission Unit within the Commission for the Mission of the Uniting Church in Australia (Synod of Victoria and Tasmania), Island Press, Kevin Mayhew Publishers, the Kon-Tiki Museum, Kurama-dera Temple (Kyoto, Japan), Medical Mission Sisters, Missionary Sisters of St. Charles Borromeo (Honduras), National Council of Churches in the Philippines, the Nobel Foundation, Orbis, Orion Magazine, Oxford University Press, Parallax Press, Penguin Random House, Plon, Presbyterian Church in Canada, Reconstructionist Press, Rowman and Littlefield Publishers, SPCK, SYNDESMOS, United Church of Christ and Pilgrim Press, the United Nations, Uniting Church in Australia, University of Chicago Press, University of Nebraska Press, Upper Room Books, World Prayers Project, Writers Workshop (Calcutta, India), and Yale University Press.

We are grateful to the members of United Church of Santa Fe, New Mexico, who invited us to lead an environmental weekend on the theme "Sing for Earth, Pray for Earth, Act for Earth." This lively weekend fired our imaginations and sowed the seeds for what has now become *God's Good Earth*.

We are greatly indebted to Mary Evelyn Tucker, co-director of the Forum on Religion and Ecology at Yale University, for her generous encouragement throughout the compiling of this book and for writing the foreword.

The Overseas Ministries Study Center in New Haven provided a hospitable and inspiring living and writing space. The Yale Institute of Sacred Music and its director, Martin Jean, provided access to the Yale University Libraries. Gregory Sterling, dean of Yale Divinity School, generously funded a work-study student, Brendan Dempsey, and a research assistant, Marie Hause. Marie was invaluable in checking the many references in the book, in obtaining copyright permissions, and so much more. This was tedious and exhausting work, but Marie handled it with skill, dedication, and grace. With energy and enthusiasm Ellen Little helped in the early stages of the book. Carolyn Hardin Englehardt opened up the treasures of the Ministry Resource Center at the Yale Divinity School Library, time and again leading us to invaluable materials.

We are greatly indebted to the Episcopal Diocese of Connecticut and especially to Companions in Mission for Publishing and Communication and Bill Schrull, chair of CMPC, for generous help toward covering the cost of copyright permissions. Virginia Army, chair, and her committee awarded us a Jack Spaeth Care for Creation Environmental Grant. We are grateful for friends and colleagues at St. John's Abbey in Collegeville, Minnesota, and in particular Donald Ottenhoff, director of the Collegeville Institute, who introduced us to Liturgical Press. We thank Peter Dwyer, publisher of

Liturgical Press, and Barry M. Hudock, former publisher for Parish Market, for undertaking to publish *God's Good Earth*. We also thank Michelle Verkuilen for her work in promoting this book, Cathy Broberg and Stephanie Lancour for their editorial work, and Colleen Stiller and Julie Surma for their production work.

We are overwhelmed by your kindness, creativity, skill, hard work, and imagination and we heartily thank you.

Every effort has been made to identify all the texts used in this book and to secure permission to publish and/or reprint. If we have nonetheless erred in the acknowledgments or infringed on any copyrighted material, we offer our apologies.